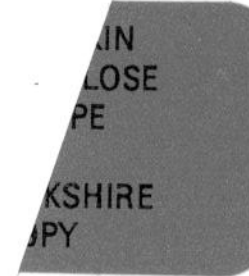

Creative TASSELS

Madeleine Willingham and Julie Neilson-Kelly

A J.B. Fairfax Press Publication

CONTENTS

EDITORIAL
Managing Editor: Judy Poulos
Editorial Assistant: Ella Martin
Editorial Coordinator: Margaret Kelly
Photography: Andrew Elton, John Venus
Styling: Kathy Tripp
Illustrations: Malcolm Kelly

DESIGN AND PRODUCTION
Manager: Anna Maguire
Design: Jenny Nossal
Cover Design: Jenny Pace
Layout: Sheridan Packer
Picture Editors: Stacey Strickland, Cheryl Dubyk-Yates

Published by J.B. Fairfax Press Pty Limited
80-82 McLachlan Ave
Rushcutters Bay NSW, 2011 Australia
A.C.N. 003 738 430

Formatted by J.B. Fairfax Press Pty Limited

Printed by Toppan Printing Company, Singapore

JBFP 419

CREATIVE TASSELS
ISBN 1 86343 250 7

CONTENTS

ABOUT THE AUTHORS

MADELEINE WILLINGHAM

Madeleine Willingham has been running a successful folk art studio, known as Maddie's Corner Cottage, in Mooroolbark, Victoria for the past seven years. Maddie's interest in tassel-making was aroused by her good friend, textile artist Marijke Owen. She has been conducting tassel-making workshops in Victoria for four years and, as a result of the increasing popularity of tassels, also produces many associated products which are distributed Australia-wide.

Madeleine has travelled extensively with her workshops and is in constant demand to share her knowledge. She is well known in Victoria for her Special Weekends of art and craft exhibitions and sales at her English cottage on the famous Edna Walling Bickleigh Vale Estate.

JULIE NEILSON-KELLY

Julie Neilson-Kelly operates Artistic Renditions Studio in Adelaide, South Australia. Various tassel-making projects are just one aspect of the extremely successful workshops run by Julie over the past few years. She is a designer of gift wrapping and découpage paper and is one of Australia's foremost decorative artists, as well as a fine art painter in acrylics. Her first book *Inspirations in Paint* is also published by J.B. Fairfax Press.

Julie and her husband Malcolm are both extremely creative artists and they have combined their work for the first time, with Malcolm illustrating the step-by-step instructions in this book.

DEDICATION

We would like to dedicate this book to our dear friend Sue Schirmer and her kitchen table.

INTRODUCTION

This book is for all those people who ask 'What do you do with a tassel?'

It is not our intention to take you through the traditional, historical or cultural significance of tassels, but to simply approach our subject in a more frivolous manner to entice you to make your own decorative statements to enhance your decor.

You will discover many varied and innovative uses for tassels, as we have presented them in many scenarios within this book. We hope to encourage you to create as many uses as your heart desires.

Like us, you will be captivated by the evocative effects of colour dyeing from bold vibrant patterns through to softly shaded and blended tones. You can create gorgeous combinations of colour you never believed possible and yet the process is so simple.

Constructing our tassels is extremely easy. Whether you are an accomplished embroiderer or 'can only sew on a button', you will be equally delighted with how easily the tassels are made.

The most difficult part will be deciding which one to make first, which colour to use, whether to bead or not to bead. Don't hesitate – just begin and your life will never be the same again! You will never be able to pass a haberdashery shop without diving in to inspect their range of laces, braids and trims. Start collecting today.

Above all, we would like to wish you days filled with creativity and fun.

Good luck.
Madeleine and Julie

The authors would like to thank all those artists who have contributed their work to this photograph.

BASIC CLOTH TASSEL

This is an opportunity to create a total look with a tassel made from the same material as the item being decorated.

As the name suggests, this tassel is made from fabric. Any fabric is suitable, as long as it has been woven, so choose from cotton, linen, shantung, silk, hessian, tapestry and so on. Knitted fabrics, such as interlock and jersey, are not suitable. Some materials will fray more easily than others and some require a little more patience for a successful result.

Cloth tassels can be any size: tiny, for use on pincushions or as trimming on a garment, or medium or large to be used on soft furnishings.

MATERIALS

Woven cloth, a 30 cm (12 in) square will make a 15 cm (6 in) tassel
Clear craft glue
Length of cord for the hanger

METHOD

STEP ONE

Remove either the warp or the weft threads from opposite ends of the fabric piece until approximately 2.5 cm (1 in) of fabric remains in the centre (Figs 1 and 2). This amount can vary, depending on the size of the fabric being used.

STEP TWO

Spread the glue along the remaining unfringed fabric, then fold it in half so that both fringed edges come together. Now you have a double-thickness header with a fringe attached.

STEP THREE

Neaten one end of the header by dabbing it with glue and folding it in tightly.

STEP FOUR

Double the cord over and knot the ends together. Spread glue along the full length of the header. Place the knotted end of the cord over the header at the raw end (Fig. 3).

STEP FIVE

Roll the header firmly and evenly, with the knotted cord inside the roll and the loop protruding (Fig. 4). Roll until the full length has been used up and the neatened edge stuck down. You now have a cloth tassel to decorate as you wish or leave plain, depending on the fabric and the use to which the tassel will be put.

Fig. 1

Fig. 2

Fig. 3

Fig. 4

BASIC YARN TASSEL

This tassel is made by wrapping yarn around cardboard. Any yarn is suitable for this method, including rayon, embroidery cotton, silk, wool, ribbon, string, raffia, jute, cord etc.

For all the tassels and cords pictured which require rayon yarn, we have used Maddie's 100% Rayon Tassel and Embroidery Yarn. The tassels can be made large or small simply by varying the length of the cardboard used.

MATERIALS

Quantity of yarn
Tapestry needle
Firm cardboard
Large scissors

METHOD

STEP ONE

Cut the cardboard to the length of the tassel required. Wrap the yarn over and over in the centre of the cardboard until the desired thickness is reached.

STEP TWO

Thread the tapestry needle with a length of yarn, double it over and knot the ends together. Push the needle under the wrapped yarn on one side and pull it through (Fig. 1). Loop the needle through the knotted end of the yarn and pull firmly (Fig. 2).

STEP THREE

Pinching the wrapped yarn tightly together, push the needle through a couple of times to secure the bundle, then fasten off.

STEP FOUR

Remove the bundle from the cardboard and hold with the 'seam' uppermost (Fig. 3).

STEP FIVE

Using the needle threaded with yarn, take a couple of back stitches in the folded bundle to create a head (Fig. 4). Wrap the yarn around the neck four or five times, pulling it firmly, but not tugging (Fig. 5).

STEP SIX

Work a couple of back stitches to secure the thread (Fig. 6), then push the needle down through the length of the tassel, cutting the sewing thread at the bottom of the tassel (Fig. 7).

STEP SEVEN

Holding the looped tassel by the head, place a blade of the large scissors through the bottom of the looped bundle (Fig. 8). Pull down, then snip through to free the tassel (Fig. 9). You may need to snip several times.

STEP EIGHT

Attach the cord by oversewing the centre of the cord to the centre seam at the top of the tassel (Figs 10 and 11). See page 18 for how to make a twisted cord. Fasten off, push the needle through the length of the tassel and cut the thread at the bottom of the tassel (Fig. 12).

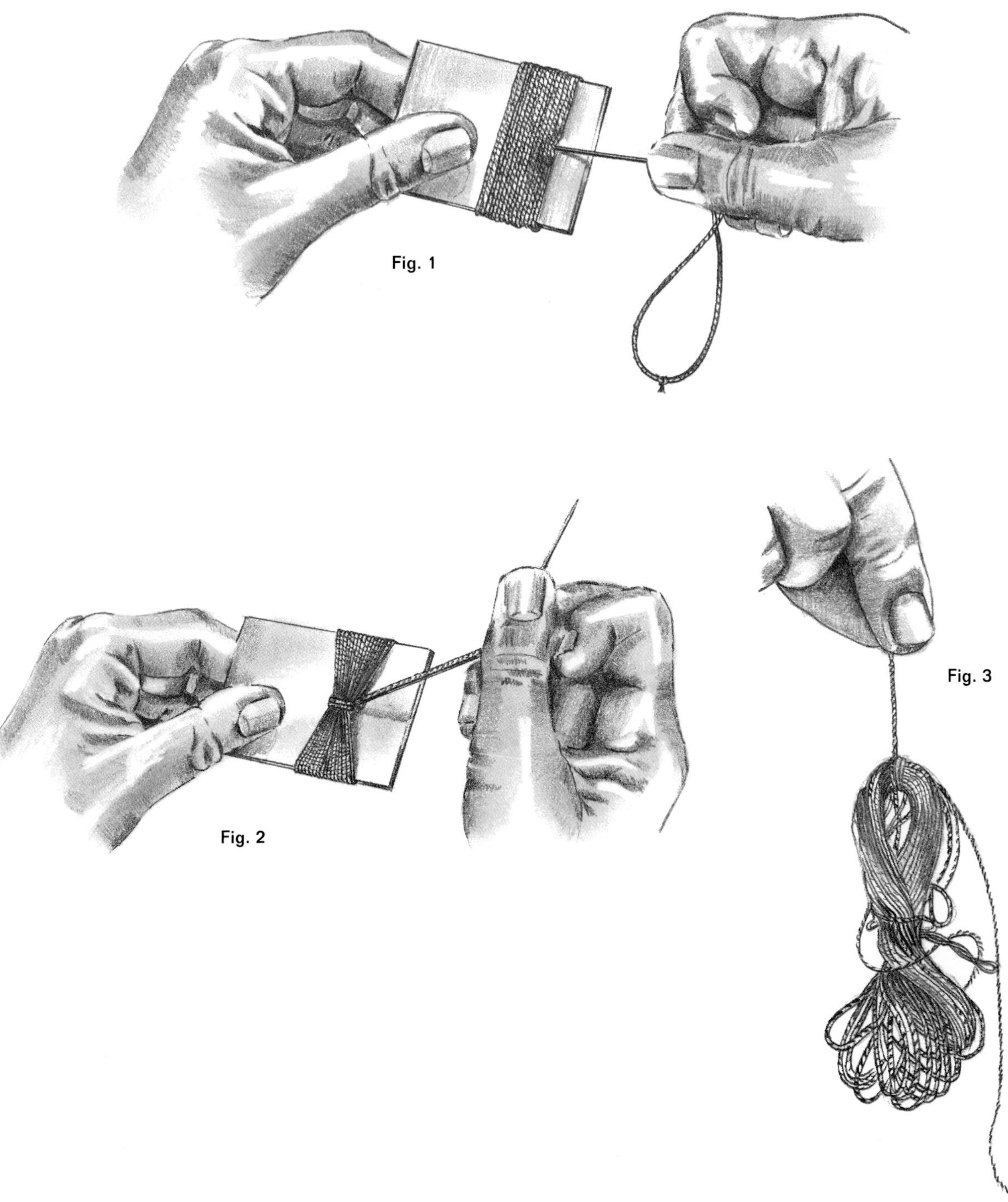
Fig. 1
Fig. 2
Fig. 3

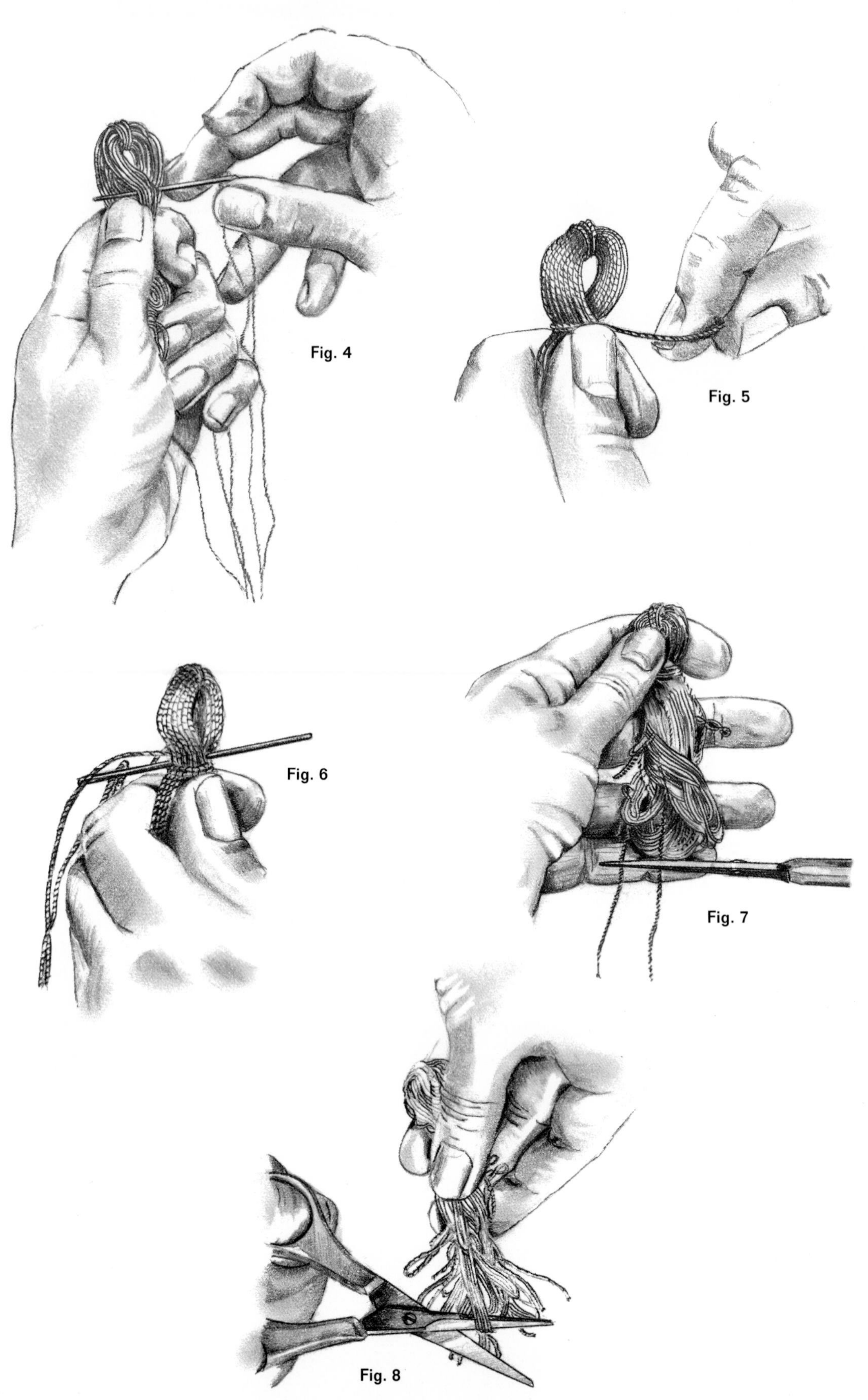
Fig. 4
Fig. 5
Fig. 6
Fig. 7
Fig. 8

Fig. 9
Fig. 10
Fig. 11
Fig. 12

BASIC WOODEN FORM TASSEL

For this type of tassel, fringe is wrapped on the spindle at the base of a wooden form, the rest of which is wrapped in cord or decorated in some way.

Forms of varying shapes and sizes are used and tassels made in this way can be tiered, multilayered or have inverted layers added. Embellish the tassel with laces, braids, ribbons, beads, buttons, flowers, charms or embroidery. The creative possibilities are endless.

MATERIALS

Wooden form
85-100 cm (34-39 in) of rayon fringe
2 m (2¼ yd) of purchased rayon cord
Clear craft glue
Satay stick
Scissors

METHOD

STEP ONE

Spread glue right around the spindle and the base of the form (Fig. 1). Wrap the fringe onto the spindle for two or three turns, dab on a little glue, then continue wrapping. Continue to wrap, dab and wrap until the fringe is fully wound (Fig. 2).

STEP TWO

Smear glue all over the wooden form, paying special attention to the top edge of the fringe. Begin to lay the cord touching the top edge of the fringe, then winding it around the form (Fig. 3). Work the cord gently into place with your finger to make sure there are no gaps between the wrapped layers. Do not pull the cord – let it work its own way.

STEP THREE

Keep winding, covering the surface completely, until only the hole at the top of the form is showing. Cut the cord at a sharp angle and work the end of the cord against the previous layer. Allow the glue to set for five minutes.

STEP FOUR

Pour some glue down into the hole in the top of the form. Cut a length of cord, approximately 30 cm (12 in). Using the satay stick, push one end of the cord into the hole, then the other end (Fig. 4). Allow the glue to set for five minutes, then decorate and embellish to your heart's content.

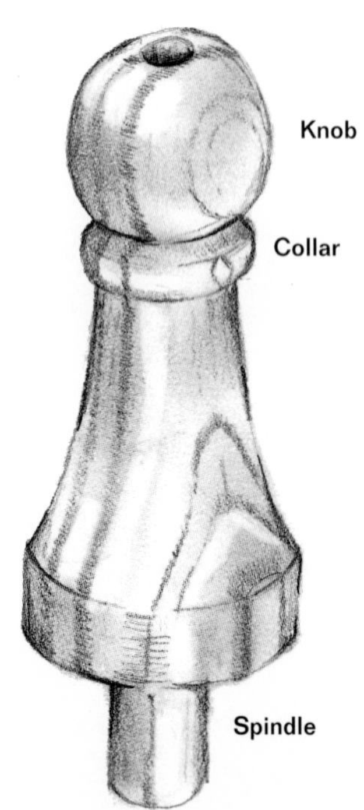

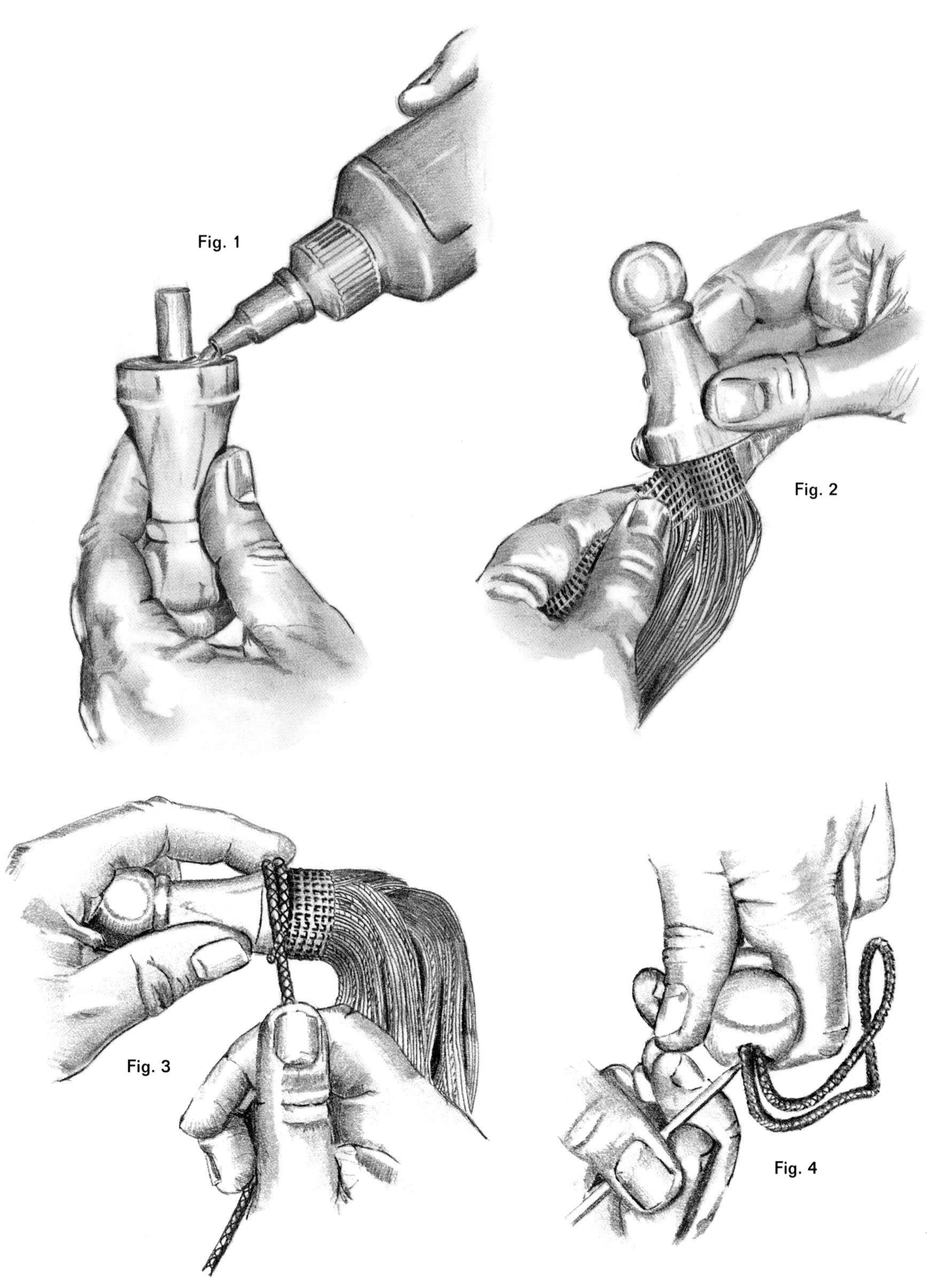
Fig. 1
Fig. 2
Fig. 3
Fig. 4

BASIC SOFT-BODIED FRINGED TASSEL

This tassel is constructed from commercially made rayon fringe which comes in a variety of widths. The most commonly used widths for tassels are 150 mm (6 in) and 75 mm (3 in).

This tassel is very quick to make. It can be decorated with a second layer of shorter fringe and embellished to suit anything from berets to bolsters, keys to candelabra.

MATERIALS

30 cm (12 in) of 150 mm (6 in) wide rayon fringe
30 cm (12 in) of rayon cord
Needle
Ordinary sewing cotton
Clear craft glue
Scissors

METHOD

STEP ONE

Apply the glue along the full length of the header of the fringe. Double the cord and knot the ends together. Place the knotted end of the cord at one end of the header, with the knot protruding (Fig. 1).

STEP TWO

Using your fingers, roll up the fringe firmly and evenly, directly under the knot of the cord (Fig. 2).

STEP THREE

Turn the fringe bundle upside down. Holding it firmly by the base of the looped cord with one hand, grasp the fringe with the other hand and tug hard to pull up the head of the tassel. Holding the neck of the tassel, smooth and even out the strands (Fig. 3).

STEP FOUR

Thread the needle with the cotton, then double it over and knot the ends. Secure the yarn into the neck of the tassel with a couple of back stitches (Fig. 4). Wrap the yarn around the neck four or five times (Fig. 5). Push the needle through the tassel from the front to the back, then to the front again. Secure the yarn with a back stitch, then fasten off.

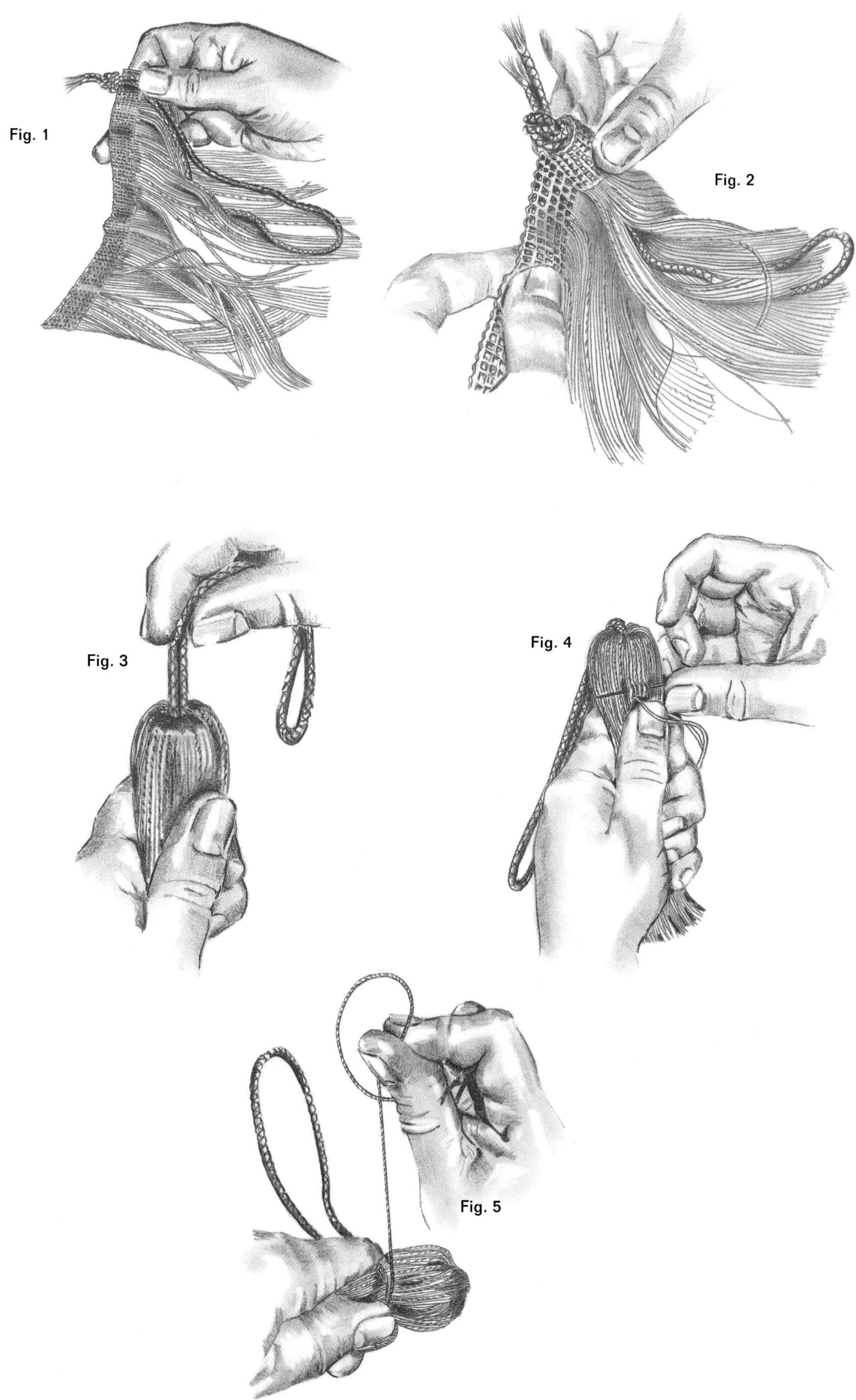
Fig. 1
Fig. 2
Fig. 3
Fig. 4
Fig. 5

BASIC CORD-MAKING

Most tassels hang from a twisted cord which is made by twisting two or more strands of yarn together. These could be strands of the same yarn or an assortment of different yarns. Try mixing wool, cotton, ribbon, cord or string for a very textural effect.

These strands are twisted, doubled and allowed to twist against themselves to form the cord.

MATERIALS

Assorted yarns
Small and large scissors
Tape measure
Pencil
Hook on a wall or some similar anchor

METHOD

STEP ONE

Choose the number of strands required, allowing for the fact that this amount will double once the cord is finished. This determines the cord thickness.

STEP TWO

Decide how long you want the finished cord to be, using this example as a guide: If you want 1 m (1 1/8 yd) of finished cord you will need a 3 m (3 3/8 yd) length of each strand.

STEP THREE

Knot all the strands together at each end. Attach one knotted end to the hook or other anchor. Push the pencil between the strands on the other knotted end.

STEP FOUR

Standing away from the anchor and keeping the yarn taut, pinch the strands of yarn against the pencil with one hand and wind the pencil with the other (Fig. 1). This will cause the yarn to twist. Keep winding the pencil until the yarn starts to firm up, then do a test in the following way:

Release the tension on the yarns momentarily by moving your hand toward the anchor. The yarns should very quickly twist (Fig. 2). If they are slow to react, pull the yarn taut again and twist a few more times, then test the twist again.

STEP FIVE

Pull the yarns taut, then remove the pencil and slip the yarns through the handle of the small scissors. With the yarns in one hand and the scissors in the other, walk towards the anchor, keeping the tension on the scissors and doubling the yarns. Once the scissors are in the centre of the cord, unhook the yarns, maintaining the tension, then let go of the scissors. The yarns will now twist against themselves (Fig. 3).

STEP SIX

Once the cord stops spinning, tie a knot at the end you are holding, then, using the other scissors, cut the other end and knot it as well (Figs 4 and 5). Trim the ends to neaten them.

Note: We have used thirty-one strands of thread in 5 m (5 1/2 yd) lengths to make the luxurious thick cord on page 20 and have wound together a combination of two lots of fringe (blue and taupe) to get this variegated effect in the skirt of the tassel.

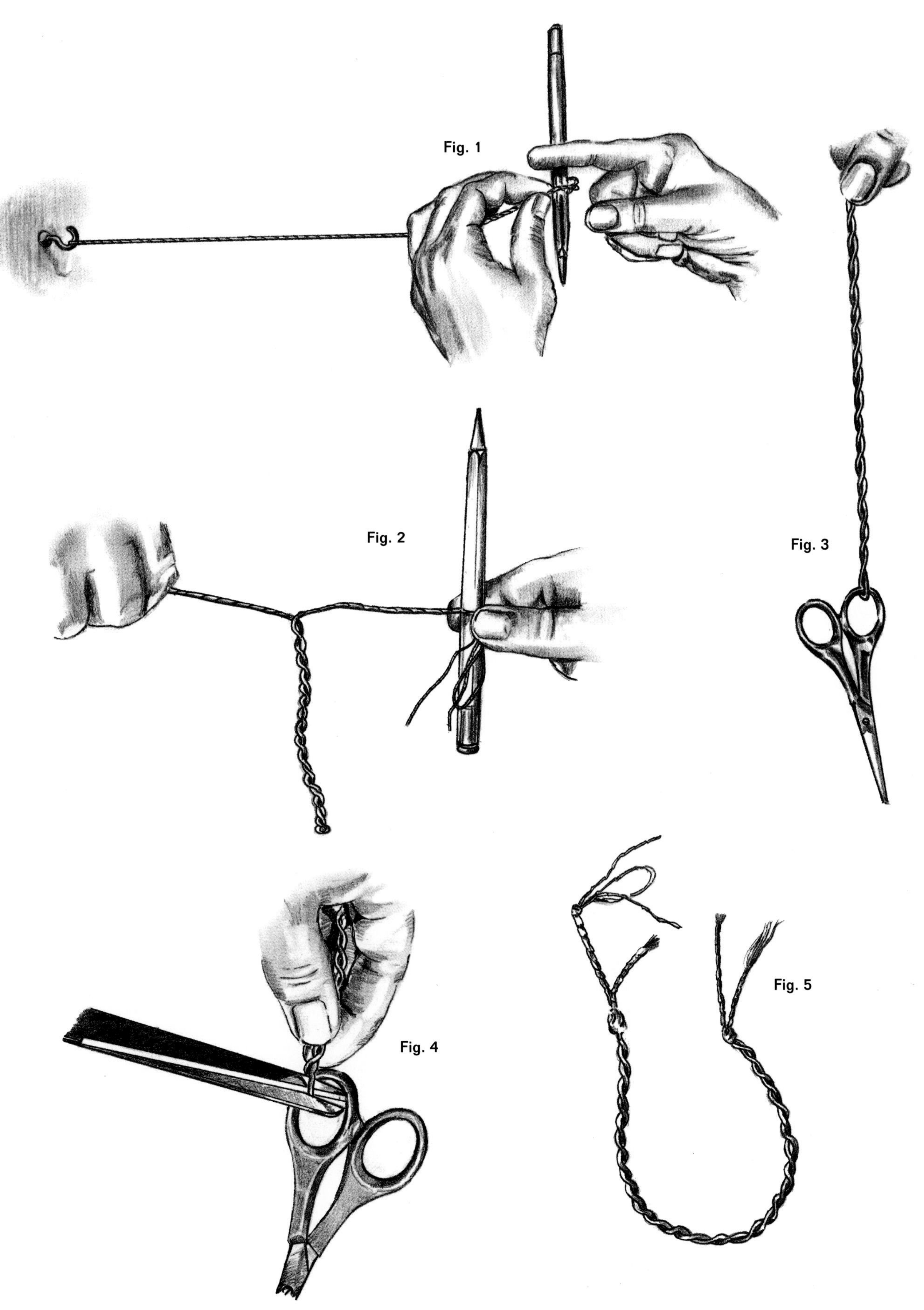
Fig. 1
Fig. 2
Fig. 3
Fig. 4
Fig. 5

Fabric from Boyac, Sydney

DYEING

Making tassels which are quite unique is a simple matter of dyeing.

You can create exciting colours to suit any mood or colour scheme with Maddie's Craft Dye. Follow these easy instructions and you will be delighted with the results.

MAKING UP DYES

You will need:

4-cup measuring jug
Maddie's Craft Dye: Red, Blue and Yellow
Tablespoon
Three empty plastic bottles
Pine O Cleen disinfectant
Rubber gloves
Stick-on labels

Empty the contents of one container of dye into the measuring jug. Add four cups of hot water from the tap. Add one tablespoon of Pine O Cleen to the jug. Stir the dye mixture, then pour it into a plastic bottle. Attach a label. Repeat the process with each colour.

Note: Adding the Pine O Cleen helps preserve the dye, if you wish to keep it for a long time.

MIXING COLOURS

You will need:

Dye
Small pieces of white cotton cloth to make colour swatches (an old sheet is suitable)
Empty margarine containers with lids for making and storing mixed colours
Large white ice cream container lids to use as palettes
Eyedropper or teaspoon
Satay stick
Paper and pen
Container of water

Using one margarine container for each colour, half-fill the container with dye. Using the eyedropper or teaspoon, place small amounts of the colours to be mixed onto the palette. For example, three teaspoons of red and one teaspoon of blue gives four teaspoons of burgundy. Mix them with the stick. Dip a piece of cloth into this mix to give you a sample of the colour. Write down the combination of colours for future reference and store it with the swatch.

Note: Make sure you wash the eye-dropper or spoon each time before changing to another colour, otherwise your recipes will not be accurate.

Experimenting with small amounts of dye in this way will give you the information you require without wasting large amounts of dye. When you are satisfied with the result, you can make larger quantities of the colour simply by exchanging your eyedropper for a tablespoon, cup or jug – the ratios will be the same: three cups of red mixed with one cup of blue makes four cups of burgundy. To make softer or paler colours, add varying amounts of water.

Experimentation is the key.

DYEING FRINGE

STEP ONE

Cut the fringe to the desired length and fold it neatly. Dip one end of the folded fringe into the dye, allowing it to soak only the area you want to colour – for example, just the tip or halfway up. Squeeze out any excess dye.

STEP TWO

Holding the dyed end of the fringe, dunk the undyed end into another colour for a two-colour effect. Twist the fringe to remove the excess dye and to allow the two colours to merge.

If you want a paler result, dip the folded fringe into water before you dip it into the dye, wring out the excess water, then dip it as described above. The water allows the colours to blend gently, creating a very soft result.

STEP THREE

Place the dyed fringe on a towel to remove any excess water. After a few minutes you can peg the fringe on a clothes airer in a warm environment, or dry it on cake racks, but keep it away from any direct heat source or sunlight. Do not blow dry it or place it in a windy location, because the fringe could become tousled and messy-looking.

CREATING PATTERN

To create an interesting pattern in your dyeing, cut a piece of fringe to the desired length, fold it in half and lay it on an old towel. Using a teaspoon or eyedropper, pour, dab or trickle patches of colour in a random fashion onto the fringe. Allow a few minutes for the dye to be absorbed, then hang up the fringe to dry.

DYEING LACES AND BRAIDS

Cut laces and braids to the desired length, then dip them in the dye. Leave them on an old towel to absorb any excess dye, then dry them on cake racks. If a lighter shade is required, wet the laces and braids first, before dunking them into the dye.

Note: Maddie's Craft Dye is not colour-fast. The colours will run if the material gets wet. Tassels are not meant to be

COLOUR RECIPES				
TO MAKE	**RED**	**BLUE**	**YELLOW**	**WATER**
Lavender	4 tsp	8 tsp		1/2 cup
Plum Pink	6 tsp	2 tsp		1/4 cup
Scottish Green		6 tsp	4 tsp	1/2 cup
Pale Blue		4 tsp		1/2 cup
Old Gold	2 tsp	2 tsp	10 tsp	1/2 cup
Taupe	4 tsp	4 tsp	4 tsp	1/2 cup
Bright Pink	4 tsp			1/4 cup
Moss Green	1 tsp	2 tsp	8 tsp	1/4 cup
Violet	4 tsp	4 tsp		1/2 cup
Teal Green		4 tsp	2 tsp	1/4 cup
Tan	5 tsp	3 tsp	10 tsp	
Rich Burgundy	4 tsp	2 tsp	2 tsp	
Apricot	2 tsp		4 tsp	1/2 cup
Salmon	4 tsp		2 tsp	1/2 cup
To make Cream, dilute two teaspoons of Old Gold mixture with half a cup of water.				

washed. However, if you wish to change the colour of your tassel or fringe, rinse it in water to remove excess colour, then dye with another colour. Because dye is transparent, it will take over the colour underneath, changing both colours. If you have dyed your tassel yellow, then dunk it into blue dye, it could turn green; a yellow tassel dipped in purple could turn brown. Generally, you cannot dye over dark colours and expect to see a difference.

You can get some surprising results if you experiment. Remember, the dyed fringe looks very much better dry than wet. Don't be discouraged if you think you've made a mistake with colour, wait for it to dry – you may be surprised. If you wish, you can soak the fringe in water, then dye again, perhaps in a darker colour.

Dyeing can add delicate shading to a tassel

PINE O CLEEN
DISINFECTANT
HOSPITAL GRADE
500mL
ALPINE FRESH
Tassel and Embroidery
100 percent Rayon
2 CUPS
500ml
1 CUP
METRIC CUPS
Maddie's
Craft Dye

THE PROJECTS

The projects on the following pages have been developed using one or more of the basic methods described on pages 8-23. Read these pages carefully and refer back to them as you work.

As the perception of colour is a very personal matter, we have not given dye recipes for individual projects. Instead, use the dye chart on page 22 to create colours that suit your home and reflect your own imagination and creativity. Finally, feel free to embellish your tassels as richly or as simply as pleases you.

We hope you find as much pleasure from your beautiful tassel creations as we did designing them for you.

Bread dough ornaments from Judith and Kathryn, Adelaide

GILDED TASSELS

Made from soft cotton yarn, stiffened with glue, these tassels are painted, then brushed with gold paint for a stunning effect. Not only can they be used on pots, such as these, the same method could be applied to an urn, vase, lamp base or statue.

MATERIALS

Terracotta pot
One ball of Patons 4-ply Gem Cotton
Large-eyed needle
Scissors
15 cm (6 in) long piece of cardboard
Aquadhere or other PVA glue
Container for glue
Sealer
Black paint
Gold paint or a gilding kit
Antiquing or French Wash (optional)

METHOD

STEP ONE

Make two basic yarn tassels, as shown on page 10.

STEP TWO

Using the Patons cotton, make a plaited cord to place around the top of the pot.

STEP THREE

Pour the Aquadhere or other PVA glue into the container. Immerse the tassels and the cord in the glue, removing any excess glue by squeezing it back into the container. The tassels and cord should be covered evenly with glue, but not have glue running from them.

STEP FOUR

While the tassels and cord are still saturated with glue, attach them to the pot, arranging them in a pleasing way. Allow them to dry out thoroughly, then seal the entire surface of the pot, tassels and cord with the sealer. When the tassels dry, they will be solid.

STEP FIVE

Paint the pot, the tassels and the cord with the Black paint and brush them with the Gold paint when they are dry. If you are using a gilding kit, gild the tassels for a richer effect. Antiquing or French wash can then be added after gilding, if you wish.

Note: The second pot pictured is decorated with a cotton mop yarn, tied into knots to form the head of the tassel. The cord is simply twisted or plaited and it is then treated in exactly the same way as the other pot.

VICTORIAN LADY

This is an elegant tassel which can be purely decorative, hung on a special display cabinet, holding back delicate lace curtains or securing a special key.

MATERIALS

Porcelain figurine
Maddie's Craft Dyes in your chosen colours (see below)
80 cm (32 in) of 150 mm (6 in) wide fringe
Assorted laces and braids
80 cm (32 in) of purchased cord
Craft glue
1/4" square shader brush
Liner brush
Soft cloth
Acrylic paints in colours to suit your chosen colour scheme (see suggested colour schemes below)
FolkArt Peach Perfection
Matisse Professional Artists Acrylic Colours, Burnt Sienna
Acrylic sealer, matte
Antiquing Medium, FolkArt Wooden Bucket or Jo Sonja's Retarder and Antiquing Medium (optional)
Gold metal filigree toggles (optional)

SUGGESTED COLOUR SCHEMES

Pink and green fringe – paint the bodice in Matisse Antique Green, the bodice trim in Jo Sonja's Rose Pink, the hair in a combination of FolkArt Tapioca and Matisse Raw Sienna

Peach and green fringe – paint the bodice in Matisse Antique Green, the bodice trim in FolkArt Peach Perfection, the hair in a combination of FolkArt Tapioca and Matisse Raw Sienna

Burgundy and teal fringe – paint the bodice in Jo Sonja's Burgundy, the bodice trim in Matisse Antique Green, the hair in Burnt Sienna

Blue and copper fringe – paint the bodice in Jo Sonja's Paynes Grey, the bodice trim in Matisse Copper, the hair in Matisse Black

Similar paint colours to those listed are available in other acrylic paint brands.

PAINTING

STEP ONE

To paint the body of the porcelain figurine, first outline the edges of the bodice and hair with your choice of colour using the liner brush, then block in the colour with the flat brush. Make sure the paint application is even – two coats of paint may be necessary. Paint in the bodice trim with a contrasting colour, using the liner brush.

STEP TWO

As the porcelain is pink, it is not necessary to paint the flesh colour onto the face of the figurine. To create a soft shadow around the hairline, the base of the arms and the chest area, paint with a combination of Burnt Sienna and FolkArt Peach Perfection.

Paint in the cheeks with Peach Perfection. Detail the eye, eyeline and eyebrows with the liner brush, using the hair colour. Paint the lips pink or peach using the liner brush.

STEP THREE

Allow the figurine to dry, then seal with the clear sealer.

STEP FOUR

If desired, antique with the Antiquing Medium (FolkArt Wooden Bucket) or by adding Jo Sonja's Retarder and Antiquing Medium to Burnt Sienna paint. When the sealer has completely dried, apply the antiquing medium to the entire surface of the figurine with the shader brush. Immediately wipe back the medium with the soft cloth, removing it from the high and flat areas. The antiquing medium will be left in all the grooves, giving your figurine an aged look. Allow it to dry thoroughly before proceeding.

TASSEL

STEP ONE

Dye the fringe, laces and braid to complement your colour scheme.

STEP TWO

Using the craft glue, roll and glue approximately 50 cm (20 in) of the fringe. Insert this part of the fringe firmly into the base of the figurine.

STEP THREE

Apply glue to the hip area of the figurine. Continue to roll the fringe around the hips, gluing as you go.

STEP FOUR

Apply glue to the pieces of lace and braid, then attach them around the hips, pulling firmly. Bring the braid down slightly at the back to form a V to ensure a snug fit, and to create a bustle.

STEP FIVE

Loop the handle cord through the arms of the figurine, then tie it in a knot at the length required. The ends of the cord can be fringed or neatened with gold metal filigree toggles.

ROMANTIC TASSEL

This tassel would be a beautiful accessory for a bride to carry with her bouquet or to embellish a delicate lingerie bag. Almost natural in colour, only the ends of the fringe and some of the lace have been dipped in a pale taupe colour.

MATERIALS

Small wooden form with a knob
85 cm (34 in) of 150 mm (6 in) wide rayon fringe
Clear craft glue
Elastic band
30 cm (12 in) of purchased rayon cord
Sufficient rayon yarn to make a 150 cm (60 in) 10-strand handmade cord
Satay stick
Sewing needle
Ordinary sewing cotton
Scissors
Sticky tape
Assorted laces and braids
Flower motif for top of tassel
Maddie's Craft Dyes in the colours of your choice

PREPARATION

Dye the fringe, laces and braid, following the instructions on pages 21-23.

METHOD

STEP ONE

Make a ten-strand cord, using five strands of rayon yarn and following the directions for cord-making on page 18.

STEP TWO

Hold the wooden form upside down and apply glue to the entire spindle. Wind the fringe onto the spindle, dabbing with glue as you go, until all the fringe is glued in place.

STEP THREE

Hold the tassel right way up. Smooth down the inverted fringe and secure it with the elastic band at the waist.

STEP FOUR

Apply glue to the lower portion of the form and wrap it with the handmade cord, finishing under the collar. Dab a little glue on each end of the cord to stop the ends unravelling.

CURLY TOP

STEP ONE

Tape one end of the remainder of the handmade cord to the end of the satay stick, then wrap the stick with the cord until it is fully wound and all the cord is used. Put a little tape at the end to prevent it unravelling.

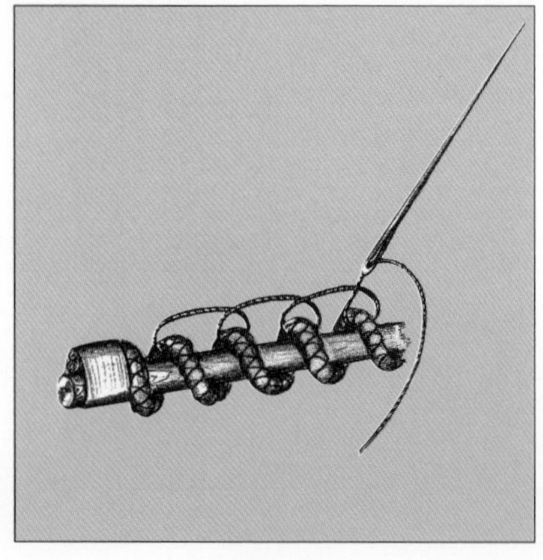

Fig. 1

STEP TWO

With the sewing needle and cotton, sew each coil firmly to the other with an over stitch (Fig.1).

STEP THREE

Remove the tape and the stitched coil from the stick. Don't worry if it looks a bit scraggly.

STEP FOUR

Apply glue all over the knobby head of the wooden form. Wrap the stitched coil around the head, starting on the collar and covering the knob to create the curly top. Leave a small space at the very top near the hole.

MAKING UP

Cut a small hole in the centre of the flower motif, then glue it onto the top of the wooden form. Attach the hanging cord as shown for the basic wooden form tassel on page 14.

Prayer book from Louella Kerr and Lorraine Reed, Sydney

RECLINING TASSEL

This tassel is simply achieved, using an ordinary household mop and some rope. It is ideal for tying back casual curtains or to enhance a cane chair, hammock or deck chair.

MATERIALS

Basic floor mop
1 m ($1^1/_8$ yd) of rope
1 m ($1^1/_8$ yd) of sash cord
Hot glue gun

METHOD

STEP ONE

Cut enough rope to surround the base of the head of the tassel twice; the remaining length is used to create the hanger.

STEP TWO

Coat the inside edge and the bottom of the plastic end of the mop with hot glue and insert both ends of the rope. This length can be adjusted, depending on the use for the tassel.

STEP THREE

Using the hot glue gun, apply glue around the surface of the head of the mop. Starting from the bottom of the header, press the sash cord into the glue, winding it as you go. When you reach the top of the header, force the end of the cord into the hole for the handle.

STEP FOUR

Add the remaining rope around the bottom of the sash cord ensuring that the ends meet and intertwine so there are no rough edges showing.

STEP FIVE

Add additional interest to the tassel by tying knots in the cotton fibre around the top of the tassel.

Hammock from Australis Partners, Mittagong NSW; Cushions from Freedom Furniture, Sydney

TASSEL WITH A VIEW

This classical tassel was designed as a curtain tie-back but it is very versatile. Try hanging it from a standard lamp or as a bell pull.

MATERIALS

Bell-shaped wooden form
Two 85 cm (34 in) lengths of 150 mm (6 in) wide rayon fringe
Maddie's Craft Dyes in the colours of your choice
2 m ($2^{1}/_{4}$ yd) of purchased rayon cord
Satay stick
Elastic band
Clear craft glue
Assorted laces and braids
Beads (optional)
Scissors

PREPARATION

Dye the fringe, laces and braid, following the general instructions on pages 21-23.

METHOD

STEP ONE

Wind one piece of fringe on the spindle, gluing as you go. See the instructions for the basic wooden form tassel on page 14.

STEP TWO

Secure the bottom of the fringe with the elastic band to stop it from moving about and allowing you to complete the next step.

STEP THREE

Holding the tassel upside down, glue the end of the header of the second piece of fringe immediately below the header of the first piece. Wrap the fringe, dabbing with glue, until the fringe is fully wound and secure.

STEP FOUR

Turn the tassel over, holding it the right way up. Remove the elastic band. Smooth down the fringe, then secure it again with the elastic band. Decorate with the laces and braids to cover the elastic band.

STEP FIVE

Cover the wooden form with the cord and attach the hanging cord as shown for the basic wooden form tassel on page 14.

Candlestick from Mosman Antique Centre, Mosman

SPIRAL TASSEL

This rather bold little tassel has been wrapped with alternating bands of two colours of gold cord. The fringe has been dyed red, then dipped in burgundy for a truly dramatic effect. It is ideal for looping onto the key of a desk or an elegant box.

MATERIALS

1 m ($1\frac{1}{8}$ yd) of 75 mm (3 in) wide rayon fringe
Maddie's Craft Dyes in the colours of your choice
Clear craft glue
40 cm (16 in) of purchased rayon cord
Assorted laces and braids
Sewing needle
Ordinary sewing cotton
Selection of silk roses, motifs, cord, old jewellery, buttons, bows, beads (optional), gold cord

PREPARATION

Dye the fringe, laces and braid, following the general instructions on pages 21-23.

METHOD

STEP ONE

Fold the rayon cord in half and glue or stitch the ends together.

STEP TWO

Commence gluing the fringe, starting about 3 cm ($1\frac{1}{4}$ in) up from the bottom of the cord. Wind the fringe in place with three turns, then begin to wrap, gradually spiralling downwards and gluing as you go. Don't glue more than about 8 cm (3 in) at a time or you may get into a mess. Take it slowly.

STEP THREE

When you get to the last 50 cm (20 in) of the fringe, stop spiralling, but continue to wrap the fringe around until it is used up.

STEP FOUR

Embellish the fringe, using scraps of laces or braids, wrapped and glued into place. You could add silk roses or motifs, some wound cord, pieces of old jewellery, an odd earring, buttons, bows or beads. Be creative.

Découpage box by Nerida Singleton; Candlestick from Mosman Antique Centre, Mosman

POETS' PANSY

This pansy-painted tassel was inspired by some of the wonderful verse written about this charming flower. It could find a place in a den or library, surrounded by beautiful books, or even as an old-fashioned light pull.

MATERIALS

Large wooden form, made from a curtain rod finial
One ball of 8-ply Panda Carnival Courtelle, Colour 10 yarn
Needle
Acrylic paints
Sealer
Cardboard
Scissors
Clear craft glue
Purchased tassel braid
Gilding kit or Gold paint (optional)
Black paint (optional)
Masking tape or sticky tape
½" flat brush
Liner brush, size 0

PREPARATION

Drill a hole through the centre of the finial, then seal it with the sealer.

PAINTING

See the painting design on page 40. Base paint the form. Paint the design onto the wooden form, using your own colour scheme. Seal the piece again. If you wish, you can gild the bottom section of the finial or paint it with Gold paint, then antique it with Black paint.
Note: Full instructions for painting pansies and other flowers are in Julie Neilson-Kelly's first book in the same series, *Creative Inspirations in Paint.*

TASSEL

STEP ONE

Using the yarn, make four basic tassels using two hundred winds for each tassel, as shown for the basic yarn tassel on page 10.

STEP TWO

Loop a handle made from four lengths of yarn through each tassel. The length will depend on how long you require the completed handle to be. Tape the ends of the group of handles together with the masking tape or sticky tape and pull them through the hole in the finial. Tie a knot in the end close to the finial so that the cords cannot slip back. The strands of the handle are now hanging freely through the end of the wooden form.

STEP THREE

Make a twisted cord for the handle by dividing the yarn strands into two sections. Twist one group of strands until it is firm enough to pull back on itself. Hold it securely in one hand, then twist the other strands in the same direction. Hold the ends of both cords together and tie a knot. Slowly release the cords up the length of the wool. They will twist together as you release, forming a thick cord. This method can be used as an alternative to the basic cord-making described on page 18. It is ideal for a situation like this where you cannot double back the yarn to form a thick cord.

STEP FOUR

Using the craft glue, attach the tassel braid around the edge of the finial.

The head of the tassel, painted with pansies

LITERARY TASSELS

Tassels have long been used to decorate bookmarks. Beautiful as well as practical, a tasselled bookmark makes a superb gift for the person who has everything.

LACE BOOKMARK

MATERIALS

20 cm (8 in) of lace or braid, approximately 2.5 cm (1 in) wide
Acrylic paint, Gold
Maddie's Craft Dyes in the colours of your choice
Fabric stiffener or PVA glue
Clear craft glue
Metal bell cap or brass book corner
Small pair of pliers
8 cm ($3^1/_8$ in) of 75 mm (3 in) wide fringe
Plastic bag
Soft paintbrush
Two gold motifs or buttons

PREPARATION

Dye the fringe, laces and braids, following the general instructions on pages 21-23.

METHOD

STEP ONE

Neaten both ends of the lace or braid, forming a point at one end. Stitch or glue the ends to secure.

STEP TWO

Mix some Gold paint with a little fabric stiffener or PVA glue and apply the mixture to both sides of the lace or braid with a stippling, dabbing movement. Allow it to dry on the plastic bag.

STEP THREE

When the paint is dry, dab a little glue on the pointed end of the lace and fit the bell cap or brass corner over the glued area, then pinch the cap or corner together, using the pliers.

STEP FOUR

Apply glue to both sides of the lower end of the lace or braid. Wrap the fringe around the glued lace or braid, dabbing with the glue as you wrap. Attach the gold motifs or buttons, one on each side.

TWISTED CORD BOOKMARK

MATERIALS

Three 30 cm (12 in) pieces of purchased rayon cord in three different colours
Three jewellery bell caps, all different or all the same
Small pair of pliers
Three beads
Clear craft glue
Needle
Ordinary sewing cotton
Maddies 100% Rayon Yarn
7.5 cm (3 in) of cardboard
Maddie's Craft Dyes in the colours of your choice

PREPARATION

Dye the fringe, laces and braids, following the general instructions on pages 21-23.

METHOD

STEP ONE

Lay the three pieces of cord alongside each other. Dab glue on top of each of the cords at one end, then roll all three cords between your fingers so that the ends stick together.

STEP TWO

On one end, dab a little more glue on the top of the joined cords, then push the bell cap on, pinching firmly with the pliers.

STEP THREE

Plait the cords together and sew firmly at the end to secure. Using a length of doubled sewing cotton, string a bell cap, three beads, another bell cap, then fasten off (Fig. 1).

STEP FOUR

Wind the rayon yarn around the cardboard eighty times. Complete the tassel, following the instructions for the yarn tassel on page 10.

STEP FIVE

Dab a little glue into the first bell cap. Push the plaited cords into it, using the pliers to pinch the bell cap around the cords. Dab a little glue into the last bell cap, push the end of the small tassel into it, then pinch with pliers.

THE SECOND FLEET.
THE SECOND FLEET.
69
1793
Payment by results.
Effect of the new regulations.
Case of the Queen, transport.
Defrauding convicts of their food.

ILLUMINATED TASSEL

Tassels are often associated with lamps and lampshades. Slender tassels with beaded tops have been added to this silk shade for an air of opulence.

MATERIALS

Suitable lampshade
12 cm (5 in) of 150 mm (6 in) wide fringe for each tassel
Maddie's Craft Dyes in the colours of your choice
Ordinary sewing cotton
Needle
Clear craft glue
Scissors
Assorted beads, three medium and one small bead for each tassel
Assorted narrow laces or braids

Note: Make the appropriate number of tassels for the lampshade you have chosen – one for each peak.

PREPARATION

Dye the fringe, laces and braids, following the general instructions on pages 21-23.

METHOD

STEP ONE

Apply glue along the full length of the fringe header, then roll up the fringe tightly and evenly.

STEP TWO

Turn the fringe roll upside down. Take hold of the fringe around the neck, smoothing and evening out the strands on the head. Using the needle, secure a thread into the neck of the tassel, wrap it around the neck three or four times, then fasten off.

STEP THREE

Glue lace or braid around the neck to cover the thread.

STEP FOUR

Repeat steps one to three for the other tassels. Now, you are ready to attach the tassels to the lampshade.

MAKING UP

STEP ONE

Thread the needle, double the cotton and knot the ends. Push the needle up under the lace or braid trim until it comes up through the top of the tassel. Secure the thread with a couple of small neat stitches on top of the tassel.

STEP TWO

Pick up three medium beads and one small bead on the needle, then sew the tassel to the lampshade with the same cotton.

CELESTIAL TASSEL

The angel figurine makes an ideal centrepiece for a table, especially for celebrations. It would look equally beautiful on a mantelpiece, enhanced with long slender beeswax candles.

MATERIALS

Wooden form
Acrylic paint: Black, Gold
Porcelain angel figurine with a hollow bottom
80 cm (32 in) of 150 mm (6 in) wide fringe
30 cm (12 in) of 75 mm (3 in) wide fringe
Cold water dye, Black (optional)
Maddie's Craft Dye: Red, Blue, Yellow
Thick black-and-gold twisted cord
Thin gold cord
Black beads, various shapes and sizes
Needle
Ordinary sewing cotton
Clear craft glue
Black iron candelabra
Beeswax candles
Hot glue gun

Allow the skirt of tassel to fan out elegantly

PREPARATION

STEP ONE

Remove the knob of the wooden form to allow you to insert the tassel into the hollow base of the porcelain figurine.

STEP TWO

Dye the fringe Gold and Black, following the instructions on page 21. Use the dyeing colour chart on page 22 to mix the Old Gold, however it will be necessary to purchase a Black cold water dye as black cannot be mixed.

TASSEL

STEP ONE

Make a basic tassel over the wooden form, using the dyed fringe, following the instructions for the basic wooden form tassel on page 14.

STEP TWO

Thread the black beads and arrange them around the tassels in loops. It is effective to have a large or unusually shaped bead at the lowest point of the loop.

MAKING UP

STEP ONE

Paint the figurine Black, then brush over it with the Old Gold. Using the hot glue gun, insert the completed tassel into the hollow figurine.

STEP TWO

Wind the thick cord around the base of the figurine and down onto the top of the wooden form to make a nice neat edge. Finish the join neatly.

STEP THREE

Using the thin gold cord, make a handle by pulling the cord under the wings of the figurine and tying them behind her back. Extend the cord over and through the iron candelabra to hold the figurine in place. When positioning the angel, consider the length of the skirt so it can drape down onto the table and fan out. Tie a knot in the cord. You can secure the cord more firmly by adding some hot glue.

GOURMET TASSELS

These tassels have a country feel and are ideal for decorating bottles of homemade vinegar, jars of preserves, jams or sauces. Decorated with a sprig of the appropriate herb, they make welcome gifts or you can use them to enhance your own kitchen. We have included a simple recipe for herb vinegar – so enjoy!

MATERIALS

Raffia
Dried lavender or dried herbs
White wine vinegar
Clear craft glue
Scissors
Hot glue gun
Decorative clear glass bottle with a cork

VINEGAR

Place the lavender flowers and leaves or fresh herbs to taste in the decorative glass bottle. Boil some white wine vinegar and, while it is still hot, pour it over the lavender or herbs. Allow the vinegar to cool, then seal the bottle with the cork. It is important that the bottle is airtight. Allow the vinegar to sit for several weeks to develop flavour before using it.

LARGE KNOT TASSEL

STEP ONE

Make a plaited raffia strip long enough to loop around the neck of the bottle.

STEP TWO

Tie a knot in the middle of a bundle of raffia, but before pulling the knot tight, loop one end of the raffia through the knot again, as if tying a non-slip knot. Thread the handle of plaited raffia through the knot (head of the tassel) and pull firmly.

STEP THREE

Tie a band of raffia around the neck of the tassel, securing it at the back. Trim the tassel to the desired length. Decorate with heads of dried lavender and bunches of dried herbs.

STEP FOUR

Form a small wreath with the plaited handle which has been threaded through the knot, big enough to slide over the neck of the bottle. Wind it back on itself, until it is worked back to the head of the tassel, then using the hot glue gun, glue the raw edges down behind the head of the tassel.

STEP FIVE

Slide the circle of plaited raffia over the neck of the bottle. Position the tassel, then hold it in place, using a small dob of hot glue. Apply the glue to the back of the tassel, then press it onto the bottle.

LARGE BRAIDED TASSEL

For the large braided tassel, make a plait of raffia and leave long loose ends to make the tassel fringe. Loop the plait around in a small wreath shape and wind it back on itself. Use a thinner plait of raffia to wrap around it, creating the neck of the tassel. Decorate it with sprigs of herbs. Slide the wreath over the neck of the bottle and secure it in place, using the hot glue gun.

HERE'S-MY-HEART TASSEL

For the truly romantic, this tassel is the finishing touch for this heart-shaped cushion which features a hand-painted design of roses. The fringe for this tassel is available commercially, but a special tassel seems appropriate for such a special cushion.

MATERIALS

50 cm (20 in) square of cream silk for the cushion front
Two pieces of calico, each 25 cm x 40 cm (10 in x 16 in) for the cushion back
80 cm (32 in) of calico for the cushion insert
Polyester fibre fill
28 cm (11 in) cream zipper
Ordinary sewing cotton, Cream
Acrylic paints in the appropriate colours
Textile medium
$^1/_2$ " flat paintbrush
Liner brush, size 0
Pencil
Embroidery hoop
Assorted embroidery threads, including stranded cotton, silk ribbon and wool, in colours to complement the painting
Embroidery needles
1.2 m ($1^1/_3$ yd) of 4 cm ($1^1/_2$ in) wide purchased cotton fringe
One ball of Patons 4-ply Gem Cotton
7.5 cm (3 in) wide piece of cardboard
Needle with a large eye
Scissors

CUSHION

See the painting design on page 53.

STEP ONE

Using the pencil, draw the heart shape onto the cream silk. You may find this easier to do if you first make a paper pattern to follow.

STEP TWO

Mix the acrylic paints with the textile medium, following the manufacturer's instructions. Paint the rose design into the centre of the heart. Fix the paint by heat-setting with an iron on the back of the painting. If you are not confident with the painting, Julie Neilson-Kelly's first book *Creative Inspirations in Paint*, published by J.B. Fairfax Press 1995 may help you.

STEP THREE

Secure the square of silk in the embroidery hoop. Embroider the heart shaped garland of flowers around the painted centre. Use a variety of stitches (including bullion roses, wool roses, French knots, lazy daisy stitch and stem stitch) and yarns to create the garland. Finally, satin stitch the bow at the point of the garland.

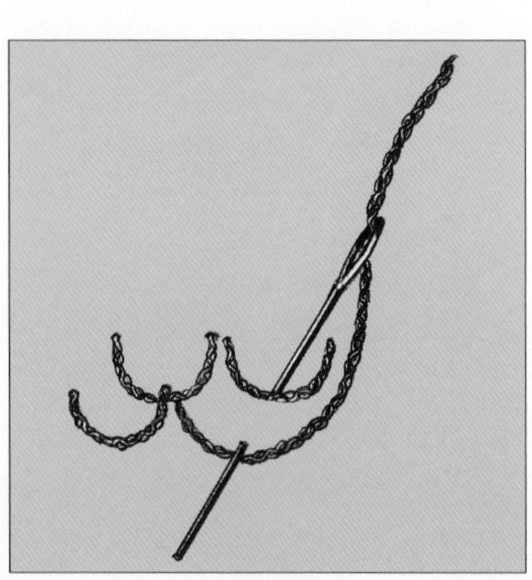

Fig. 1

STEP FOUR

Remove the fabric from the hoop and cut out the heart, 1 cm ($^3/_8$ in) outside the pencil line. Stitch the purchased fringe around the right side of the heart, on the pencil line, beginning and ending at the point of the heart.

STEP FIVE

Place the two pieces of fabric for the cushion back together with the right sides facing. Join them along one 40 cm (16 in) side, leaving an opening in the centre for the zipper. Sew the zipper into place.

STEP SIX

Using the same heart pattern as for the front, cut out the cushion back, taking care to centre the zipper.

TASSEL

STEP ONE

Wind the cotton yarn around the cardboard two hundred times. Construct the tassel as for the basic yarn tassel on page 10.

STEP TWO

Make a twisted cord using twelve strands of cotton yarn following the instructions on page 18. Attach it to the top of the tassel.

STEP THREE

Thread a strand of the cotton yarn through the needle and double it over. Bring the needle up through the head of the tassel to the top, near the handle.

STEP FOUR

Work Y stitches (Fig. 1) around and around the head of the tassel, catching the previous line of stitches as you work. Cover the whole head of the tassel, creating a textural effect.

STEP FIVE

Knot twelve strands of yarn at each end. Work along the length of the yarn tying knots as close together as possible. Trim the ends. Twist the knotted yarn back on itself as you take it around the neck of the tassel and form a loop. Feed the ends through and neaten them off. Secure the cord in place with several stitches around the knotted trim.

STEP SIX

Attach the tassel into the cotton fringe at the peak of the cushion.

MAKING UP

STEP ONE

Open the zipper. Place the cushion front and back together with the right sides facing. Stitch around the outside edge, taking care not to catch the fringe or the tassel into the seam. Turn the cushion cover through to the right side through the zipper opening.

STEP TWO

From the calico, cut out two heart shapes, using the same pattern as before. Place the two hearts together and stitch around the outside edge, leaving a small opening for turning. Turn through to the right side. Stuff lightly with the fibre fill, then slipstitch the opening closed. Place the insert inside the completed cushion cover.

Embroider a garland of roses to complement the painting

Painting Design

TASSELLED FOR COMFORT

Plump little tassels nestle into the curves of this little footstool. They would look equally charming on a desk key or suspended from a decanter.

MATERIALS

Footstool, purchased or hand-made (see below)
Small wooden form with a knob
Paint or dye
50 cm (20 in) of 75 mm (3 in) wide rayon fringe
Maddie's Craft Dyes in the colours of your choice
15 cm (6 in) cord for a hanger
Clear craft glue
Assorted braids and laces
Ordinary sewing cotton

Note: These quantities are for making one tassel. The number of tassels you need will depend on the design of your footstool.

PREPARATION

Dye the fringe and lace, following the general instructions on pages 21-23.

TASSELS

STEP ONE

Paint or dye the knob on the end of the wooden form. Allow it to dry.

STEP TWO

Apply glue to the spindle on the wooden form and wind the fringe onto the spindle, dabbing with glue as you go, until 30 cm (12 in) of fringe remains, then continue to glue the next section of the form, under the collar.

STEP THREE

Take the fringe up to this section, creeping up gradually until all the fringe is used and the fringe sits under the collar.

STEP FOUR

Glue the laces and braids over the collar. Add the cord to the top for a hanger as shown on page 14.

STEP FIVE

Form a loop at the top of the cord and stitch the tassel to the footstool, using the matching sewing cotton.

FOOTSTOOL

This footstool has been made, using a quite ingenious method. A plywood base and top are cut to the shape of six empty Milo or 1 litre ($1^{3}/_{4}$ pt) paint tins arranged in a flower shape. The tins are securely taped together, then they are covered with wadding. A strip of fabric is wrapped around the wadding with the raw edges turned under. The fabric is glued to the top and bottom of the tins. Stubby feet are screwed into the base, before it is glued into place. The plywood top is padded with wadding before a fabric cover is added with the edges glued to the underside of the plywood. The top is then glued to the tins. Trim the upper and lower edges with rayon cord and you have a Victorian footstool, ready for the tassels.

The small tassels nestle in the curves of the footstool

Lamp from Mosman Antique Centre, Mosman

THE HUNTER'S DEN

You can set the scene for this very masculine tassel, coordinating dramatic colours and textures. This wonderfully creative tassel can lead you on a journey of imagination.

MATERIALS

Note: These quantities will make one tassel.

Large wooden form
Small square of leopard skin fabric (faux)
1 m (1 1/8 yd) of 150 mm (6 in) wide fringe
Maddie's Craft Dyes in the colours of your choice
Purchased braid
Purchased cord
Cardboard for the template
Clear craft glue
Tracing paper
Pencil

METHOD

STEP ONE

Dye the fringe, cord and braid to an appropriate colour to match the fabric (see pages 21-23 for dyeing instructions).

STEP TWO

Trace the patterns below. Stick them to the cardboard, then cut them out. You will have a circle for the top, an open circle for the base of the form (determined by measurement) and a strip for the raised area around the middle of the form.

Note: If you need to adapt the patterns to suit your wooden form, measure the diameter of the base of the form and the length and the size of the top. Make a paper pattern and cut trial pieces from calico to ensure that they fit snugly around the form.

STEP THREE

Using the patterns, cut the pieces from the fabric. Apply glue to the surface of the wooden form. Firmly press the fabric pieces into place. The strip is applied last as it also neatens the joins of the other pieces. Be very careful not to allow the glue to catch on the 'fur' side of the fabric and make sure the joins are neat.

STEP FOUR

Attach the fringe by winding and gluing as you go. Finally, glue the braid in place, covering the header of the fringe and capping the edge, covering the join between the fringe and the fabric.

STEP FIVE

Insert the cord for the hanger into the top of the wooden form as shown for the basic wooden form tassel on page 14.

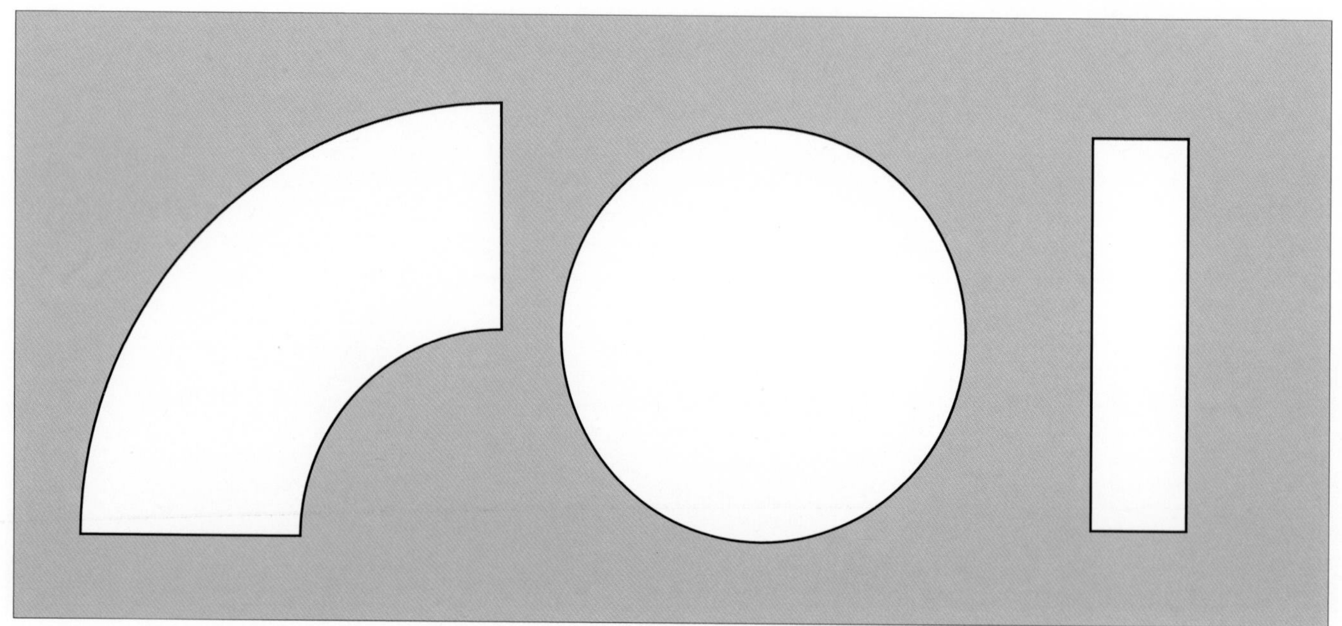

Wooden bowl and Shuva mats from Inyaka, Sydney; Fabric from Boyac Decorative Furnishings, Sydney

LADY DAVENPORT

This is a multi-tassel, which is to say that it consists of many small tassels grouped together to make a single tassel. The finished item is quite small and is ideal to hang on the key of a fine piece of furniture, jewel box or china cabinet.

MATERIALS

- Small wooden form with a hole right through the centre
- Rayon yarn
- Maddie's Craft Dyes in your chosen colours
- Gold paint
- Paintbrush
- Gold dimension paint
- Purchased ruffed braid
- Gold cord
- Sticky tape
- Needle
- Clear craft glue
- 7.5 cm (3 in) of cardboard
- Scissors

METHOD

STEP ONE

Dye the rayon yarn, following the general directions for dyeing on pages 21-23.

STEP TWO

Make ten yarn tassels, each wound eighty times, as shown for the basic yarn tassel on page 10.

STEP THREE

Thread several strands of yarn individually through the top of each tassel. The yarn should be long enough to feed through the wooden form and be wound together to make the hanging cord. Tape the ends of all of the cords together and thread them through the hole in the wooden form.

STEP FOUR

Pull the cords firmly until the bunch of ten tassels fits snugly into the base of the wooden form, then firmly tie the cords together at the top of the wooden form. The knot should be big enough to act as a stop, keeping the tassels in place and creating a small crown on the top of the form. The remaining lengths of cord can then be wound or plaited together to form the hanger.

STEP FIVE

Paint the wooden form with the Gold paint. Allow it to dry, then glue on the ruff and the gold cord around the edges.

STEP SIX

Using the dimension paint, create a weblike surface by forcing out the dimension paint over the wooden form, extending the design down over the top of the corded area.

Dimension paint adds interest to the head of the tassel

1853
1864
OF
ENGLAND
MACAULAY
VOL. II.
1789—1794.
INK

ON THE FRINGE OF LIBERTY

We have used a Liberty linen to create this tassel, which is fringed directly from the linen itself. Depending on whether you fringe the warp or weft threads, the effect of the design on the fringe will vary. Experiment with a small piece of fabric to determine which you prefer.

MATERIALS

1 m ($1^1/_8$ yd) of 115 cm (45 in) wide Liberty print tapestry fabric for the bolster and tassels (less, if you are using 150 cm (60 in) wide fabric)
2 m ($2^1/_4$ yd) of purchased or self-bias strip for the piping
2 m ($2^1/_4$ yd) of narrow piping cord
30 cm (12 in) zipper
Matching sewing thread
Clear craft glue
Scissors
Cord

BOLSTER

STEP ONE

Cut a 75 cm ($29^1/_2$ in) square of fabric and two pieces 14 cm x 75 cm ($5^1/_2$ in x $29^1/_2$ in) for the ends.

STEP TWO

Make the piping by stitching the piping cord inside the bias binding, using the zipper foot on your sewing machine. Stitch the piping to the right side of two opposite sides of the fabric square.

STEP THREE

Fold the fabric square in half with the right sides together with the piping at the ends. Sew the seams, leaving an opening in the centre for the zipper. Sew the zipper into place.

STEP FOUR

Gather one long side of each end piece. Stitch the ungathered side to the body of the bolster, with the right sides together, stitching in the piping stitching line.

TASSELS

STEP ONE

Cut two strips of fabric each approximately 20 cm x 60 cm (8 in x 24 in). Fringe the two long sides of the fabric. Make two tassels, following the instructions for the basic cloth tassel on page 8. As you roll the fringe, spiral the top edge downwards as you go.

STEP TWO

Pull up the gathering on the ends of the bolster and secure it. Insert the cord into the centre of each end of the bolster and stitch it in place to secure it.

Sheets by Actil, available nationally

DRAPED BY DESIGN

This tassel is useful if you want to extend the use of fabric you've chosen for curtains, pelmets, canopies or to hold back a net feature over a bed. We have used Dupion silk, but any fabric, either matching or complementary to your decor is suitable.

MATERIALS

25 cm (10 in) of 115 cm (45 in) wide Dupion silk
Scissors
Needle
Ordinary sewing cotton
Craft glue or hot glue gun
Cord for the handle
25 cm (10 in) of 75 mm (3 in) wide rayon fringe
Maddie's Craft Dyes in the colours of your choice

METHOD

STEP ONE

Dye the fringe to match the fabric, following the general instructions for dyeing on pages 21-23.

STEP TWO

Cut a piece across the full width of the fabric, following figure 1. Fold the fabric over double, lengthwise (Fig. 2).

STEP THREE

Keeping the raw edges together, slightly gather the piece along the length.

STEP FOUR

Start to roll the fabric into a cone shape, folding over the raw edges as you go. Continue to roll until only about 5 cm (2 in) of fabric remains. Secure the roll in place by sewing.

STEP FIVE

Using the craft glue or the hot glue gun, force the raw edges of the cord into the folds of material at the top (the narrow end).

STEP SIX

Wrap the remaining unfolded piece of material around the top 5 cm (2 in) of the fabric cone to form the head of the tassel, pulling it firmly around the corded handle to make a neat top. Fold the end of the fabric inside the roll and sew it in place.

STEP SEVEN

Cut a 5 cm x 20 cm (2 in x 8 in) strip of fabric for the rose. Fold it over double, then twist it into the shape of a rose. Stitch it to the front of the tassel.

STEP EIGHT

Fold the length of fringe and secure it beneath the rose with a few stitches.

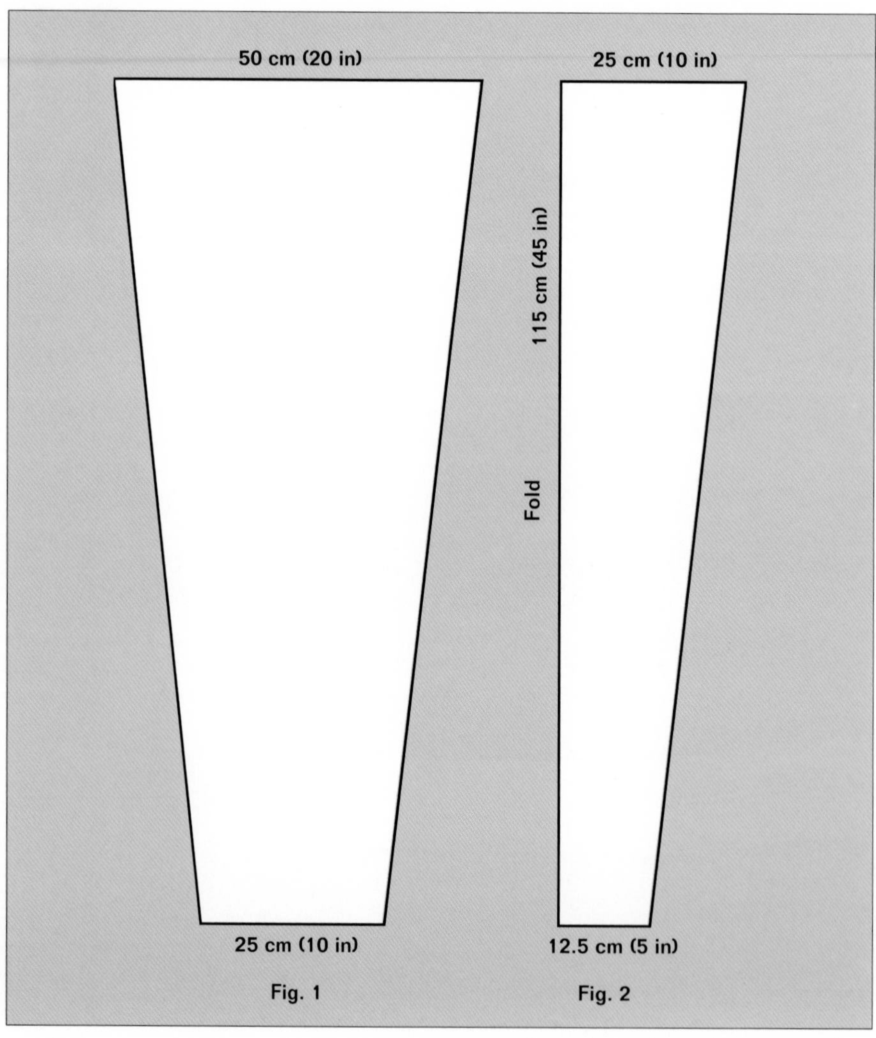

Fig. 1 Fig. 2

PLEATED TASSEL

Create this elegant tailored tassel using a piece of silk rather than fringe. The crisp fabric lends itself to concertina pleating and the charming rose is the perfect finishing touch.

MATERIALS

25 cm (10 in) of Dupion silk
Purchased cord for the handle
Needle
Ordinary sewing cotton
Clear craft glue or hot glue gun
Iron

METHOD

STEP ONE

Fold the fabric over double to be 12.5 cm (5 in) wide. Fold the fabric along its length, concertina-style, with folds approximately 4 cm ($1^1/_2$ in) apart. Press the pleats as you go. You will find that approximately 90 cm (36 in) of folded fabric will be enough to give a nice tassel shape to your fabric. When you have pleated the desired amount of fabric, catch the pleats together at the top (the raw edge) with a few stitches.

STEP TWO

Fold the cord for the handle in half and attach the ends on either side of the fabric at the top of the tassel. Secure the handle with stitching or with the hot glue gun.

STEP THREE

Fold and drape the remaining fabric around the pleated section to form the top of the tassel. Remember to pull it in close to the cord handle for a neat appearance. On this tassel, we have twisted and knotted the fabric around to form a rose and secured it in place with stitching.

ALFRESCO TASSEL

Imagine a garden urn, basket or garden chair adorned with this rustic tassel. You might replace the natural hessian and wooden beads with dyed hessian trimmed with gumnuts or shells.

MATERIALS

Large bell-shaped wooden form
30 cm x 40 cm (12 in x 16 in) of hessian
5 cm x 12 cm (2 in x 5 in) of hessian for embellishment
Clear craft glue
Satay stick
Ball of jute or twine
Four 10 mm (3/8 in) wooden beads
Assorted beads, buttons, shells, gumnuts etc for decoration
Ordinary sewing cotton (optional)

METHOD

STEP ONE

Using the jute or twine, make a 30 cm (12 in) stranded cord (see instructions for cord-making on page 18).

STEP TWO

Fray the two longest sides equally on the large piece of hessian, until there is only 4 cm (1 1/2 in) of woven material left in the centre as shown for the basic cloth tassel on page 8. Apply glue right along this centre piece, then double it over to form the fringe.

STEP THREE

Apply glue to the spindle and the underside of the form. Wind 20 cm (8 in) of the hessian fringe onto the spindle, dabbing with glue as you go.

STEP FOUR

Apply glue to the next section of the wooden form and take the rest of the hessian fringe over it, creeping up gradually until you reach the top of the section.

STEP FIVE

Apply glue to the entire top of the wooden form, then wind the jute or twine on until it is covered, except for the hole in the top.

STEP SIX

Make a twisted cord from the jute or twine and glue the centre of it into the top of the wooden form. Tie the ends into a knot.

STEP SEVEN

Make four simple tassels using the leftover frayed strands. Take a bundle of the strands and secure them in the middle with jute or twine. Fold the bundle in half and secure it around the neck with the jute or twine, as for the basic yarn tassel on page 10. Trim the tassels to an even length.

STEP EIGHT

Attach a double thread of jute or twine to the top of each tassel. Thread a wooden bead on the twine, leaving a length of twine to allow the tassel to dangle. Glue the end of the twine to the top of the hessian fringe.

STEP NINE

Fray the two longest sides of the small piece of hessian evenly until about 1.5 cm (5/8 in) of woven fabric remains in the centre. Glue this frayed strip to the top of the hessian fringe, covering the twine ends of the tassels.

STEP TEN

Stitch or glue on buttons, beads, shells, gumnuts or other suitable decorations.

ENTER THE TASSEL

When you see a tassel on a doorknob, doesn't it give you a feeling of anticipation and entice you to enter? This tassel will do just that. It is softly shaded, painted with forget-me-nots, trimmed with braid and lace scattered with pearls.

MATERIALS

Large wooden bell form
85 cm (34 in) of 150 mm (6 in) wide rayon fringe
Maddie's Craft Dyes in the colours of your choice
30 cm (12 in) of rayon lacing cord for the hanger
Assorted laces and braids
Tiny sew-on pearls
Clear craft glue
Ordinary sewing cotton
Needle
Scissors
Satay stick
Acrylic paints, including Gold
Sponge
Hair dryer
Paintbrush (optional)

PREPARATION

Dye the fringe and lace, following the general instructions on pages 21-23.

METHOD

STEP ONE

Paint the top section of the wooden form in the colour of your choice. Remember, you can mix acrylic paints to get the colours you desire. Lightly sponge on some paint, dry it with a hair dryer, then sponge again with a lighter shade. Dab on a little Gold paint or paint some simple flower shapes or patterns.

STEP TWO

Apply glue to the spindle, then attach the fringe by wrapping it onto the spindle, dabbing it with glue as you go. Continue to wrap until only 40 cm (16 in) of the fringe remains.

STEP THREE

Apply glue to the next section of the wooden form. Take the fringe up to this section, creeping gradually upwards until all the fringe is used. The fringe should reach the top of this section.

STEP FOUR

Attach the hanging cord as instructed on page 14.

TWISTED BRAID

STEP ONE

Lay the tassel in your right hand (left hand, if you are left-handed). With your left hand, pick up a bunch of approximately twenty strands of the tassel and twist them quite firmly. Pass the twisted strands into your right hand. Pick up another bunch of strands next to the first bunch and make another twist like the first one.

STEP TWO

Take both bunches in your left hand and let go of the tassel. The tassel will twirl around, creating a lovely twisted braid. Fasten the ends by wrapping them with thread. Make three twisted braids, spaced around the tassel.
Note: If your braids are not tight enough, begin again. It can sometimes be helpful to moisten your fingers.

MAKING UP

Attach the laces and braids to the tassel. Sew on the pearls as shown. Cover the wrapped ends of the braids with scraps of lace decorated with pearls.

SCENTED TASSEL

Scents are most evocative. Use this tassel as a pomander and enjoy the scent every time you open your wardrobe, or you can tuck it away with your precious keepsakes.

MATERIALS

Wooden form with a knob
85 cm (34 in) of 150 mm (6 in) wide rayon fringe
Maddie's Craft Dyes in the colours of your choice
110 cm (44 in) of purchased cord
Clear craft glue
Needle
Ordinary sewing cotton
Length of lace
Narrow braids, one with a flower motif
Tiny sew-on pearls
Glass beads
15 cm (6 in) diameter circle of tulle
Satay stick
Potpourri
Scissors

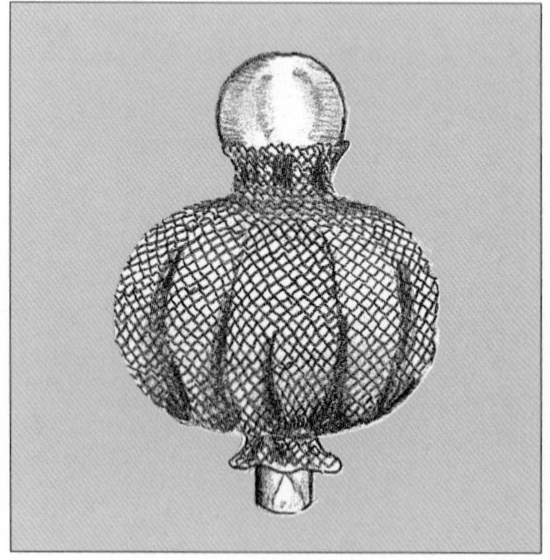

Fig. 1

PREPARATION

Dye the fringe and lace, following the general instructions on pages 21-23.

METHOD

STEP ONE

Cut a circle of tulle with a diameter of approximately 13 cm (5 in). Sew a line of running stitches just in from the edge of the tulle and leave the needle attached.

STEP TWO

Make a small slit in the shape of a cross in the centre of the tulle. Place a little glue right around under the collar of the wooden form. Push the wooden form up through the slit in the tulle so the tulle sits against the glue, under the collar.

STEP THREE

Slightly gather the tulle by pulling on the needle and holding the wooden form upside down. Fill the tulle with approximately two tablespoons of potpourri, then gather the skirt in tightly around the spindle. Fasten off the thread (Fig. 1).

STEP FOUR

Continue to construct the tassel, following the instructions for the soft-bodied fringed tassel on page 16.

STEP FIVE

Wind the cord around the top of the wooden form and attach the hanger as for the basic wooden form tassel on page 14.

STEP SIX

Attach four lengths of the narrow flower braid over the ball of potpourri, then sew on a few tiny pearls. Attach the lace around the tassel, covering the ends of the narrow braid. Thread two glass beads and three pearls on a thread and attach them to the peaks of the lace. Glue narrow braid around the top of the tulle ball, covering the ends of the narrow flower braid.

Pearl box from Potpourri, Rose Bay, NSW

STATUESQUE TASSEL

A tassel adorning a statue will give it a graceful quality. This understated, but elegant tassel also looks wonderful suspended from a lamp or hallstand.

MATERIALS

Wooden form with a knob
30 cm (12 in) of 150 mm (6 in) wide rayon fringe
50 cm (20 in) of 75 mm (3 in) wide rayon fringe
Maddie's Craft Dyes in the colours of your choice
30 cm (12 in) of purchased rayon cord
Clear craft glue
Scissors
Lace edging
Acrylic paints, various colours, including Gold
Paintbrush
Satay stick
Ordinary sewing cotton
Needle
Glass beads, various sizes and shapes

PREPARATION

Dye the fringes and lace, following the general instructions on pages 21-23.

METHOD

STEP ONE

Paint the knob of the wooden form and allow it to dry. This particular one is painted first with Gold, then with a random pattern in Pinks and Greens to resemble flowers.

STEP TWO

Glue the long fringe onto the spindle and attach the cord to the top as shown for the basic wooden form tassel on page 14.

STEP THREE

Apply glue to the entire portion of the wooden form under the knob. Gradually wind the short fringe around and up the glued area until it finishes under the collar to create a layered look.

STEP FOUR

Glue the lace around the tassel, just below the knob. Attach a doubled length of cotton to the peaks of the lace and secure it firmly. Thread it with beads until you have the desired length, selecting a special bead for the drop on the end. Push the needle back up through the string of beads (except for the drop) and secure the string in the lace again. Repeat this process for all the peaks and the short strings of beads in between.

The head of the tassel is painted to suggest flowers

HOLDING THE PURSE STRINGS

These charming little tassels add a dash of style to the plainest bag or complement an extravagant one such as this. The wooden forms are painted gold, but you could gild them or découpage them for a very special look.

Note: The instructions given here are only for making the tassels. You may be lucky enough to own a patchwork bag like this or you may find one in a second-hand shop.

MATERIALS

Small wooden form with a knob
50 cm (20 in) of 75 mm (3 in) wide rayon fringe
Maddie's Craft Dyes in the colours of your choice
Clear craft glue
30 cm (12 in) of purchased rayon cord
75 cm (30 in) of handmade cord
Assorted lace or short-looped fringe
Acrylic paint, Rich Gold
Paintbrush
Black antiquing gel
Soft cloth
Satay stick
Scissors
Note: The quantities given here are for making one tassel.

PREPARATION

Dye the fringe and lace, following the general instructions on pages 21-23.

METHOD

STEP ONE

Paint the wooden form with the Rich Gold paint. When it is dry, apply the antique gel. Rub the antique gel off with a soft cloth, until you are pleased with the finish.

STEP TWO

Apply glue to the entire spindle. Wrap the fringe onto the spindle, dabbing with glue as you go, until all the fringe is used up.

STEP THREE

Glue the short-looped fringe and any other laces you wish to add, just under the header on top of the rayon fringe.

STEP FOUR

Make the curly ruff, using the hand-made cord dyed to suit the tassel, as for the curly top on the romantic tassel on page 30. Glue the curly ruff to the header, winding it around over and over until the header is covered.

Gloves, mirror and silver boxes from Mosman Antique Centre, Sydney

SENTIMENT AND SILK RIBBONS

Delicate hues of pink and blue are entwined in this beautiful ribbon tassel. Display it with your mementos or attach it to a family album or photograph frame.

MATERIALS

One ball of Next Edition Mosaics knitting ribbon
15 cm (6 in) piece of cardboard
Elastic band
Large scissors

METHOD

STEP ONE

Using five strands of the ribbon, make 1 m (1 1/8 yd) of finished cord, following the directions for cord making on page 18.

STEP TWO

Cut the cord into two pieces: one measuring 35 cm (13 3/4 in) and the other measuring 65 cm (26 in). Knot the ends firmly immediately after cutting to prevent the cord unravelling.

STEP THREE

Wrap the ribbon around the cardboard approximately one hundred and fifty times as shown for the basic yarn tassel on page 10.

STEP FOUR

Insert the shorter cord under the wound ribbon on one side of the cardboard. Pull the cord through until it is centred. Tie the ends of the cord firmly together with a double knot, enclosing the ribbon. Tie the ends together to form the hanger.

STEP FIVE

Remove the ribbon bundle from the cardboard and cut through the bottom with the large scissors (Fig. 8, page 12).

STEP SIX

Even out and smooth down the ribbons, then slip the elastic band over the head of the tassel to form the neck.

STEP SEVEN

Wrap the remaining cord around the neck of the tassel, covering the elastic band. Secure the cord with a looped bow.

70
F. Carulli
Fine
Var. III
D.C.

TREASURED TASSELS

We couldn't resist sharing these gorgeous antique tassels and trimmings with you. They have been lent to us by Robert Dodridge who was fortunate enough to acquire these priceless pieces. Originally from Buckingham Palace, these pieces decorated the palace during the reign of Queen Victoria.

All of the tassels are made from pure silk. The pearl drop tassels were used to trim a chaise longue. The red tassel and braided trim were used for curtains and draping, as can be seen in the photograph, and are still in use today. The remainder of this trim, which was discovered in the basement of the palace, was apparently sold in 1973 to an Arab sheik for one thousand dollars per metre.

This page: Antique tassels from Buckingham Palace

ACKNOWLEDGMENTS

Madeleine Willingham

I wish to thank my darling Norm and my gorgeous boys Jeremy and Joshua for their love and support and to my family for their enthusiasm; dear Melissa Whitehead and Marian Cate for all their work in preparation of materials and for giving me free space to co-write this book; Malcolm Kelly, for his beautiful drawings, attention to detail and patience; to Easycraft for producing my dyes and distributing my products; to Maurie and Denise for their sleepless nights in the garage; to Julian and Loretta, Erika, Damien and Marge from Shamrock for their advice and support; to my students and friends, for urging me on; and to Melissa Langford from The Amelia Bloomer Store, Malvern for creating a diversion.

Julie Neilson-Kelly

I would like to acknowledge and thank my husband, Malcolm Kelly, for his contribution to this book and his many hours spent on the beautiful illustrations, and my wonderful family for their continued support. I would also like to thank the following people: Freda Kaplan, for her assistance with the production of the Hunter's Den tassel and the beautiful blue tassel shown in the cord-making section; Jane Smith, for her expert sewing skills; Susie Kisajukian, from The Gilding Supply Company, Queen Victoria Building, Sydney, for the gilding products used in all my publications; Robert Dodridge for allowing us to photograph his priceless treasures from Buckingham Palace; my students who have helped make the many varied workshops so successful; and Sue Schirmer for her friendship and inspiration.

COPYRIGHT

Oxford AQA GCSE History

Conflict and Tension: First World War 1894–1918

AUTHOR & SERIES EDITOR
Aaron Wilkes

OXFORD

OXFORD
UNIVERSITY PRESS

Great Clarendon Street, Oxford, OX2 6DP, United Kingdom

Oxford University Press is a department of the University of Oxford. It furthers the University's objective of excellence in research, scholarship, and education by publishing worldwide. Oxford is a registered trade mark of Oxford University Press in the UK and in certain other countries.

First published in 2018

British Library Cataloguing in Publication Data Data available

978-0-19-842900-5

Kerboodle Book: 978-0-19-842901-2

10 9 8 7 6 5 4 3 2 1

MIX
Paper from responsible sources
FSC www.fsc.org FSC® C007785

Paper used in the production of this book is a natural, recyclable product made from wood grown in sustainable forests. The manufacturing process conforms to the environmental regulations of the country of origin.

Printed in Great Britain by Bell and Bain Ltd., Glasgow

Approval message from AQA

This textbook has been approved by AQA for use with our qualification. This means that we have checked that it broadly covers the specification and we are satisfied with the overall quality. Full details of our approval process can be found on our website.

We approve textbooks because we know how important it is for teachers and students to have the right resources to support their teaching and learning. However, the publisher is ultimately responsible for the editorial control and quality of this book.

Please note that when teaching the AQA GCSE History course, you must refer to AQA's specification as your definitive source of information. While this book has been written to match the specification, it cannot provide complete coverage of every aspect of the course.

A wide range of other useful resources can be found on the relevant subject pages of our website: www.aqa.org.uk.

From the author: Sincere thanks to the brilliant team at OUP – Becky DeLozier, Kate Buckley, Janice Chan, Melanie Waldron and Sarah Flynn – who have once again provided such sound advice and support. Thank you also to Jon Cloake whose good humour and practical suggestions have been invaluable. I am also indebted to my incredible family – Emma, Hannah and Eleanor – who make all the hard work worthwhile.

The publisher would like to thank the following people for offering their contribution in the development of this book: J.A. Cloake, Fran Robertson, Ellen Longley and James Helling.

Contents

Conflict and Tension: First World War 1894–1918

Introduction to the Oxford AQA GCSE History series

The Oxford AQA GCSE History series has been specially written by an expert team of teachers and historians with examining experience to match each part of your AQA course. The chapters which follow are laid out according to the content of the AQA specification. Written in an interesting and engaging style, each of the eye-catching double-pages is clearly organised to provide you with a logical route through the historical content.

There is a lively mix of visual **Sources** and **Interpretations** to enhance and challenge your learning and understanding of the history. Extensive use of photographs, diagrams, cartoons, charts and maps allows you to practise using a variety of sources as evidence.

The **Work** activities and **Practice Questions** have been written to help you check your understanding of the content, develop your skills as a historian, and help you prepare not just for GCSE examinations, but for any future studies. You can develop your knowledge and practise examination skills further through the interactive activities, history skills animations, practice questions, revision checklists and more on *Kerboodle**.

Conflict and Tension: First World War 1894–1918

This book guides you through one of AQA's Wider world depth studies, *Conflict and Tension: First World War 1894–1918*. Wider World Depth Studies investigate a time of international conflict. This book focuses on the causes, nature and conclusion of the First World War and seeks to show how and why conflict occurred, and why it proved difficult to bring the war to a conclusion. This book also considers the role of key countries and key individuals in shaping change and how they were affected by and influenced international relations.

Understanding history requires not just knowledge, but also a good grasp of concepts such as causation, consequence and change. This book is designed to help you think historically, and features historical **Sources**. These sources will encourage you to question critically the content and context of visual and textual evidence of the time.

We hope you'll enjoy your study of the First World War–

Aaron Wilkes

Series Editor

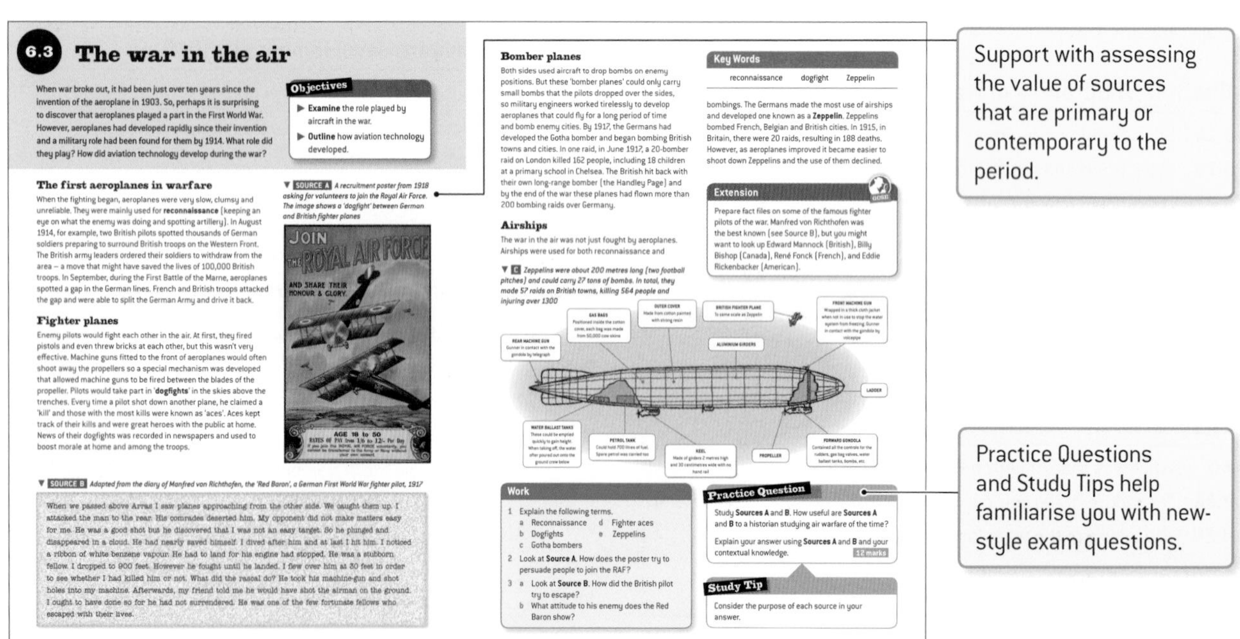

6.3 The war in the air

When war broke out, it had been just over ten years since the invention of the aeroplane in 1903. So, perhaps it is surprising to discover that aeroplanes played a part in the First World War. However, aeroplanes had developed rapidly since their invention and a military role had been found for them by 1914. What role did they play? How did aviation technology develop during the war?

Objectives

- **Examine** the role played by aircraft in the war.
- **Outline** how aviation technology developed.

The first aeroplanes in warfare

When the fighting began, aeroplanes were very slow, clumsy and unreliable. They were mainly used for **reconnaissance** (keeping an eye on what the enemy was doing and spotting artillery). In August 1914, for example, two British pilots spotted thousands of German soldiers preparing to surround British troops on the Western Front. The British army leaders ordered their soldiers to withdraw from the area – a move that might have saved the lives of 100,000 British troops. In September, during the First Battle of the Marne, aeroplanes spotted a gap in the German lines. French and British troops attacked the gap and were able to split the German Army and drive it back.

Fighter planes

Enemy pilots would fight each other in the air. At first, they fired pistols and even threw bricks at each other, but this wasn't very effective. Machine guns fitted to the front of aeroplanes would often shoot away the propellers so a special mechanism was developed that allowed machine guns to be fired between the blades of the propeller. Pilots would take part in '**dogfights**' in the skies above the trenches. Every time a pilot shot down another plane, he claimed a 'kill' and those with the most kills were known as 'aces'. Aces kept track of their kills and were great heroes with the public at home. News of their dogfights was recorded in newspapers and used to boost morale at home and among the troops.

▼ SOURCE A *A recruitment poster from 1918 asking for volunteers to join the Royal Air Force. The image shows a 'dogfight' between German and British fighter planes*

▼ SOURCE B *Adapted from the diary of Manfred von Richthofen, the 'Red Baron', a German First World War fighter pilot, 1917*

When we passed above Arras I saw planes approaching from the other side. We caught them up. I attacked the man to the rear. His comrades deserted him. My opponent did not make matters easy for me. He was a good shot but he discovered that I was not an easy target. So he plunged and disappeared in a cloud. He had nearly saved himself. I dived after him and at last I hit him. I noticed a ribbon of white benzene vapour. He had to land for his engine had stopped. He was a stubborn fellow. I dropped to 900 feet. However he fought until he landed. I flew over him at 30 feet in order to see whether I had killed him or not. What did the rascal do? He took his machine-gun and shot holes into my machine. Afterwards, my friend told me he would have shot the airman on the ground. I ought to have done so for he had not surrendered. He was one of the few fortunate fellows who escaped with their lives.

68 Chapter 6 The wider war

Bomber planes

Both sides used aircraft to drop bombs on enemy positions. But these 'bomber planes' could only carry small bombs that the pilots dropped over the sides, so military engineers worked tirelessly to develop aeroplanes that could fly for a long period of time and bomb enemy cities. By 1917, the Germans had developed the Gotha bomber and began bombing British towns and cities. In one raid, in June 1917, a 20-bomber raid on London killed 162 people, including 18 children at a primary school in Chelsea. The British hit back with their own long-range bomber (the Handley Page) and by the end of the war these planes had flown more than 200 bombing raids over Germany.

Airships

The war in the air was not just fought by aeroplanes. Airships were used for both reconnaissance and bombings. The Germans made the most use of airships and developed one known as a **Zeppelin**. Zeppelins bombed French, Belgian and British cities. In 1915, in Britain, there were 20 raids, resulting in 188 deaths. However, as aeroplanes improved it became easier to shoot down Zeppelins and the use of them declined.

Key Words

reconnaissance dogfight Zeppelin

Extension

Prepare fact files on some of the famous fighter pilots of the war. Manfred von Richthofen was the best known (see Source B), but you might want to look up Edward Mannock (British), Billy Bishop (Canada), René Fonck (French), and Eddie Rickenbacker (American).

▼ C *Zeppelins were about 200 metres long (two football pitches) and could carry 27 tons of bombs. In total, they made 57 raids on British towns, killing 564 people and injuring over 1300*

Work

1. Explain the following terms.
   a. Reconnaissance
   b. Dogfights
   c. Gotha bombers
   d. Fighter aces
   e. Zeppelins
2. Look at **Source A**. How does the poster try to persuade people to join the RAF?
3. a. Look at **Source B**. How did the British pilot try to escape?
   b. What attitude to his enemy does the Red Baron show?

Practice Question

Study **Sources A** and **B**. How useful are **Sources A** and **B** to a historian studying air warfare of the time?

Explain your answer using **Sources A** and **B** and your contextual knowledge. 12 marks

Study Tip

Consider the purpose of each source in your answer.

Conflict and Tension: First World War 1894–1918 69

Conflict and Tension: First World War 1894–1918

**Kerboodle* is not approved by AQA.

How to use this book

Written for the new AQA specification, the features in this book include:

Objectives

At the beginning of the topics, you will find a list of learning objectives. These are based on the requirements of the course – so you can ensure you are covering what you need to know.

Work

The activities and questions aim to develop your knowledge, understanding and key history skills. They are designed to be progressive in terms of difficulty, and to get you to think about the topic, become familiar with the history, and apply what you have learned.

▼ SOURCE ▼ INTERPRETATION

Sources introduce you to material that is primary or contemporary to the period, and **Interpretations** provide you with different people's perspectives on the past.

Extension

This is an opportunity to challenge you to investigate the history more deeply through independent research and reflection.

Practice Question

These are focused questions to help you practise your history skills, including evaluating sources or interpretations and essay writing. They give you an idea of the types of questions you might get in an examination.

Key Words

The important phrases and terms are highlighted and are also defined in the glossary. Learn what they mean – and how to spell and use them correctly.

Study Tip

These are hints to highlight key parts of **Practice Questions** and will help you answer the questions.

Timeline

A short list of dates identifying key events to help you understand chronological developments.

Fact

Fascinating references, facts or anecdotes that will make you think and add to your knowledge and understanding.

Key Biography

Details of a key person to help you understand the individuals who have helped shape history.

Timeline

Conflict and Tension: First World War 1894–1918

The First World War started in June 1914 and ended in November 1918. In total, more than 9 million people died and over 21 million were wounded in the fighting. The war started in Europe when two countries, Serbia and Austria-Hungary, started fighting each other. Within a few weeks, some of the most powerful countries in Europe had joined in. The war was fought on land, at sea and in the air, using the latest tactics and weapons technology that were available at the time. This book explores the causes, nature and conclusion of the First World War and shows how and why the conflict occurred, and why it proved difficult to bring the war to a conclusion.

1895 | 1900 | 1905 | 1910

1879
The Dual Alliance between Germany and Austria-Hungary

1882
Italy joins Germany and Austria-Hungary to form the Triple Alliance

1892
The Franco-Russian Alliance is formed

1897
Germany begins formulating the Schlieffen Plan

1902
Anglo-Japanese Alliance between Britain and Japan

1904
Britain and France sign an agreement called the Entente Cordiale, meaning 'friendly understanding'

1905–6
The Tangier Crisis (or the First Moroccan Crisis)

1906
The British announce the creation of a new, improved type of warship called the Dreadnought

1907
Britain, France and Russia become allies – The Triple Entente 1907

1908–9
The Balkan Crisis

1911
May - The Second Moroccan Crisis

September - The Black Hand is formed

1915

February - The Gallipoli Campaign begins in Turkey

April - The first use of poisoned gas. Also, Italy joins the conflict on Britain and France's side

May - German U-boat sinks a British passenger liner called the *Lusitania*, sailing from New York to Liverpool

December - General Sir Douglas Haig takes control of British forces on the Western Front. The Gallipoli Campaign ends

1916

February - the Battle of Verdun begins

May - The Battle of Jutland

July - The Battle of the Somme begins

September - Tanks first used in battle, during the Somme Offensive

1918

March - The Treaty of Brest-Litovsk between Russia and Germany, which officially ends Russia's role in the war. Also, Ludendorff's Spring Offensive begins

April - French Army leader, Ferdinand Foch, becomes supreme Allied commander

August - The Allied counter-attack (later known as the 'Hundred Days') begins

October - German sailors based in Kiel refuse to follow orders. News of their mutiny begins to spread to other German ports and towns

November - Germany is now fighting alone after the surrender of its allies. The German Emperor, abdicates. The government that replaces him asks for an armistice (ceasefire), which begins at 11am on 11 November

1912–13

The Balkan Wars

1920

1915

1914

June - Assassination of Archduke Franz Ferdinand, heir to the throne of Austria-Hungary by members of the Black Hand

July - Austria-Hungary declares war on Serbia; the first countries are now at war in what would become the First World War

August - Germany, Russia, France and Britain join the conflict within a week of each other

September - Stalemate at the Battle of the Marne kick-starts the 'race to the sea'

November - British declare the North Sea a 'War Zone' and that any ships entering it do so at their own risk

December - The British coastal towns of Scarborough, Hartlepool and Whitby are bombed by German ships

1917

February - German submarines restart a series of U-boat attacks on Allied shipping

March - The first of two Russian revolutions take place

April - The USA joins the conflict on Britain and France's side

July - The Battle of Passchendaele (or the Third Battle of Ypres) begins

November - Second Russian Revolution

Who were the great powers of Europe before the war?

The five most powerful countries in Europe in the years building up to the First World War were Britain, Germany, France, Russia and Austria-Hungary. To understand the origins of the First World War, you need to examine these countries in detail, and consider each country's ruler, the issues each country faced, the relationships between them, and their positions as military, industrial and **imperial** nations.

Objectives

- **Examine** key features of the most powerful European nations before the First World War.
- **Assess** the strengths and weaknesses of the key European nations.

Britain – the largest empire

In the years before the First World War, the British people had many reasons to be proud. Most British people were better fed, better clothed, healthier and more educated than many in other countries. Britain had been the first country in the world to have an industrial revolution, in the late 1700s and 1800s. As a result, Britain became an industrial power and, by 1900, was the world's richest country. Shops in towns and cities contained a wide range of goods, either made in British factories or brought in from parts of the British **Empire** – the largest the world had ever seen.

Ruling Britain

It was during the reign of Queen Victoria (1837–1901) that Britain had become one of the richest and most powerful nations on Earth.

- Through Victoria's marriage to Albert, a German duke, and the marriages of her children, the British royal family was directly connected to the rulers of Russia, Germany, Spain, Norway, Denmark, Sweden, Greece and Romania.
- Before the end of Victoria's reign, some people had started to call Queen Victoria the 'Grandmother of Europe'.
- By the time of George V's reign (1910–36) the role of the monarch was largely symbolic. The King had very little political power. The British Parliament, like today, made all the laws, and members of Parliament were voted into power by the people of Britain who were eligible to vote.

▼ **SOURCE A** *A souvenir postcard from the time of George V's coronation in 1910*

The British Empire

By 1914, Britain ruled over 400 million people living in 56 different places all over the world. This amounted to approximately one quarter of the world's population and one quarter of the earth's total land area. The size of the British Empire was one of the reasons why an island as small as Britain was viewed as such a powerful nation.

▼ **B** *The British Empire before the First World War; some historians argue that the British made positive changes in many of the lands they conquered, whilst others argue that there were many negative impacts on the colonies and the people within them*

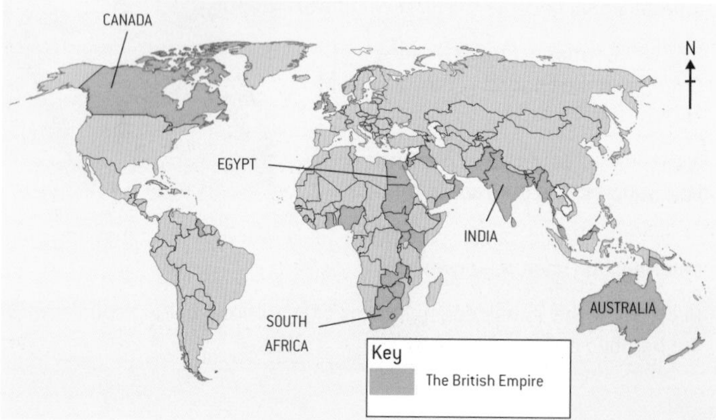

Key Words

imperial empire

Britain's issues

Despite having wealth and power, Britain was a divided nation. In the late nineteenth century, the politician Benjamin Disraeli (who went on to become Prime Minister) had claimed that that the lives led by the rich and poor were so different that Britain was like two nations – a poor one and a rich one. About 3 per cent were very rich, 25 per cent were relatively wealthy (middle-class bankers, doctors, and so on) and the rest, the working class, were poor. The richer people enjoyed a life of luxury. They owned land, homes and many didn't have to work at all because they made so much money out of investments and rents. On the other side, the majority of poor people earned only enough money to get by, and often nowhere near enough to feed their families. There was no state sick pay, pensions or unemployment benefit. The injured and sick paid for their own medical care – if they could afford it.

Essential statistics: Britain in 1914	
Population of Britain	41 million
Size of army	710,000
Battleships	122
Submarines	64
Air force	110 fighter and bomber planes, 6 airships
Number of colonies	56
Population of colonies	400 million
Size of the colonies	27 million square kilometres
Coal production per year	300 million tonnes
Steel production each year	11 million tonnes

There were also signs that Britain's status as a world economic leader was under threat. The USA, for example, was making more goods than Britain and Germany. Britain still had the largest shipbuilding industry in the world, but was outperformed by Germany in the production of coal, iron and chemicals. Other nations, such as Canada, were also making lots of their own goods – and buying less from Britain.

▼ **SOURCE C** *A picture about British involvement in Africa published in an American magazine in 1902; it had the title, 'From the Cape to Cairo'; 'Britannia' is shown carrying a large white flag with British soldiers and colonists behind her*

Work

1. Explain why Queen Victoria was given the nickname 'Grandmother of Europe'.
2. Outline why Britain was a 'divided nation' in the early 1900s.
3. Create a mind-map that shows the position and status of Britain in the years before the First World War. In the centre, write 'Britain before the First World War' and include branches called:
   - British society
   - Ruling Britain
   - The British Empire
   - Britain's problems
   - Military power
   - Economic power.

Practice Question

Look at **Source C**. It supports the British Empire. How do you know? Explain your answer using **Source C** and your contextual knowledge.

4 marks

Study Tip

Study the image carefully. How does it show the British Empire in a positive way? What does the artist want you to think about Britain?

Who were the great powers of Europe before the war?

France – a rival empire

In the early 1800s, under Napoleon, France was one of the strongest and most feared military powers in Europe. Many French people had been very proud of this history, but by the late 1800s much of this national pride had been lost. In 1870 the French were beaten by German forces in the Franco-Prussian War. After this defeat, Germany took two areas of land from France – the rich coal, steel and glass production regions of Alsace and Lorraine. These areas were not just valuable pieces of land, but their loss was a bitter blow to French pride. From this point on, many French people wanted revenge against the Germans.

By the early 1900s, farming was still one of France's main industries and around 40 per cent of the population were farmers. Although there were also many factories producing goods that were traded all over the world, France could not match the industrial output of Germany and Britain.

▼ **SOURCE D** *Paris became centre stage in 1889 for the 'Exposition Universelle'; world fairs, such as this one, are large international exhibitions designed to display a nation's achievements; a new 324-metre tall steel arch – the Eiffel Tower – was built as an entrance to the exhibition*

However, France rivalled any country in the world in science, technology and culture:

- Paris was the centre of the world fashion industry.
- Many of the world's most famous writers, painters and musicians lived and worked in France.
- French food was viewed by many as the finest in the world.
- Frenchman Louis Pasteur made remarkable breakthroughs in the causes and prevention of diseases; whilst working in France, Pierre and Marie Curie did pioneering work on radioactivity, paving the way for scientists in later years to work on cancer treatments.
- France led the world in the development of cinema, aeroplanes, motorcars and motorcycles.

▼ **SOURCE E** *Adapted from an official report by W.B. Franklin to the members of the United States Congress after visiting the 1889 Exposition; Franklin was one of America's official representatives in Paris*

> The event was organized perfectly – the magnificent show of industrial and agricultural products, the fine art exhibits, which have never been equalled, the splendid works of engineering and agriculture, the intelligent historical exhibits and the colonial exhibits. In fact, everything connected with the event convinces me that the nation which could organize such a grand exhibition must be an equal of any other modern nation.

Ruling France

France did not have a ruling royal family like many of the other leading European powers. It was a republic – a nation ruled by an elected president with the help of elected politicians. Many of France's army generals also had lots of political power and not only held high-ranking positions in the Army, but held important jobs in the government too.

Many French politicians had a long-standing hatred for Germany and wanted revenge for the Franco-Prussian War. Some government policies brought in during the early 1900s were concerned with increasing the size of France's army and navy. These policies were a result of a long-standing fear of German attack.

The French Empire

The French Empire was the second largest behind the British Empire. At the outbreak of war in 1914, after years of expansion in the late 1800s, the French controlled around 11 million square kilometres of land and nearly 60 million people, mainly in West and North Africa and in South East Asia.

France's issues

France was one of the world's leading trading nations as a result of the size of its empire, but it was beginning to fall behind many other nations, including Britain and Germany, in the production of goods and materials such as iron, coal, steel, ships and food. Also, despite being twice the size of Britain and around the same size as Germany, France's population was less than both of those nations – and was shrinking every year.

Essential statistics: France in 1914	
Population of France	41 million
Size of army	1,250,000
Battleships	46
Submarines	73
Air force	132 fighter and bomber planes
Number of colonies	29
Population of colonies	58 million
Size of the colonies	11 million square kilometres
Coal production per year	40 million tonnes
Steel production each year	5 million tonnes

▼ **F** *The French Empire at the outbreak of the First World War*

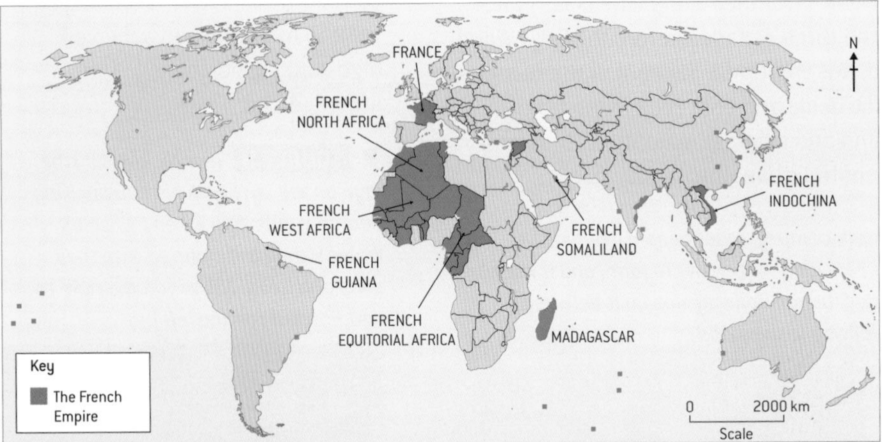

Extension

France's president from 1913–20 was named Raymond Poincare. Find out about Poincare's background. What region of France was he from? Suggest why he may have had strong anti-German feelings. Do you think this influenced his dealings with other European countries?

Work

1 France, like Britain, had a huge overseas empire.
   a What are the advantages of having a large empire?
   b Can you think of any disadvantages?
2 What impact did the Franco-Prussian War have on the French attitude to Germany?
3 Read **Source E**. In your own words, sum up what the visitor says about:
   - The 1889 Exposition
   - The French nation.
4 In what ways was France a leader in science, technology and culture by the early 1900s?

1.1C Who were the great powers of Europe before the war?

Russia – the world's largest nation

Russia is by far the largest country in the world. Russia has vast amounts of valuable natural resources (such as oil, coal and gold) but in the years before the First World War much of this lay undiscovered or unworked. Vast areas of land cannot be used for farming because it is too cold. Although the country has a long coastline, much of it is frozen for long periods of time every year.

In the early 1900s:

- Russia had a huge population of nearly 160 million people, most of whom lived in the western (European) part of the country
- the population was very ethnically mixed, with over 200 different ethnic groups, speaking many different languages
- most Russians were members of the Russian Orthodox Church (one of the three main Christian groups, the others being Roman Catholic and Protestant), but there were also 5 million Jews and around 23 million Muslims. Sometimes violence erupted between the different ethnic groups and many wanted to gain their independence.

Russia was a nation of both great wealth (for the ruling, elite class) and extreme poverty (for the rest). In the three decades before the First World War, oil and coal production trebled, but around 85 per cent of the Russian people continued to live in the countryside and earn their living from farming. The rich owned the best land and the vast majority of Russians were illiterate peasants under the control of wealthy landowners.

▼ **G** *Russia at the turn of the twentieth century; most people lived in the south-western corner of the country where land was easier to farm, and it wasn't covered in forest or mountains; the Trans-Siberian Railway was built between 1891 and 1916; it remains the longest railway in the world*

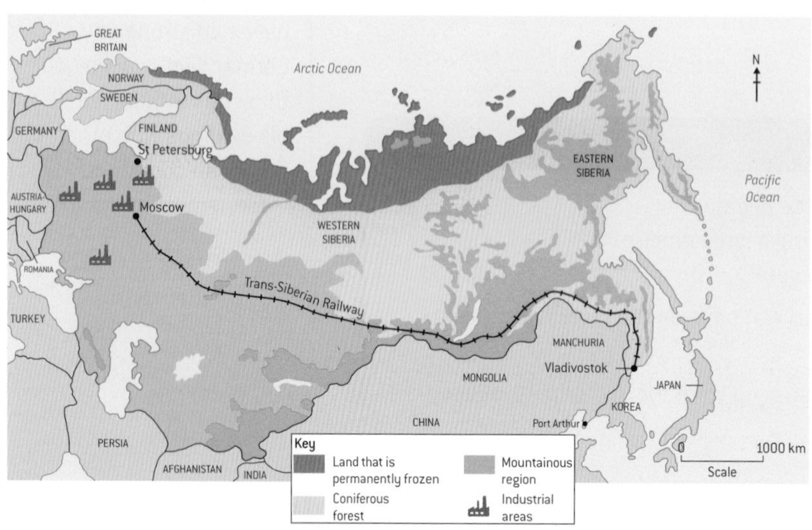

Ruling Russia

Since the sixteenth century, Russia had been ruled by an emperor (known as a **tsar**). In 1894 Tsar Nicholas II took power. Nicholas and his wife Alexandra were distant cousins of both Kaiser Wilhelm II, the German Emperor, and King George V of Great Britain.

Nicholas had absolute control of Russia and believed that God had chosen him to be ruler. However, he was not a good judge of character. He often appointed family members and friends to important positions, even though most of them were not qualified to do the job, or were corrupt. Other key jobs usually went to men who had achieved high-ranking positions in the armed forces.

▼ **SOURCE H** *Tsar Nicholas II (the man on the left) with his cousin, King George V of Britain (then Prince of Wales); they are pictured with their sons and heirs, Alexei (on the right) and Edward (on the left)*

Essential statistics: Russia in 1914	
Population of Russia	159 million
Size of army	1,200,000
Battleships	26
Submarines	29
Air force	360 fighter and bomber planes, 16 airships
Number of colonies	0
Population of colonies	0
Size of the colonies	0
Coal production per year	36 million tonnes
Steel production each year	4 million tonnes

The Russian Empire

Russia didn't have any overseas **colonies**. However, the Tsar was keen to acquire areas next to Russia, such as Manchuria (in China), Persia (modern-day Iran) and the Balkans, an area in south-eastern Europe that was ruled by Turkey in the early 1900s. These areas are to the south of Russia, and the oceans and seas near to them do not freeze during the winter months.

Russia's issues

There was extreme poverty, and living conditions in the countryside were often harsh. A poor harvest could mean the deaths from starvation of thousands of people. Living and working conditions were not much better in the towns, and working hours were generally much longer than in other European countries. There was little concern for the workers' health and safety, and **trade unions** were illegal in Russia, so industrial workers found it difficult to improve their conditions. Strikes were also banned, and if they ever did take place, they were ended brutally when the Russian Army was called in.

Key Words

trade union   tsar   colony

From 1904–5, Russia fought and lost a war with Japan (the Russo-Japanese War). Following this loss, there were riots in Russia's capital city, St Petersburg, and the Tsar was persuaded to accept a reduction in his power. He formed a new Russian parliament called the Duma, but the Tsar often rejected any new laws that the Duma proposed. As a result, the country remained very unstable; strikes became more and more frequent and the Tsar responded with an increasing use of force.

▼ **INTERPRETATION I** *Adapted from* Strategic Observations of the Russo-Japanese War *by Andrew Torelli, 2004; Torelli is an American defence analyst and former US Air Force officer*

> Port Arthur [in Manchuria] was a symbol of national solidarity. Its fall to the Japanese resulted in a huge psychological blow which led to widespread protests and strikes in Tsarist Russia, 'Bloody Sunday', and ultimately the Tsar's reputation and standing within the Russian empire.

Work

1 a What areas of the world did Russia hope to take over?
  b Why do you think Russia was interested in these areas?
2 a Russia was a huge nation with a large population and lots of natural resources. What are the advantages of this if Russia was to go to war?
  b Suggest reasons why Russia's size, its large population and geographical position might not help Russia in a time of war.
3 Some historians have described Russia as a 'weak giant' in the years before the First World War. Do you think this is a suitable description? Give reasons for your answer.
4 Read **Interpretation I**. What does it tell you about the impact of Russia's defeat in 1905 by the Japanese? Explain your answer.

Who were the great powers of Europe before the war?

Germany – a new nation

Before 1870 there was no such country as Germany. Instead, there was a collection of small states or areas that were loosely linked together – the people shared similar customs and spoke the same language (German).

One of the states, Prussia, was bigger than the others and the King of Prussia wanted to join all the other states together to make a stronger and more powerful state. Nearby France, Austria and Denmark felt threatened by this and tried to stop it. A series of wars were fought against all of these countries, that Prussia won, and in 1871 all the states were united together to form the new nation of Germany. As a result of the victory over France, Germany also gained the valuable areas of Alsace and Lorraine. The King of Prussia became the new German Emperor (or Kaiser).

- The new Germany made rapid social, military and economic progress. Much of the workforce was highly skilled, and the German people were generally well-educated and well-fed.
- Workers had the security of government-provided sickness pay, accident insurance and old age pensions, long before any of the other European powers.
- Germany's industrial development at this time was probably the fastest in the world. Between 1880 and 1910, Germany's coal production quadrupled and other industries such as steel, chemicals, engineering and armaments also grew rapidly.
- By 1913, Germany was producing more iron and steel and nearly as much coal as Britain. In industries such as electrical goods and chemicals, German companies dominated Europe.

Ruling Germany

In 1888, Wilhelm II became Germany's Kaiser. He was the grandson of Britain's Queen Victoria and the cousin of Britain's future king, George V. The Kaiser had spent most of his youth in the Army and dreamed of creating an army and navy to rival any other in the world.

In ruling Germany, the Kaiser had help from the parliament, or **Reichstag**, which was elected by the people. However, it was the Kaiser who introduced laws, selected people for important government jobs, declared war and made peace. He only allowed the Reichstag to change laws occasionally. In fact, he once called the politicians in the Reichstag 'a troop of monkeys, blockheads and sleepwalkers'. In short, Kaiser Wilhelm was a dictator with complete power.

▼ **SOURCE J** *Born with a badly deformed left arm, the Kaiser became an excellent horse rider, swimmer and shooter*

Essential statistics: Germany in 1914	
Population of Germany	65 million
Size of army	2,200,000
Battleships	85
Submarines	23
Air force	246 fighter and bomber planes, 11 airships
Number of colonies	10
Population of colonies	15 million
Size of the colonies	2.5 million square kilometres
Coal production per year	277 million tonnes
Steel production each year	14 million tonnes

Key Words

Reichstag

Germany's empire

Germany's empire was small compared with both the British and French empires. However, in the late 1800s Germany claimed several areas in Africa and the Far East. The Kaiser was determined that Germany should continue to build an empire, and by the beginning of the twentieth century Germany was recognised as having the finest army in the world.

Germany's issues

The success of German industry had made many landowners, businessman and factory owners very rich. Working with the Kaiser, these people made all the key decisions in Germany at this time. But things were changing. Many of the workers in the new factories, mines and workshops were unhappy because their wages and working conditions did not seem to be improving, despite all the progress German industry was making. More and more working-class people joined trade unions and organised strikes in the hope that this might force the Kaiser, his advisers and the politicians in the Reichstag to try and improve their conditions. Several new political parties were being formed in Germany at this time too. Some wanted to rebel against the Kaiser's rule, start a revolution and take control of the country.

Extension

A series of Navy Laws were introduced between 1898 and 1912. Research why they were introduced and what impact they had on the German Navy – and international relations.

K *The German Empire before the outbreak of war*

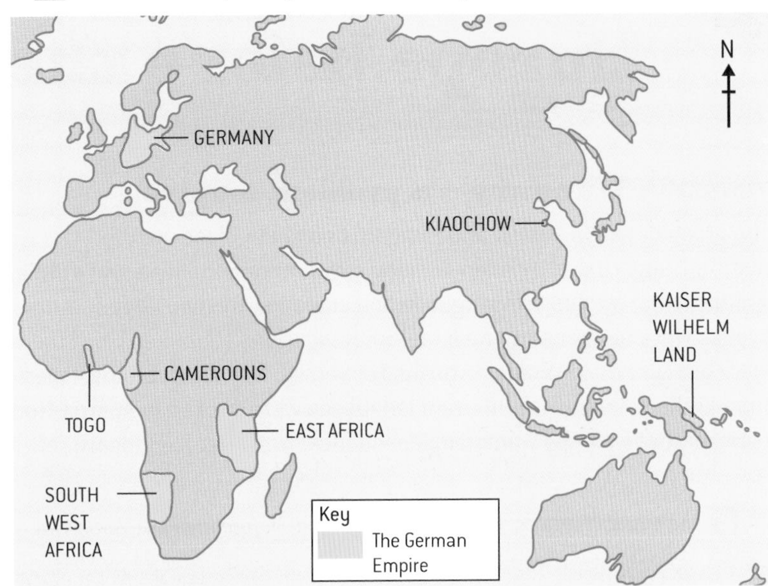

Work

1. Outline how the state of Germany came into being.
2. Explain why many Germans joined trade unions in the early 1900s.
3. You have been asked to work on a TV show about the great European powers at the beginning of the twentieth century. Your task is to write a 2-minute script called 'Germany before the First World War'. Remember to include:
   - some background information on Germany in the years before the War
   - details about the German political system
   - information on the German Empire
   - Germany's military and economic power
   - the problems Germany faced.

Practice Question

Write an account of how Germany became a powerful and ambitious European state. **8 marks**

Study Tip

There are two elements for you to look at here: how Germany became both powerful *and* ambitious.

1.1E Who were the great powers of Europe before the war?

Austria-Hungary – a problem empire

The union between Austria and Hungary had taken place in 1867. Austria-Hungary was a nation of many different nationalities and **ethnic groups**, each with its own language and customs. The two largest ethnic groups were Germans (10 million) and Hungarians (9 million), but there were also Czechs, Slovaks, Serbians (or Serbs), Bosnians, Croats, Poles and many others. Overall, 15 different languages were spoken in Austria-Hungary. Many of these groups wanted independence from Austria-Hungary.

▼ **L** *The ethnic divisions within Austria-Hungary before the First World War*

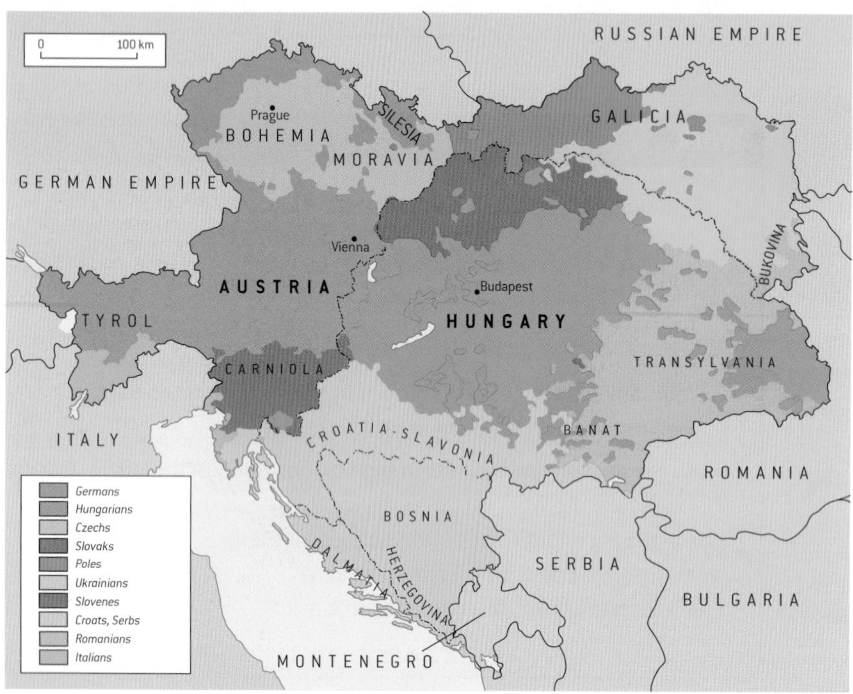

▼ **SOURCE M** *Franz Josef, Emperor of Austria-Hungary; the Emperor's personal life was a tragic one; his son committed suicide and his younger brother, Karl Ludwig, died of typhoid fever; this left Ludwig's son, Archduke Franz Ferdinand, as heir to the throne*

Ruling Austria-Hungary

Austria and Hungary shared the same currency, but they had separate elected parliaments based in Vienna (the Austrian parliament) and Budapest (the Hungarian parliament). However, Austria and Hungary acted together (as Austria-Hungary) when dealing with other nations. Overall political authority was held by the Emperor Franz Josef – and he was particularly proud of his skills in foreign policy. At 84-years-old when the First World War broke out, he was the oldest of all the European rulers. He was a well-liked emperor, but the government officials who ran Austria-Hungary on a day-to-day basis were not popular.

The Austro-Hungarian Empire

Austria-Hungary did not have any overseas colonies. Perhaps the fact that so many of the ethnic groups *within* the country wanted their independence meant that the Emperor had enough to do to keep the country unified without the added complication of extra territories.

Austria-Hungary's issues

While the ageing Emperor himself was popular, the people he put in control of the various regions were generally hated. There were regular riots and demonstrations about new laws and rules that the government imposed.

There was also tension between the different ethnic groups. In December 1897, for example, ten people were killed and 200 wounded when violence erupted in Prague between Germans and Czechs.

The task of keeping Austria-Hungary unified was one of the government's biggest problems in the years leading up to the First World War. The Czechs in the north and the Croats in the south-west of Austria-Hungary wanted to rule themselves; and Serbs living in the south wanted to join with the neighbouring country of Serbia. Serbia itself was becoming increasingly more powerful – and was a strong ally of Russia.

▼ **SOURCE N** *Adapted from a report from the British government's officials in Dalmatia, a southern mainly* ***Slav*** *province of the Austro-Hungarian Empire, 1911*

> Most of the population here dislike being part of the Austro-Hungarian Empire because they think the empire is anti-Slav. They think that the Emperor is really a German and favours Germans and is completely out of touch with his Slav subjects. The Dalmatian Slavs feel they are treated as an inferior race and that their region has been entirely neglected by the Emperor's government. The peasants have no affection for an emperor they blame for this.

Work

1 a Describe the ethnic mix of Austria-Hungary.
  b Austria-Hungary faced problems caused by ethnic groups and nationalities that wanted independence. Why might this be a serious problem for Austria-Hungary?

2 a Create your own table to compare the strengths of the great powers of Europe, using the 'Essential statistics' table as a guide. Add columns for each country: Britain, France, Russia, Germany, Austria-Hungary. Look back at all the Essential Statistics tables in this chapter to help you fill in the details.
  b. Now write a paragraph explaining which country you think was the leading European power before outbreak of war in 1914. Give reasons for your choice.

Key Words

ethnic group   Slav

Essential statistics: Austria-Hungary in 1914	
Population of Austria-Hungry	50 million
Size of army	810,000
Battleships	24
Submarines	6
Air force	35 fighter and bomber planes, 1 airship
Number of colonies	0
Population of colonies	0
Size of the colonies	0
Coal production per year	47 million tonnes
Steel production each year	5 million tonnes

Extension

Italy was another European nation that was to feature in the build-up to the First World War and the war itself. Using the same headings as the countries you have already examined (ruling the country, the empire, issues within the country, and so on), carry out some research on Italy. Also, think about where Italy would be placed in your list of Europe's most powerful nations.

1.2 Europe splits into two armed camps

In the years building up to the First World War, some of the most powerful countries in Europe had divided into two opposing sides (or **alliances**). In one alliance were Germany, Austria-Hungary and Italy. The other group consisted of France, Russia and Britain. The countries within each alliance had large populations and an increasing amount of military force. How and why did these countries split into these two alliances?

Objectives

- **Define** and explore the origins of the Triple Alliance and the Franco-Russian Alliance.
- **Describe** relations between the 'Entente' powers.

The alliances begin

Agreements, deals, **treaties** and alliances between countries had been taking place in Europe for hundreds of years. Indeed, the alliances that were in place at the beginning of the First World War originated over a long period of time. In 1873, for example, the emperors of Germany, Austria-Hungary and Russia formed the 'Three Emperors' League' in which the countries agreed to go to each other's aid in a time of war. However, Germany disagreed with Russia taking control of the Balkan area of southern Europe in 1879, and signed a new deal with Austria-Hungary agreeing that they would help each other if either of them was attacked. This was called the Dual Alliance and was the first in a series of new alliances in the years before the outbreak of war. The diagram below shows how some of the most powerful countries of Europe formed into two rival camps.

1879

Alliance 1: Dual Alliance

Who? Germany and Austria-Hungary

Why? They were natural allies given their shared language, culture and history.

1882

Alliance 2: Dual Alliance becomes Triple Alliance

Who? Germany, Austria-Hungary and Italy

Why? Each country promised to provide military support to the others if one was attacked by two other powers. Italy had the weaker military forces and was viewed as a minor partner.

1892

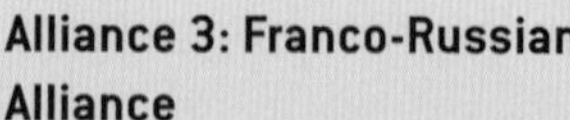

Alliance 3: Franco-Russian Alliance

Who? France and Russia

Why? After the Franco-Prussian War, France was determined to protect itself against Germany. France had developed a close friendship with Russia and they signed a deal to help each other out if either of them was attacked. This would mean that Germany would be attacked from opposite sides because it is wedged between France and Russia.

1904

Alliance 4: Entente Cordiale ('Friendly understanding')

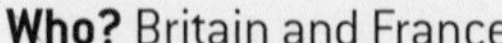

Who? Britain and France

Why? Britain was becoming increasingly concerned about the threat of Germany's growing army and navy and in one of its colonies, South Africa, Britain had fought a war against a group of settlers who wanted their independence (the Boers). Germany had supported the Boers. As a result, Britain looked for an ally in Europe and signed this agreement with France.

1907

Alliance 5: The Triple Entente

Who? France, Russia and Britain

Why? France and Russia were already in the Franco-Russian Alliance and this was strengthened in 1907 when Britain joined the deal.

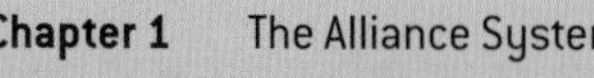

By 1907 the most powerful nations in Europe were divided into two groups. Although the aim of these alliances was to keep the peace, this 'Alliance System' meant that if a disagreement started between any two nations in opposite alliances, then the others could quickly get dragged into the conflict.

▼ A *The Triple Alliance (the beginnings of the 'Central Powers') and the Triple Entente (the beginnings of the 'Allied Powers'); note the size of each side's armies and navies in 1914; Italy did not fight with the Central Powers when war broke out and later joined the Allies*

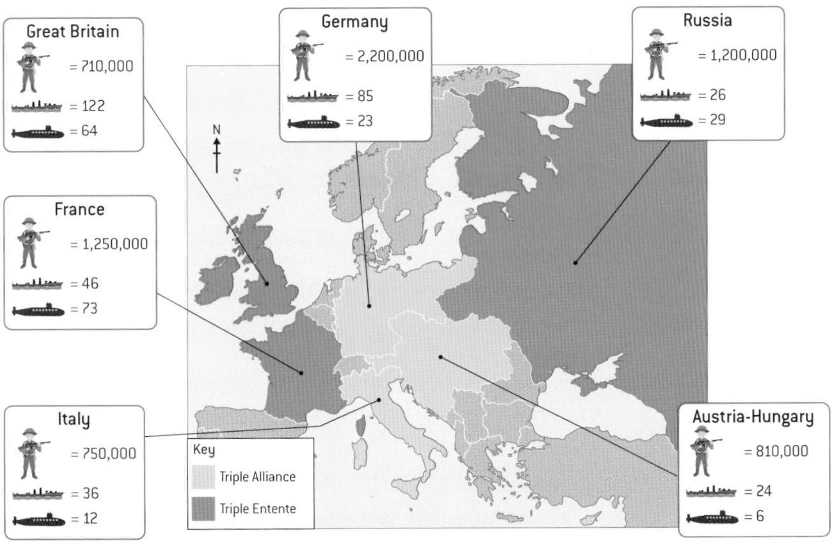

▼ SOURCE B *A French cartoon showing Kaiser Wilhelm being kicked by Russia, France and the United Kingdom, 1907*

▼ SOURCE C *The Kaiser's son (Crown Prince Wilhelm) writing that Germany must be ready for 'attack'; from his book, published in 1913*

> Our country is obliged more than any other country to place all its confidence in its good weapons. Set in the centre of Europe, it is badly protected by its unfavourable geographic frontiers, and is regarded by many nations without affection. Upon the German Empire, therefore, is imposed the sacred duty of watching carefully that its army and its navy be always prepared to meet any attack from the outside. It is only by reliance upon our brave sword that we shall be able to maintain that place in the sun which belongs to us, and which the world does not seem very willing to accord us.

Key Words

alliance treaty

Work

1 Make a list of the countries in:
   - **a** the Triple Alliance
   - **b** the Triple Entente.

2
   - **a** If the Triple Alliance attacked France, how could Russia's friendship help France?
   - **b** If Austria-Hungary attacked Russia, how could France's friendship help Russia?
   - **c** If Russia attacked Germany, how could Austria's friendship help Germany?

3 Look at **Source B**.
   - **a** Which countries are represented by the three boots?
   - **b** Who is being kicked?

Practice Question

Study **Source B**. The cartoon supports the Triple Entente. How do you know?

Explain your answer using **Source B** and your contextual knowledge. **4 marks**

Study Tip

Try to identify all of the elements in a cartoon, then explain what the cartoonist wants you to think when they are all connected together.

1.3 The Moroccan crises

When the great powers of Europe divided themselves into two major alliances, each alliance began to build up their armies and navies and make plans for war, just in case they needed to go to the aid of an ally. As tension increased between the alliances, two serious disagreements developed over the north-west African nation of Morocco. Why was Morocco at the centre of European arguments? Which countries were involved? How close did the countries come to all-out war at this time?

Objectives

- **Explore** the first and second Moroccan crises of 1905–6 and 1911.
- **Assess** the impact of these crises on European relations.

Morocco and the Entente Cordiale

Morocco was one of the few areas of Africa that had not been colonised by a European country. As part of the 1904 deal between France and Britain (the Entente Cordiale), the British agreed to support France's attempts to take over Morocco. Spain and Italy both said they had no objection to France's plans. However, Germany's Emperor, Kaiser Wilhelm II, was determined to prevent this from happening and visited Tangier to pledge his support for Morocco's ruler, the Sultan Abdelaziz.

▼ **SOURCE A** *Kaiser Wilhelm II (circled) during his visit to Tangier in April 1905, accompanied by soldiers and a military band; he told the Sultan that he would protect German business interests in Morocco and stop the French takeover*

▼ **SOURCE B** *Adapted from a report on the Kaiser's visit to Morocco in 1905, written by Councillor von Schoen, a high-ranking German official*

> His Majesty remarked that he looked upon the Sultan as the ruler of a free and independent empire subject to no foreign control; that he expected Germany to have advantages equal to those of other countries in trade and commerce; and that he himself would always negotiate directly with the Sultan.

The first crisis in Morocco, 1905–6

The German Emperor's support for Morocco was a direct challenge to France's ambitions. As news spread of the crisis, many wondered whether this would lead to war between Germany and France. It seems that the Kaiser had several aims:

- He wanted to test the French to see how far they could be pushed. Would they really declare war on Germany?
- He wanted to test the Entente Cordiale. Would France's new ally, Britain, come to France's defence?
- He wanted to demonstrate that Germany intended to become fully involved in world affairs and was very interested in the expansion Germany's empire.

The Algeciras Conference, January 1906

War between Germany and France was looming – but it never happened. An international conference, attended by all the major European nations (*and* the USA), was held in Algeciras (southern Spain) to settle the conflict.

However, the conference was humiliating for Germany. Only Austria-Hungary supported the Germans and it was decided that France could have special rights in Morocco. Although the French were stopped from colonising Morocco and including it as part of their empire, they gained a foothold in the country by being given joint control of the Moroccan police. More importantly, Britain and Russia had stood firm against Germany in their support for France. The Kaiser could now be in no doubt that the Entente Cordiale was more than just a 'friendly understanding'. Furthermore, in the wake of this crisis, the relationship between Britain and Russia improved and soon Britain, Russia and France formed the Triple Entente (see page 18).

Another crisis in Morocco, 1911

Five years later there was a second crisis in Morocco. In 1911 a rebellion against the ruling Sultan of Morocco broke out in Fez, the capital city. The Sultan asked the French for help and the French government sent 20,000 soldiers to fight the rebels. Germany's Kaiser accused the French of invading Morocco and sent a warship named *Panther* to the port of Agadir as a show of strength.

The British were worried about the arrival of the warship in Morocco. Britain had a navy base nearby in Gibraltar (see the Map **C** below) and it looked like Germany might be trying to create a navy base in Agadir. The British prepared for war.

A solution is found

A series of meetings between German, French and British politicians were held and eventually a peaceful solution was found. Britain and France again stood firm against Germany, and the Kaiser decided to back down and order the warship to leave Agadir. Other countries, such as Italy, also opposed the Germans. After a tense few weeks, the French took control of Morocco, but Germany was given some land in central Africa as compensation.

The results of the second Moroccan crisis were far-reaching:

- Germany was humiliated – and was unlikely to back down again from an international crisis.
- Many German people fully supported the Kaiser and his actions. When he talked of war, they would support him on this matter too.
- Britain was now convinced that Germany was a threat to European peace. It is no coincidence that Britain began to build more and more battleships after this crisis.
- Britain and France grew closer. They reached a secret agreement that French warships would patrol the Mediterranean Sea whilst British warships would defend the north coast of France.
- Italy had not supported Germany, and this weakened the Triple Alliance. From now on, Germany would look to Austria-Hungary as their main ally in the Triple Alliance.

▼ **C** *The Moroccan Crises of 1905–6 and 1911*

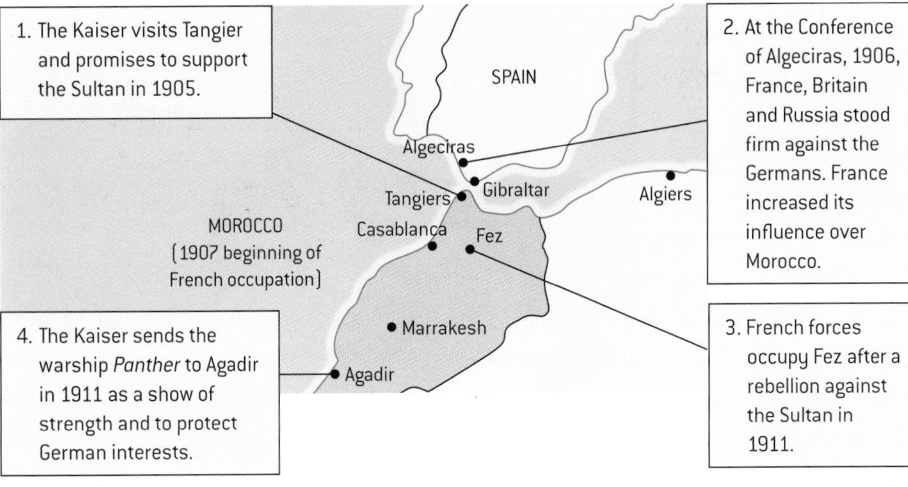

Work

1. Look at **Source A.** Why do you think the Kaiser wore his finest military uniform, rode a white horse and was accompanied by soldiers and a military band?
2. Why was the Algeciras Conference:
   a. a success for France?
   b. a humiliation for Germany?
3. How was the Entente Cordiale affected by events in Morocco between 1905 and 1911?

Practice Question

Write an account of how events in Morocco became an international crisis in 1905 and 1906.

8 marks

[AQA 2016 Paper 1 specimen material]

Study Tip

This question is not simply asking you to write about the Moroccan crisis of 1905 and 1906, it asks you to write about the impact of the crisis. It is as much about the *results* of the crisis as it is about the events of the crisis itself.

1.4A Problems in the Balkans

Map **A** shows a region of south-eastern Europe known as the Balkans. In the years leading up to the First World War, the Balkans became the focus of great tension between some of the most powerful nations in Europe. This tension was one of the main reasons why the war eventually broke out in 1914. Why was there a crisis in this region? Which countries were involved? How did problems in the Balkans affect relations between the great powers of Europe?

Objectives

- **Identify** why many powerful European countries were so interested in the Balkans.
- **Examine** the reasons why tension built up in this region.

▼ **A** *The Balkans in 1900*

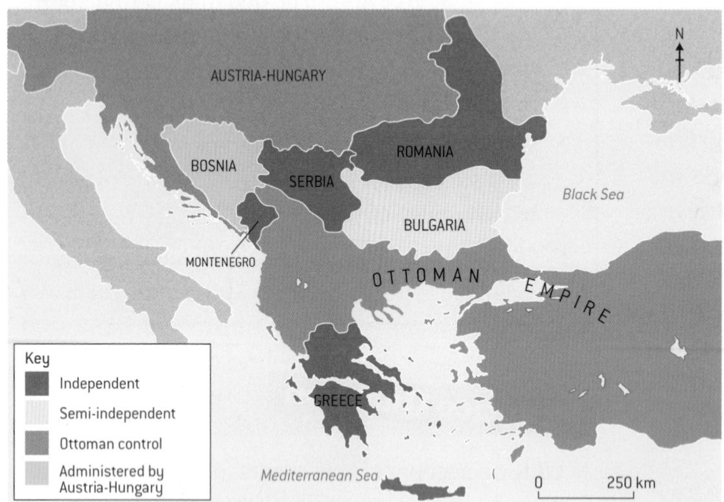

Russian Tsar: The Russians wanted to gain land in coastal areas in the Balkans to make trade easier and ensure that in times of war Russian battleships could get into the Mediterranean Sea from ports in the Black Sea.

▼ **SOURCE B** *The cover of a French magazine in 1908; the Emperor of Austria-Hungary (on the left) and the Russian Emperor (in the centre) are shown seizing parts of the Balkans, whilst the Turkish Emperor looks on powerless*

The end of an empire

The Balkans consists of several small countries. For many years, Turkey controlled these countries and they were part of the Turkish Empire (also known as the Ottoman Empire). However, by the early 1900s, the Turkish Empire was weak and different countries within the Balkans had rebelled against Turkish rule. Some, such as Greece and Serbia, had won their freedom and become independent of Turkish rule. Others, such as Bulgaria, had become **semi-independent**. This meant that Bulgarian politicians controlled everything *within* Bulgaria, but the country itself had to support Turkey in times of war. As a result of Turkey growing weaker, some of the larger nations that surrounded the Balkans (such as Austria-Hungary and Russia) saw this as an opportunity to gain land themselves and increase their influence (see Source B).

Slavs

Many of the people in the Balkans belong to an ethnic group called Slavs, which meant they all spoke similar (Slavic) languages. Many people in Serbia and Bulgaria were Slavs, for example. Serbia was the leading Slav state in the Balkans at this time and wanted to unite all Slavs into one nation (this idea was known as **pan-Slavism**).

The Balkans Crisis, 1908–9

In 1908 there was a rebellion in Turkey. Austria-Hungary took advantage of this and seized control of Bosnia, one of the small Slav states that had been under Turkish control. Nearby Serbia was angered by Austria-Hungary's invasion of a fellow Slav nation and asked Russia to take action. Russia had strong cultural and religious links to Serbia and had been a supporter of Serbia for a long time. Russia called for an international conference to discuss Austria-Hungary's actions.

The German position

Germany and Austria-Hungary were close allies, but the German Kaiser was unhappy that Austria-Hungary had taken over Bosnia. However, he promised to fully support Austria-Hungary. After all, Austria-Hungary had fully supported Germany at the Algeciras Conference in 1906 (see pages 20–21). Now Russia faced a dilemma: stand up for Serbia and Bosnia and take on both Austria-Hungary and Germany, or back down?

For now, Russia backed down. It was not prepared to risk war at this time because it felt that it was not strong enough to take on the Germans. The Bosnian Crisis of 1908–9 (sometimes known as the Balkans Crisis) had a major effect on the countries involved:

- Most people in Bosnia resented Austro-Hungarian rule and wanted to join with Serbia.
- Several secret societies were formed in Serbia and Bosnia. Their main aim was to get rid of Austro-Hungarian influence in the Balkans. Many were prepared to use violence to achieve this.
- Russia had been forced to back down against Germany. They vowed this would not happen again and began building more weapons.
- Austria-Hungary felt it now had the full support of Germany, which would affect how Austria-Hungary acted in the years to come.
- Italy was unhappy with Austria-Hungary's expansion into the Balkans. As a result, this weakened the relationship between the two countries – and the Triple Alliance.

Key Words

pan-Slavism
semi-independent

Work

1. Write out the following events, putting them in the correct chronological order:
   - Austria-Hungary takes over Bosnia
   - The Turkish Empire begins to break apart
   - Russia calls for an international conference to discuss the invasion
   - Russia backs down, unprepared to take on Germany
   - There is a rebellion in Turkey
   - Serbia asks Russia to take action against the invasion of Bosnia
2. Look at **Source B.**
   a. Who are the three men pictured in the source?
   b. What are each of the men doing?
   c. Why do you think the figure on the right is so unhappy?
   d. Why were Austria-Hungary and Russia so keen to take over parts of the Balkans? Try to divide these reasons into categories. Can you identify:
      - political reasons for wanting to control the Balkans
      - military reasons
      - economic reasons?
3. How did both the Moroccan Crises *and* these tensions in the Balkans
   - weaken the Alliance System
   - strengthen the Alliance System?

Emperor of Austria-Hungary: Austria-Hungary was difficult to rule because several different ethnic groups within it wanted their independence. One of the largest groups was the Slavs. Nearby Serbia contained many Slavs too, and the Serbian Slavs encouraged those in Austria-Hungary to rebel. As a result, Austria-Hungary wanted to control Balkan Slav areas (like Serbia and Bosnia) so they could squash this independence movement.

1.4B Problems in the Balkans

War in the Balkans

Turkey grew weaker in the first few years of the 1900s and gradually lost more and more of its empire. In fact, Turkey was known as 'the sick man of Europe'. In 1911, Italy beat Turkish forces in the Italian-Turkish War and took control of Turkish land in north Africa (Libya) and islands in the Aegean Sea. Several countries in the Balkans now saw this as a chance to finally drive the Turks completely out of Europe and gain full independence from Turkish rule. Four nations – Greece, Serbia, Bulgaria and Montenegro – joined forces and prepared to fight the Turks. They were known as the Balkan League.

The Balkan League

The Balkan League was initially set up to expel the Turks from the Balkans. However, the creation of the League was also encouraged by Russia, who felt that a strong group of mainly Slav nations would be a great ally for them – and perhaps deter any ambitions that Austria-Hungary might have in the region!

▼ **SOURCE C** *A Greek poster from 1912; the four countries in the League are represented by their flags (across the top of the poster) and soldiers in their respective uniforms; the flags are, from left to right, Bulgaria, Greece, Montenegro and Serbia; which country is represented at the feet of the soldiers?*

The First Balkan War, October 1912 to May 1913

In October 1912, the war began when Turkey was attacked. It was a quick and brutal war, lasting just 50 days, in which around half a million soldiers fought. Turkey lost and, at a peace conference in London in May 1913, agreed to withdraw from all the areas in Europe that it had controlled. Albania, a nation in the Balkans formerly under Turkish control, gained its independence. The remaining land was shared amongst the countries of the Balkan League.

The aftermath

Soon after the First Balkan War ended, the Balkan nations began to argue over the amount of land they had each taken from Turkey. The King of Bulgaria felt his country should have had more, and declared war on Serbia and Greece in order to get it.

The Second Balkan War, June to August 1913

Turkey joined in this Second Balkan War and fought against Bulgaria. Romania joined in too, also against Bulgaria, hoping to gain land from Bulgaria. The war was a disaster for Bulgaria and, by the end of another fast and brutal conflict, Bulgaria had lost almost all its gains from the First Balkan War.

Results of the Balkan Wars

The country that gained most from the Balkan Wars was Serbia. The country almost doubled in size and was by far the strongest of all the Balkan nations.

- Serbia became even more determined to be the leader of all the Slav people in the Balkans, including those living in the territory controlled by Austria-Hungary.
- Many Serbs living in Bosnia (and Bosnians themselves) were determined that their country should break free of Austro-Hungarian rule and join Serbia.
- Austria-Hungary saw the growth of Serbia as a major threat – they had a large, experienced army and were allies of Russia. They felt Serbia needed to be dealt with.
- Bulgaria came out of the wars both weaker and intent on getting revenge on Serbia.

▼ **SOURCE D** *An illustration from a French newspaper, 1913; the label from the time reads 'When Serb soldiers recapture a village from the Bulgarians, they find the buildings set on fire and the villagers massacred'*

▼ **E** *The Balkans after the First and Second Balkan Wars*

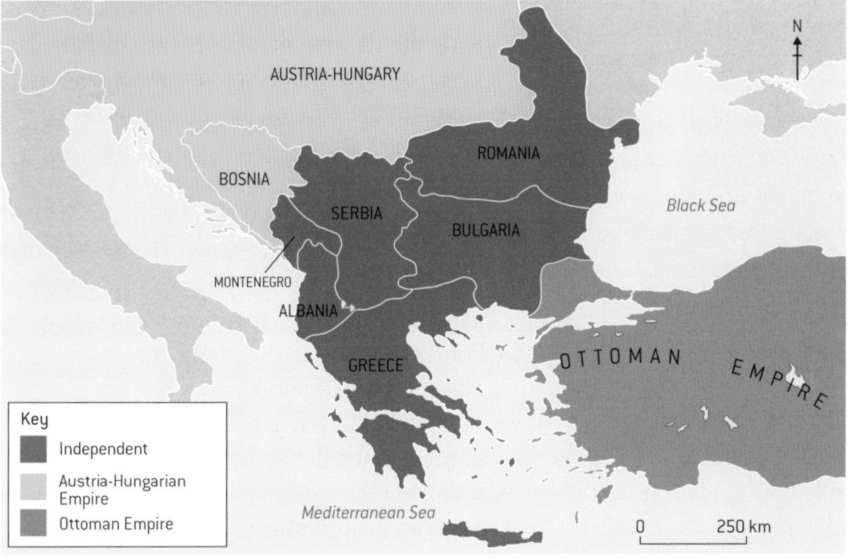

Work

1 Why do you think the Turkish Empire was known as the 'sick man of Europe' in the early 1900s?

2 a What was the Balkan League?

b Suggest reasons why the Balkan League was formed.

3 Look at **Source C**. This poster was created by a supporter of the Balkan League. How do you know?

4 a Compare Map **A** on page 22 and Map **E** on page 25. Describe how the Balkans has changed.

b Suggest reasons why these changes might increase tension in both the Balkans and amongst the European powers.

Practice Question

'The main reason for conflict in the Balkans was the weakness of the Turkish empire.'

How far do you agree with this statement? Explain your answer. **16 marks**

SPaG: 4 marks

Study Tip

Consider the word 'main' in the statement. While this may have been a reason, were there other reasons that may have been more important factors?

What was Britain's 'Splendid Isolation'?

In the late 1800s, in the reign of Queen Victoria, Britain played little part in European affairs. It had no official alliances with any other powerful nations, sticking to a policy of **'Splendid Isolation'**. Why did Britain follow this policy? What factors led Britain to stay out of European affairs? What challenges to Splendid Isolation made Britain rethink this policy?

Objectives

- **Define** 'Splendid Isolation'.
- **Examine** the challenges to Britain's Splendid Isolation.

The journey to Splendid Isolation

Britain had spent much of the 1800s building up the British Empire, mainly in Africa and Asia. By the late 1800s the British Empire was the largest the world had ever known. Britain was the richest and most powerful nation on earth, with the biggest navy, the most colonies, and the best trade links. The security of this empire depended on the strength of Britain's navy. It was needed to protect Britain's colonies and secure its trade routes. Indeed, in 1889 a British law stated that Britain's navy should be at least equal in size to the combined strength of the next two largest navies in the world (which were France and Russia at this time). This was known as the **two-power standard**. The government made £20 million available (around £1.2 billion today) to build more new warships.

The British felt, quite simply, that they did not need any military or economic allies because they had such a huge navy and an empire that provided all the goods and resources it needed. The British attitude to their position of Splendid Isolation is perhaps best summed up in Sources A and B.

▼ **SOURCE A** *A February 1896 speech by Viscount Goschen, the British government official in charge of Britain's navy from 1895 to 1900; many people credit him as the person who first used the term Splendid Isolation*

> We are said to be isolated, but I say that which I know that we only have to hold out our hands and our isolation will terminate, and we shall be welcomed into several groups of other Powers. In the modern system of European politics we could at any moment, I believe, make such alliances as we chose. Our isolation is not an isolation of weakness, or of contempt for ourselves: it is deliberately chosen; the freedom to act as we choose in any circumstances that may arise.

▼ **SOURCE B** *A popular British song from the late 1800s*

> We don't want to fight but by Jingo if we do,
>
> We've got the ships, we've got the men, we've got the money too.

Challenges to Splendid Isolation

In the early 1900s things began to change. The most powerful European nations started to split themselves into two alliances. Britain's position began to look less splendid, as the situation in Europe unfolded, and a little *too* isolated, particularly in the face of an increasingly aggressive Germany.

- The British and French had clashed over control of colonies in north Africa, and nearly went to war in the late 1800s. However, agreements were made over the colonies, which brought the nations close together.
- From 1898, Germany began to build up its navy. The Kaiser began to talk of making Germany a global power. His naval and colonial plans were a threat to Britain's power.
- Germany and Austria-Hungary joined together in an alliance (the Dual Alliance). Italy later joined this alliance (the Triple Alliance).
- France and Russia joined together in an alliance (the Franco-Russian Alliance).
- Germany supported the Boers, a group of settlers in the British colony of South Africa who had rebelled against British rule. This angered the British.

Out of isolation

In 1903, Britain's King Edward VII, while holidaying in the Mediterranean, heard that the French president was also visiting the region. Edward sent four battleships as a mark of respect to salute the President, who was delighted with this gesture and invited Edward to Paris. The subsequent visit was a brilliant success and almost overnight the climate was set for greater cooperation between the two nations. In 1904, the Entente Cordiale ('friendly understanding') was signed between Britain and France. In 1907, Britain signed a similar agreement with Russia. Now Britain was allied to two other European powers – and was no longer in Splendid Isolation.

▼ **SOURCE C** *A cartoon showing how, by 1915, Germany viewed the Entente Cordiale that was signed between Britain and France in 1904; the eagle represents Germany*

Extension

GCSE

The security of the British Empire depended on the strength of the British navy. Create a fact file on Britain's navy. When did the British first create a navy? What major historical events has the Navy been involved in? How had the Navy grown in the years leading up to the First World War?

Key Words

Splendid Isolation   two-power standard

Fact

In 1902, Britain signed an alliance with Japan, promising to help each other if either was attacked by more than one power. But this was not a European alliance – it meant that Britain had an ally in the Far East. However, some historians point to this as the beginning of the end of Britain's Splendid Isolation.

Work

1 Define 'Splendid Isolation'.
2 Why did Britain follow a policy of Splendid Isolation?
3 Read **Source A**. In your own words, summarise the British attitude towards alliances at this time.
4 In what ways were the following a threat to Britain's Splendid Isolation?
   a Tensions with France
   b Germany's Emperor
   c The other alliances in Europe

Practice Question

Source C is critical of Britain's Entente Cordiale with France. How do you know?

Explain your answer using **Source C** and your contextual knowledge. **4 marks**

Study Tip

Try to say why the date is important. Why has the cartoonist chosen to show Britain as a spider?

The aims of Kaiser Wilhelm II

From 1871, when Germany was formed out of a group of smaller states, the King of Prussia (the largest state) became the Emperor – or Kaiser – of the new Germany. Prussian generals, army officers and tactics formed the basis of the new unified German Army – and the Kaiser was its supreme commander. What were Kaiser Wilhelm's ambitions for Germany when he came to power in 1888? How did other countries view these ambitions?

Objectives

- ▶ **Define** 'Weltpolitik'.
- ▶ **Outline** Kaiser Wilhelm's aims in his **foreign policy**.
- ▶ **Assess** the impact of the Kaiser's foreign policy.

Kaiser Wilhelm II

Wilhelm became Kaiser in 1888, aged 29. He had spent most of his adult life in the Army and as Kaiser he was determined to maintain a powerful army. He took a great interest in military tactics and had a passion for wearing military uniforms because he felt that they associated him with Germany's powerful army.

Key Biography

Kaiser Wilhelm II

- Born in 1861, grandson of Germany's first Kaiser (Wilhelm I). He was also the grandson of Britain's Queen Victoria.
- Very energetic with a strong, outgoing personality. Could be unpredictable and rude.

Weltpolitik

The Kaiser felt that Germany should be a global power. At this time, many other European countries, such as France and Britain, had large overseas empires. The Kaiser decided that Germany needed a large empire, with control over colonies in different parts of the world, in order for Germany to be a global power. This idea was known as **Weltpolitik**, meaning 'world policy'. So, in the late 1800s Germany began to conquer other nations, particularly in Africa.

▼ **SOURCE A** *Kaiser Wilhelm II (holding the stick) with German army officers in 1907*

Protecting the new empire

The Kaiser wanted a large navy of powerful battleships for several reasons.

- He thought it would help Germany take over more countries and protect the countries already in the German Empire.
- He wanted the German Navy to rival Britain's huge navy (see **Interpretation B**). Germany spent huge sums of money on increasing the size of the Navy at this time. The size of the German Army was increased too. Taxes were raised and money was borrowed to pay for it – and Germany would remain in debt for a very long time.

▼ **INTERPRETATION B** *Adapted from Kaiser Wilhelm II's autobiography, written in 1926*

> I had a peculiar passion for the navy. It sprang to no small extent from my English blood. When I was a little boy I admired the proud British ships. There awoke in me the will to build ships of my own like these someday, and when I was grown up to possess a fine navy as the English.

Consequences of the Kaiser's aims and actions

The Kaiser's aims and actions increased the tension between European nations. The desire for more colonies alarmed countries that already had empires of their own. They wondered whether the Kaiser would challenge them for their colonies, which could lead to war. The fact that the Kaiser began building up his army and navy only increased this tension. It led other nations to build up their armies and navies too. Many nations began to draw out detailed defence (and attack) plans in preparation for war. It is no coincidence that this was the time when most of the powerful European nations began to form alliances. The Kaiser himself became a very unpopular figure in Britain when he gave an interview in 1908 with the *Daily Telegraph* newspaper.

▼ **SOURCE C** *Adapted from an interview with the Kaiser, published in the* London Daily Telegraph, *28 October 1908; readers would have found the Kaiser's buildup of arms alarming*

> Germany is a young and growing empire. She has a worldwide commerce which is rapidly expanding, and which patriotic Germans will not restrict. Germany must have a powerful fleet to protect her commerce and interests, even in the most distant seas. She expects those interests to go on growing, and she must be able to champion them manfully in any quarter of the globe.

Work

1. Define 'Weltpolitik' and 'foreign policy'.
2. Suggest reasons why the Kaiser was determined to make Germany a strong military power. Use **Source C** to help you.
3. a. Look at **Source D**. Who is the man on the horse and why do you think he has been drawn carrying all the weapons?
   b. What point is the cartoonist trying to make here?
4. Look at the **Timeline**. For each event, explain how tension increased as a result. Think about the relationships between the countries involved. Look at pages 18–19 to help you.

Key Words

Weltpolitik   foreign policy

▼ **SOURCE D** *The cover from a German journal published in 1909; it indicates that European countries are scared of Germany*

Practice Question

Write an account of how the Kaiser's ambitions increased the likelihood of war.

8 marks

Study Tip

This question does not just ask you to write about what the Kaiser did – you should also try to write about the impact of what he did, and why it increased the likelihood of war.

Timeline

1899–1902	1905	1908	1911
Boer War: Germany supports the Boers in their war against Britain	First Moroccan Crisis: The Kaiser promises to support the Sultan of Morocco against France's attempts to take over the country	The Balkans: Germany supports Austria-Hungary when Bosnia is invaded. Serbia and Russia support Bosnia, but back down because they are not prepared to take on Germany	Second Moroccan Crisis: After revolution in Morocco, France sends an army to take over. The Kaiser sends the gunship *Panther*, but Britain and France force him to back down

2.3 The arms race

By 1907, Europe was divided into two groups: the Triple Alliance and the Triple Entente. Each side was highly suspicious of the other. For example, the Germans felt that the friendship between Russia (to Germany's east) and France (to Germany's west) was an attempt to surround and threaten them. France and Russia, however, felt that the Kaiser's aim of becoming a world power was a direct threat to them. These fears led to all major European nations building up their armed forces.

Objectives

- **Examine** why the major European countries rearmed in the years before the outbreak of war.
- **Explore** the military rivalry between Britain and Germany at this time.

The arms race on land

An **arms race** is when rival countries build up their armed forces in a bid to become bigger and stronger than the other. In the years before the outbreak of the First World War, the major European powers took part in an arms race, as shown by the amount of money spent on the military.

- In 1870, Britain, France, Germany, Austria-Hungary, Russia and Italy spent over £90 million on the military between them.
- By 1914, this spending had quadrupled to almost £400 million.
- Germany increased spending the most (by 73 per cent), compared to France's increase of 10 per cent and Britain's increase of 13 per cent.
- Russia's spending also increased by more than a third, mainly in response to their defeat by the Japanese in 1905.
- Except for Britain, every major European power introduced (or increased) conscription. This is when governments pass laws that force men to join the armed forces.

Fact

Britain was the only major power that had not introduced conscription by the time war broke out in 1914. Instead, Britain relied on a volunteer army until 1916.

▼ **SOURCE A** *Sir Edward Grey, British Foreign Secretary, in a speech to the British Parliament in 1909*

> There is no comparison between the importance of the German navy to Germany and the importance our navy to us. Our navy to us is what their army is to them. To have a strong navy would increase Germany's prestige and influence, but it is not a matter of life and death to them as it is to us.

Military plans

The European powers were worried about possible future conflicts, so they made detailed plans about where and how their armies would attack if war broke out:

- Britain – A highly trained army unit would travel to France at short notice to help the French.
- France – French troops would march through Alsace and Lorraine, capture these areas, then continue onto Berlin. Known as Plan 17.
- Russia – Millions of Russian troops would attack the eastern borders of Germany and Austria-Hungary. Known as Plan 19.
- Germany – Planned to attack France first, defeat it quickly, then turn and fight the Russians in the east. Known as the Schlieffen Plan.
- Austria-Hungary – Developed several different war plans that related to whether different countries joined in or not. Known as Plan B and Plan R.

Anglo-German naval race

In the 1800s, Britain had built up a huge navy to protect its trade routes and colonies around the world and, by 1900, was the world's greatest naval power. However, in 1901, Germany's Kaiser announced that he wanted an empire to rival Britain's. He needed a large navy to achieve this, so began a huge shipbuilding campaign, financed through a series of Navy Laws.

Then, in 1906, the British announced the creation of a new, improved type of warship called the dreadnought. The new ship was so much faster, stronger and more powerful than any other battleship ever built that older, German ships were referred to as *funf minuten*. This translated to 'five minutes' – the amount of time that Germans thought it would take a dreadnought to sink one of their ships.

However, almost immediately, the Germans began work on their own version of the dreadnought (known as *Rheinland*). The British responded with an improved version of a dreadnought (the 'super-dreadnought'). A 'naval race' had started (see **Source C**).

▼ **SOURCE B** *A British super-dreadnought battleship, 1914;. the ship was 177 metres long; it had fast, efficient engines, so it was both quick and able to fight at long range*

a Ten 34 cm guns
b Sixteen 10 cm guns
c 20–30 cm thick armour plating
d Three torpedo tubes, one on each side and another at the stern

▼ **C** *The number of dreadnought-type ships built by Britain and Germany between 1906 and 1914*

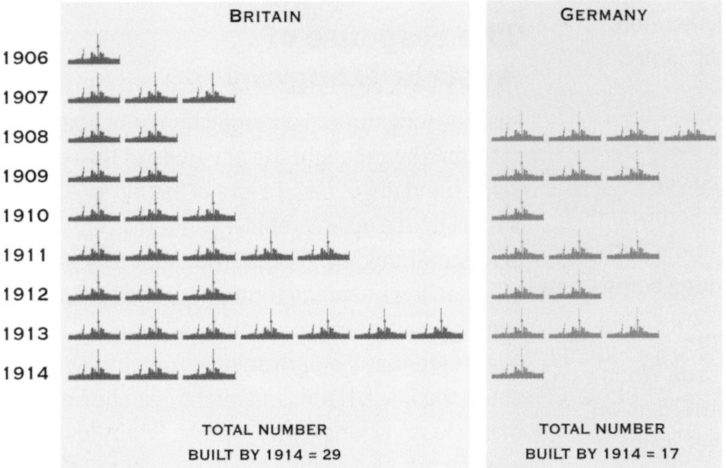

Key Words

arms race

▼ **SOURCE D** *'Why Did The Kaiser Build Dreadnoughts?', a cartoon by W. K. Haselden, published 25 September 1914*

Work

1 Test your understanding by explaining the following key terms:
   a arms race
   b Anglo-German naval race
   c dreadnought
   d *funf minuten*
   e super-dreadnought
2 Suggest reasons why the major European powers each built up their armed forces in the years before the First World War.
3 Why did Germany want a larger navy?
4 Why do you think Britain was so concerned about Germany building up their navy?
5 What effect do you think the increase in the size of the German Navy had on Britain's relationship with Germany?
6 Read **Source A**. In your own words, briefly sum up the point that Sir Edward Grey is making.

The Black Hand and murder in Sarajevo

In May 1911, a group of ten Serbian army officers formed a secret society in Belgrade, the capital city of Serbia. The group was called 'Union or Death', although it was also known as the 'Black Hand'. Its members were prepared to commit acts of terrorism to achieve their aims. Why was this group formed and what were its aims? What terror acts did its members plot – and commit?

Objectives

- **Identify** the aims of the Serbian nationalist movement.
- **Consider** the activities of the Black Hand Society.
- **Examine** the assassination of Archduke France Ferdinand.

'Greater Serbia'

In the late 1800s, several new nations (such as Italy and Germany) had been created when people with a similar culture, language and history had unified. In Serbia, there was a strong **nationalist** movement that wanted to unite all Serb areas in the Balkans into one unified country, called 'Greater Serbia'. However, this took a blow in 1908 when Austria-Hungary took over Bosnia, a country containing many Serbs. Several secret groups formed at this time with the aim of driving Austria-Hungary out of the Balkan region altogether. They had names such as 'National Defense' and 'Young Bosnia'. But perhaps the most extreme of these groups was the Black Hand. The group was mainly made of army officers, lawyers, journalists, and university professors and students. Any member had to agree that they were willing to die for the Black Hand.

The aims of the Black Hand

Its aims were simple – and brutal. They wanted 'to realise the national ideal, the unification of all Serbs. This organisation prefers terrorist action to cultural activities; so will therefore remain secret'. The leader was a 26-year-old colonel named Dragutin Dimitrijevic, code-named 'Apis'.

'Apis' soon built up a network of people loyal to the Black Hand and before long there were about 2500 members. Several members worked as guards on the border between Serbia and Bosnia, so Black Hand members could easily cross from Serbia into Bosnia to carry out terrorist acts, such as planting bombs.

In 1911, 'Apis' sent a member of the Black Hand to assassinate Austria-Hungary's Emperor, Franz Josef. When this failed, the Black Hand tried to kill an important member of the Austrian government with a poisoned dagger. This assassination attempt also failed.

▼ **SOURCE A** *Dragutin Dimitrijevic, code-named 'Apis' and leader of the Black Hand*

The response of Austria-Hungary

Austria-Hungary was outraged by these acts of terror. They thought the activities of the Black Hand might inspire lots of people in Bosnia to rise up and rebel against the rule of Austria-Hungary. They worried that this rebellion might spread throughout their empire. Leading politicians within Austria-Hungary also suspected that the Serbian government knew about the Black Hand, and might even be helping them. Austria-Hungary's Emperor, Franz Josef, was encouraged to take tough measures to crush Serbia.

A visit to Sarajevo

Austria-Hungary announced that its army would test out weapons and carry out army exercises in Bosnia next to the Serbian border. The Black Hand saw this as a very threatening move. Soon after, it was announced that Franz Josef's nephew, Archduke Franz Ferdinand, would visit Bosnia's capital city (Sarajevo) after watching the military exercises. The Archduke was next in line to the throne of Austria-Hungary. The visit to Sarajevo was scheduled for 28 June 1914 – which happened to be a National Day in Serbia, and one of the most important dates in the Serbian calendar. To many Serbs, the visit was a direct insult and confirmed to the Black Hand that Austria-Hungary was directly threatening Serbia itself. So the Black Hand decided to carry out another act of terror – kill Archduke Franz Ferdinand.

▼ **B** *The Balkans in 1914*

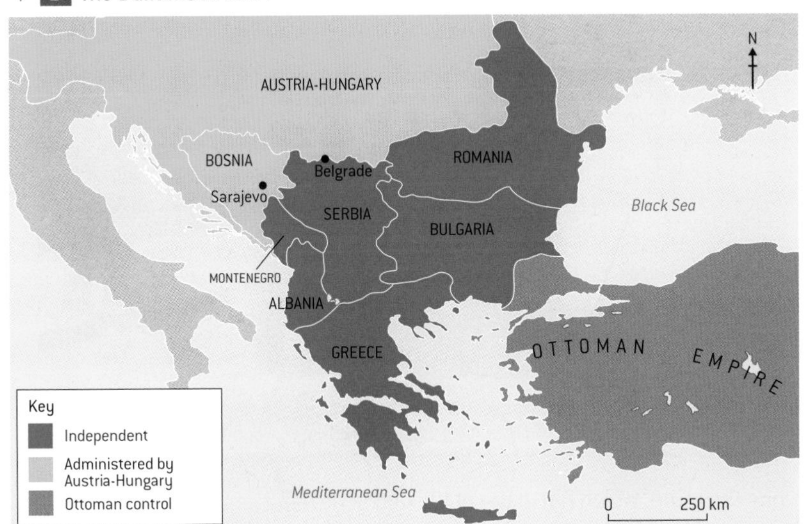

▼ **SOURCE C** *A member of the Black Hand group explains how the decision to attempt an assassination in 1914 came about; adapted from a newspaper account*

We read in a newspaper clipping that the Austrian Archduke Franz Ferdinand would visit Sarajevo, the capital of Bosnia, 28 June, to direct army manoeuvres.

How dared Franz Ferdinand, not only the representative of the oppressor but in his own person an arrogant tyrant, enter Sarajevo on that day? Such an entry was a deliberate insult. 28 June is a date engraved deeply in the heart of every Serb. It is the day on which the old Serbian kingdom was conquered by the Turks at the Battle of Amselfeld in 1389. That was no day for Franz Ferdinand, the new oppressor, to venture to the very doors of Serbia for a display of the force of arms which kept us beneath his heel. Our decision was taken almost immediately. Death to the tyrant!

Key Word

nationalist

Work

1. a What was the 'Black Hand'?
   b The Black Hand was also known as 'Union or Death'. Why do you think it chose this name?
2. Prepare a fact file on the Black Hand. Include details of its aims, leader, membership, activities and any other interesting facts.
3. Why was the government in Austria-Hungary so concerned about the Black Hand?
4. Some people have argued that it was a foolish decision to announce the Archduke's trip and travel plans in newspapers for 28 June. Do you agree? Explain your answer.

Extension

Find out about the Battle of Amselfeld (or Battle of Kosovo) in 1389 and its importance for Slav history and sense of identity. Note that the battle is dated 15 June, as the Julian calendar was used then. This date translates to 28 June using today's Gregorian calendar.

3.1B Black Hand and murder in Sarajevo

Planning for murder in Sarajevo

Black Hand quickly made plans and seven Bosnian students, living in Serbia, were selected to carry out the murder. They were trained how to use guns and bombs, and a few weeks before the visit they left Serbia and made their way across the border and into Bosnia. Look at the timeline and images relating to 28 June 1914, the day of the assassination.

1

The Archduke and his wife, Sophie, arrived at Sarajevo train station at 9.28am. They were driven towards the town hall to meet the Mayor of Sarajevo. Crowds lined the streets and the car drove slowly so the royal couple could wave to people.

▶ **SOURCE D** *Archduke Franz Ferdinand and his wife, Sophie in their open-topped car*

2

Black Hand **assassins** waited for the car along the route, which had been published in newspapers. The first member to try to kill the Archduke threw a bomb at the car. The Archduke managed to deflect the bomb and it exploded underneath the car behind, injuring several people. The Archduke's car quickly sped away to the town hall.

3

A furious Archduke cancelled the rest of his planned visit, but decided to visit those injured by the bomb before making his way back to the train station. At 11am he set off intending to take a different route to the one originally planned. However, no one had told the driver the route had changed. As they passed Schiller's Café, the driver was told about the altered route and stopped the car to turn around.

▼ **E** *The route taken by the Archduke's car; as you can see, if the driver had known about the altered return route (marked in green), instead of following the planned route (in red), then he would never have driven past his assassin*

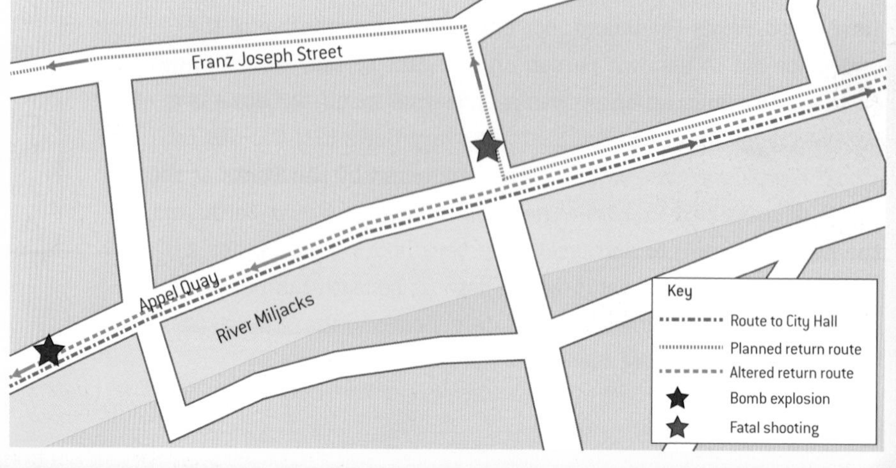

4

The car stopped in front of 19-year-old Gavrilo Princip, one of the assassins, who was on his way home thinking the plan had failed. Princip pulled out a gun and fired two shots. The Archduke was hit in the throat and Sophie was shot in the stomach. Both were killed.

▼ **SOURCE F** *An illustration from a French magazine, 12 July 1914, showing the moment Princip fired his gun*

▼ **SOURCE G** *Gavrilo Princip was arrested and sentenced to 20 years in prison; he died in 1918; this two-metre tall statue of Princip was erected in 2015 in Belgrade, Serbia, where he is viewed by many as a folk hero and freedom-fighter*

Key Words

assassin

Key Biography

Archduke Franz Ferdinand (1863–1914)

- Born in 1863 in Austria. Eldest son of Archduke Charles Louis, the brother of Emperor Franz Joseph.
- Became heir to the throne in 1896 after the suicide of the Emperor's son and his own father's death from typhoid fever.
- Married Sophie, Countess of Chotek, in 1900.
- Worked to improve relations between Austria-Hungary and Russia and tried to persuade the Emperor to make political reforms.
- From 1913 he became Inspector General of the Army. He and his wife were assassinated in June 1914 in Sarajevo after visiting army exercises.

Work

1. Why do you think the Black Hand chose lots of people for the assassination attempt?
2. Why do you think the return route from the town hall was changed.
3. Create your own timeline for 28 June 1914. You may use no more than 50 words – so choose them carefully.
4. Look at **Source G**. A similar statue was erected in Sarajevo on 28 June 2014. Why do you think Princip is viewed in such a positive way by many modern Serbs and Bosnians?

Practice Question

Write an account of how events in the Balkans during the summer of 1914 led to the assassination of Archduke Franz Ferdinand.

8 marks

Study Tip

Try to focus on several moments in the story that had a big impact on the events that followed. Explain what that impact was.

3.2 Countdown to war

Most European nations thought that the Sarajevo murders were a local matter that would be dealt with by the countries involved: Serbia and Austria-Hungary. This didn't happen. Soon the European powers became involved in a major conflict that would drag on for over four years – the First World War. How did the assassination of Archduke Franz Ferdinand escalate into world war?

Objectives

- **Examine** the immediate consequences of the assassinations in Sarajevo.
- **Explore** events that led to the outbreak of war in August 1914.

The response of Austria-Hungary

Franz Josef and his advisers thought that the Serbian government had played a role in the murders – and wanted to teach the Serbs a lesson. Conrad von Hötzendorf, a leading politician and army general (and a close friend of Franz Ferdinand) proposed that Austria-Hungary should declare war on Serbia.

▼ **SOURCE A** *Advice given by Conrad von Hötzendorf to the government of Austria-Hungary after the assassination of Archduke Franz Ferdinand, June 1914*

> This is not the crime of a single fanatic; the assassination is Serbia's declaration of war on Austria-Hungary. If we miss this chance, Austria-Hungary will break up. We must wage war to prevent this. To wait any longer means a diminishing of our chances – there must be a final and fundamental reckoning with the Serbs. It will be a hopeless fight – nevertheless it must be waged.

The July Crisis begins

In late July, after checking it had the support of Germany, Austria-Hungary sent a list of demands (known as an **ultimatum**) to Serbia. They asked that Serbia takes full responsibility for the assassinations and gets rid of the Black Hand and any other 'anti-Austrian' groups. Austria-Hungary insisted that their own police should be allowed into Serbia to make sure that the Serbs were doing all they could to get rid of these terror groups. Serbia was given 48 hours to decide whether to accept the demands.

Fact

The international crisis that began with the murder of Archduke Franz Ferdinand on 28 June 1914 and culminated in the declarations of war by all the great powers is often referred to as the **July Crisis**.

The Serbian response

Shortly before the 48-hour deadline was up, the King of Serbia accepted all the demands except the one that allowed police from Austria-Hungary into his country. He argued that this challenged Serbia's independence and was worried that it could give Austria-Hungary a foothold in his country.

The Austro-Hungarian response

When Austria-Hungary received Serbia's response, they broke off all communication and prepared their army for war. On 28 July, one month after the assassinations, Austria-Hungary declared war on Serbia and began bombing Serbia's capital city, Belgrade. This triggered a chain of events that meant that all the great powers of Europe were at war with each other in just over a week.

1914 Wednesday 29 July

Russia has supported Serbia for many years. When Russia's tsar, Nicholas II, hears that Serbia has been attacked, he orders the Russian Army to **mobilise** and prepare to go to Serbia's aid.

Thursday 30 July

Germany's alliance with Austria-Hungary comes into force. Germany's Kaiser sends a message to his cousin, Tsar Nicholas, asking him to stop getting his troops ready. There is a flurry of messages between them – but nothing is agreed.

Saturday 1 August

Tsar Nicholas refuses to stop his preparations for war, so Germany mobilises its army and declares war on Russia. The French (an ally of Russia) prepares its army for war.

Sunday 2 August

Germany begins the first part of the Schlieffen Plan. This plan details how Germany will fight both Russia and France in a war, and assumes Russian troops will take longer to mobilise than French troops. It involves the invasion of France through Belgium, a swift defeat of France within six weeks, and a redeployment of troops after this to fight Russian troops to the east. Germany sends troops towards the Belgian border, and asks for passage through Belgium to France; Belgium refuses.

Monday 3 August

Germany declares war on France and invades Belgium. This brings Britain into the conflict, as it signed a treaty in 1839 promising to protect Belgium if it was invaded. The German Kaiser believes Britain won't stick to this treaty. The British send a message to the Germans asking them to call off their invasion of Belgium.

Tuesday 4 August

The Germans do not respond to Britain's message, and German troops continue their invasion of Belgium. At 11pm Britain declares war on Germany.

Wednesday 5 August

France declares war on Germany.

Thursday 6 August

Austria-Hungary declares war on Russia.

▼ **SOURCE B** *A comic depiction of the web of alliances, published in the American newspaper, the* Brooklyn Eagle *in July 1914*

Key Words

July Crisis mobilise ultimatum

Work

1. Define:
   a. ultimatum
   b. mobilise
2. Read **Source A**. Explain in detail Conrad von Hötzendorf's reasons for wanting to declare war on Serbia.
3. The outbreak of war has been likened to a 'row of falling dominoes'. Why do you think this phrase has been used?
4. Look at **Source B**.
   a. Identify the countries in this cartoon.
   b. In your own words, explain what the cartoonist wanted the reader to understand from the cartoon.

Practice Question

'The actions of Germany were the main reason that European countries went to war in 1914.'

How far do you agree with this statement? Explain your answer. **16 marks**

SPaG: 4 marks

Study Tip

It is important that your answer isn't only about the actions of Germany but considers how other countries may have contributed to the outbreak of hostilities.

How to... write an account

Below is an example of a question that asks you to write an account of how a historical event led to particular consequences.

Practice Question

Write an account of how the assassination of Archduke Franz Ferdinand led to the outbreak of war in 1914. **8 marks**

Study Tip

This question is asking you to describe what happened as a result of the assassination of the heir to the Austro-Hungarian throne on 28 June 1914. When there are dates in a question, make sure that you pay close attention to them and only consider events that happened in those years.

Study Tip

You should try to consider the immediate effects of the assassination – and the consequences throughout the year. In other words, the question wants you to think about not just the resulting declaration of war by Austria-Hungary on Serbia, but also the events that happened after to make it an international crisis.

Over to you

This type of question asks you to write an account in which you describe, explain and analyse how an event led to further important developments. In this example, you are asked to consider how the assassination of Archduke Franz Ferdinand in June 1914 led to the outbreak of war in July and August of 1914.

1 Read the question carefully. It is not asking you to simply describe the assassination; it is more complex than that. It is asking you to write *how* the assassination led to the outbreak of war – but to write about this properly, you must outline what had happened before the assassination.

2 Consider how events *before* the assassination contributed to what happened *after* it. Think about how the following events and developments contributed to what happened after the assassination:
   - the Alliance System
   - the crises in Morocco (1905 and 1911) and the Balkans (1908–9), and their effects on international relations
   - Anglo-German rivalry
   - Serbian nationalism and relations between Serbia and Austria-Hungary before the assassination
   - the Schlieffen Plan and Britain's agreement with Belgium.

3 It is not enough to simply know about each of these events – it is important that you know how they fit into the story of the outbreak of war in July and August of 1914. To understand why the great powers of Europe went to war, a top historian should also understand how events and developments *before* the war played their part.

4 However, the question asks you to write an account of the consequences of the assassination and the outbreak of war. So, you should outline how each country reacted when war broke out:
   - 28 June – the heir to the throne of Austria-Hungary was assassinated in Sarajevo, Bosnia, by members of the Black Hand, a Serbian nationalist group with the aim of using acts of terror to drive Austria-Hungary out of the Balkan region altogether.
   - Austria-Hungary blamed Serbia. They sent an ultimatum to the Serbians asking them to take full responsibility for the murders and to get rid of the Black Hand and other 'anti-Austrian' groups.

- Serbia agreed to most of the demands of the ultimatum, but not all. Austria-Hungary broke off all communication with Serbia – and prepared their army for war.
- On 28 July, one month after the assassinations in Sarajevo, Austria-Hungary declared war on Serbia and began bombing Serbia's capital city, Belgrade.
- 29 July – The Russian army prepared to go to Serbia's aid.
- 1 August – Germany mobilised its army and declared war on Russia. The French (an ally of Russia) prepared its army for war.
- 2 August – the Germans began the first part of the Schlieffen Plan by sending soldiers towards the Belgian border.
- 3 August – Germany declared war on France and invaded Belgium. Britain asked Germany to end its invasion of Belgium.
- 4 August – the Germans ignored Britain's message and continued to invade Belgium. At 11pm Britain declared war on Germany.
- 5 August – France declared war on Germany.
- 6 August – Austria-Hungary declared war on Russia.

5. With all this in mind, what are the strengths and weaknesses of the following opening paragraphs?

On 28 June 1914, the heir to the throne of Austria-Hungary was assassinated in Sarajevo, Bosnia, by members of the Black Hand, a Serbian nationalist group. Bosnia had been conquered by Austria-Hungary in 1908 and many Serbs lived there. In Serbia, there was a strong nationalist movement that dreamed of uniting all Serbs in the Balkans into one, unified country, called 'Greater Serbia'. Several secret groups (including the Black Hand) formed at this time with the aim of driving Austria-Hungary out of the Balkan region. Many of these he groups were prepared to use acts of terror, such as this assassination, in an attempt to achieve their aims.

Austria-Hungary blamed Serbia for the assassination and sent an ultimatum asking it to take full responsibility for the murders and to get rid of Black Hand and any other 'anti-Austrian' groups. Serbia agreed to most of the demands, but not all. When Austria-Hungary received Serbia's response, it prepared its army for war. On 28 July, Austria-Hungary declared war on Serbia. On 29 July, Russia, who had supported Serbia for many years, mobilised its army and prepared to go to war to aid Serbia. The outbreak of war followed as the pre-war alliances between the great European powers came into effect.

On 1 August, Germany ...

Study Tip

The student begins by describing the event mentioned in the question.

Study Tip

The student puts the assassination in context. It is explained why the assassination took place.

Study Tip

Here, the student begins to write about the consequences of the event, which links to the part of the question that asks you to show how the assassination 'led to the outbreak of war in 1914'.

Study Tip

The student again shows good contextual knowledge before moving on to address the consequences of the assassination.

6. Now complete the answer.

4.1 What was the Schlieffen Plan?

In 1892, France and Russia signed a deal to help each other out if either was attacked (the Franco-Russian Alliance). This posed a problem for Germany – if it went to war with one of these countries, then it would face war with the other. Germany was sandwiched between France and Russia, so a war would mean that France could attack from the west and Russia from the east. This is known as a 'war on two fronts'. So how did Germany prepare for this?

Objectives

- ▶ **Outline** the origins of the Schlieffen Plan.
- ▶ **Assess** the strengths and weaknesses of the plan.

Origins of the Schlieffen Plan

Following the signing of the Franco-Russian Alliance, the Germans began working on a plan to deal with a 'war on two fronts'. It was called the Schlieffen Plan in honour of its creator, General Count Alfred von Schlieffen, head of the German Army.

Key Biography

General Count Alfred von Schlieffen (1833–1913)

- Born in Berlin in 1833.
- Son of a Prussian general, entered the Army aged 21.
- Quickly moved up the ranks in the Prussian Army and took part in the Franco-Prussian War (1870–71).
- Became head of Germany's army in 1891.
- Differed from previous German generals who thought that a 'war on two fronts' would involve an attack on Russia first. Felt that a swift sweep through Belgium (and part of the Netherlands) in the north would be best as the southern area of France was too mountainous.
- Retired in 1906. The Schlieffen Plan was adapted several times after his retirement.
- Died in 1913.

The plan was simple – but risky. Schlieffen did not want to fight France and Russia at the same time, because this would mean splitting his army in two and sending half to the west and half to the east. Instead, he planned to beat the countries one at a time.

He decided that France should be the first country to be attacked. Schlieffen knew that Russia lacked an effective road and railway system, so he assumed it would take several weeks (perhaps three to four months) for Russia to get its troops ready. This would give Germany time to beat France, who he felt would mobilise for war a lot quicker. After defeating France, German forces could then turn around and attack the Russians.

▼ A *The Schlieffen Plan involved taking the French by surprise by attacking at speed through Belgium and taking France's capital city, Paris, within six weeks*

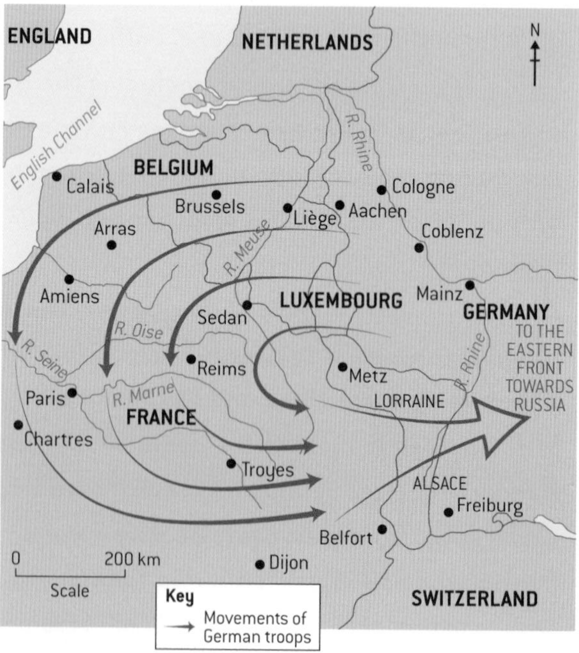

Attacking France

The plan involved several smaller groups of German soldiers entering France through its more lightly defended northern regions. However, most troops would not march directly into France; instead, they would invade France by marching through the smaller nations of Belgium, Luxembourg and the Netherlands first. These three countries lacked large military forces and Belgium and Luxembourg had borders with France that were not well protected. Once the huge force of German troops had successfully entered France, they would sweep south-west and down toward Paris. Schlieffen assumed that the French would not expect an attack through Belgium, Luxembourg and the Netherlands and that most French troops would be positioned on the German border. The Schlieffen Plan, therefore, meant that the French would be **outflanked** and surrounded. Schlieffen predicted that Paris could be taken, and the French defeated in around 40 days, giving the Germans plenty of time to turn their forces around and attack the Russians.

Problems with the plan

The plan had several flaws:

- Schlieffen assumed that Russia would take at least six weeks to get its army ready to fight. What if Russia got its army ready quickly – or France took longer than six weeks to defeat?
- The plan relied on Germany attacking France through Belgium, Luxembourg and the Netherlands. However, in 1839 Britain had signed a treaty to protect Belgium. Schlieffen didn't think the British would honour this 75-year-old deal – but what if they did? And what if Belgium put up fiercer resistance than anticipated?

There was a further issue with Schlieffen's plan. It actually made a war on two fronts even more likely. Schlieffen took it for granted that if Russia and Germany went to war, then France would join in. But what if France stayed out of the war and decided not to help Russia? The plan ensured that France would be attacked, even if it was just Germany and Russia at war. The Schlieffen Plan guaranteed a large-scale conflict.

The plan is changed

The original Schlieffen Plan was adapted. Not all German generals supported the plan because some felt it was too risky. Schlieffen was replaced in 1906 by General von Moltke. He 'downsized' Schlieffen's plan by reducing the number of troops used in the attack and he removed the Netherlands from the battle plan altogether.

The early stages of war

When the war began, in August 1914, German troops invaded Belgium and Luxembourg, in line with the modified Schlieffen Plan. The French had their own war plan (Plan 17) and invaded Alsace and Lorraine, the **provinces** that Germany had taken from France at the end of the Franco-Prussian War in 1870. The French plan relied on capturing the 'lost provinces' quickly and advancing at speed towards Germany's capital city, Berlin. Meanwhile, 120,000 highly trained British soldiers (known as the BEF – British Expeditionary Force) landed in France to help. However, within weeks, both the Schlieffen Plan and Plan 17 had gone horribly wrong!

Key Words

outflanked province

▼ **SOURCE B** *General Helmuth von Moltke speaking about von Schlieffen's plan in 1911*

> It may be safely assumed that the next war will be a war on two fronts. Of our enemies, France is the most dangerous and can prepare the most quickly. Accounts must be settled with her very soon after deployment. Should the defeat of the French be achieved quickly and decisively, it will also be possible to make forces available against Russia. This is only possible by means of an advance through Switzerland or Belgium.

Fact

The original Schlieffen Plan was so detailed that it wasn't finished until 1905 – and it was modified again several times up until the outbreak of war. Schlieffen himself died in 1913 and never saw the plan 'in action'.

Work

1. Why was the Schlieffen Plan created?
2. Make two lists. One list should contain strengths about the plan. The other list should contain weaknesses.
3. Why did Germany attack Belgium in 1914?
4. Can you suggest reasons why Germany did not think that Britain would get involved in the conflict? Don't just think about what you have learned on these pages, think about Britain's position in the world at this time.
5. If the Schlieffen Plan failed, what problems do you think Germany would face?

The failure of the war plans

The Germans advanced quickly into Belgium in the first few weeks of the war. But the speed of their advance didn't last. Before long, their progress was halted by fierce fighting against Belgian, French and British troops in the west and Russian troops in the east. Why did the war plans fail? How did the failure of these plans affect the type of war being fought?

Objectives

- **Explore** why the war plans in both the west and the east failed.
- **Examine** how the war spread to different parts of the world.

Early problems for the Schlieffen Plan

The Schlieffen Plan's success relied on the speedy defeat of Belgium, followed by a quick victory over France. After this, German troops could march eastwards and take on the Russians. But things went wrong very quickly. The Germans had underestimated the Belgians, who put up much fiercer resistance than expected. They had built a series of huge, stone forts equipped with long-range, powerful guns to protect the country from attack. This slowed the Germans down, especially at Liège where the combination of the fort and the bravery of Belgian troops delayed the German invasion of France by four or five days.

▼ **SOURCE A** *A British cartoon from* Punch *magazine, 12 August 1914*

The German advance was also slowed down at the Belgian city of Mons, near to the French border. Here the Germans faced the British Expeditionary Force (BEF), who pinned down a large number of German troops. The British rifle-fire at Mons was so fast that the Germans thought they were being machine-gunned. The Germans had been referring to British troops as 'a contemptible little army' but this showed them that the British Army was small but well trained and effective even when outnumbered. The delay in the German advance forced the Germans to abandon their plan of sweeping around Paris to capture it – thus disregarding one of the key elements of the Schlieffen Plan: the speedy capture of Paris. Also, at times the German Army marched too quickly – and their supplies of food, water and ammunition could not keep up with them. In the hot August sunshine of 1914, the German troops were already exhausted after only a few weeks at war.

The Russian surprise

The Schlieffen Plan relied on the Russians taking around six weeks to get their armies ready to fight. This six-week period would be enough, the Germans hoped, to beat France before turning their forces on the Russians. But the war against France was going badly – and the Russians took only ten days to get their armies on the march towards Germany and Austria-Hungary.

In response to the Russian threat, the Germans ordered around 100,000 soldiers to leave the war in France and take on the Russians. This slowed down the German advance in France because there were now fewer soldiers to fight the French, Belgian and British troops. Germany was now fighting a 'war on two fronts', something that the Schlieffen Plan had tried to avoid.

The Battle of the Marne

By late August, despite the setbacks, the Germans had reached the River Marne. They were weak and hungry, but were now only 40 kilometres from Paris.

However, by now there were fewer German troops heading towards Paris than was intended in the original Schlieffen Plan. Eleven divisions, for example, had been moved from Belgium to fight Russian forces in the east. As a result, a large group of German troops under General von Kluck (the German 1st Army) swerved to the southeast, away from Paris, rather than heading southwest to surround the city. This meant that they marched into the valley of the River Marne, within reach of British and French troops – and this gave the French and British an opportunity to attack.

The British and the French (under General Joffre) attacked from the west on 6 September, forcing von Kluck to stop his advance and turn westwards to meet the attack. In turning to meet the French and British, a 50-kilometre (30-mile) gap was created in the German lines between von Kluck's 1st Army and the German 2nd Army, commanded by General von Bülow, located to the east of von Kluck.

Soon, British troops began to advance into the gap between the German 1st and 2nd Armies, so the cautious Bülow ordered a retreat, forcing von Kluck to do the same. Over the next few days, British and French troops continued their advance and forced the Germans to retreat to the River Aisne. This became known as the Battle of the Marne and, in total, more than two million soldiers fought – and over half a million were either injured or killed in less than one week of fighting.

Once the German Army had started to retreat, it was clear that the Schlieffen Plan had failed. The Germans began to dig trenches in the ground to protect themselves from gunfire and bombs. They added machine guns and barbed wire to the top of their trenches. French and British troops did the same, facing the German positions. Up until now, the war had been one of movement, where large groups of soldiers had moved quickly to cover large areas of ground – but now things were about to change.

▼ **B** *Battle of the Marne (6–10 September 1914)*

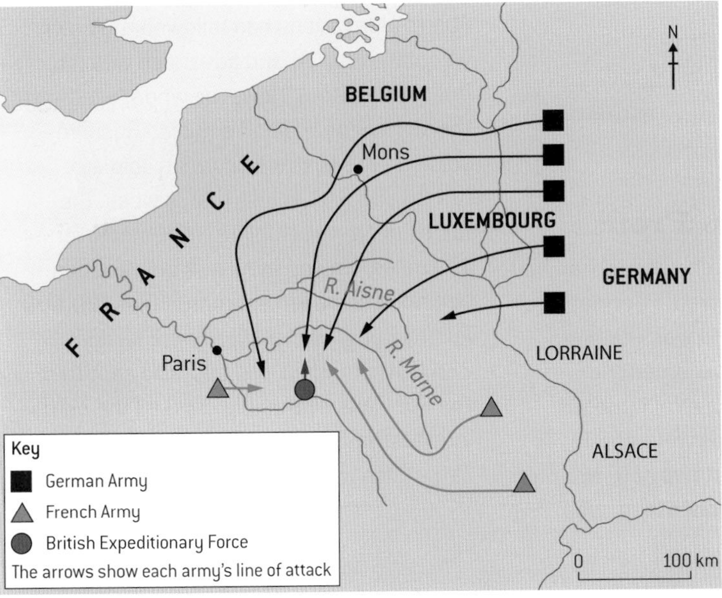

Work

1 a Look at **Source A**. Which two countries do the figures represent?
  b Can you suggest why the figures have been drawn this way?
  c What point do you think the cartoonist was trying to make?

2 In what ways did the following contribute to the failure of the Schlieffen Plan?
  a **The** Belgian resistance
  b The BEF
  c The Russians
  d German military leaders

3 The Battle of the Marne is seen as a turning point in the early part of the war. A turning point is a particular event or moment that marks an important change. Suggest reasons why the battle is viewed as a turning point.

Practice Question

'The resistance of the Allies was the main reason why the Schlieffen Plan failed.' How far do you agree with this statement? Explain your answer.

16 marks
SPaG: 4 marks

Study Tip

There were several reasons why the Schlieffen Plan failed. The question suggests one of the reasons. Write about other reasons, and say why you think one of them had more impact on the failure of the plan.

Extension

The Battle of the Frontiers is the collective name for some of the early clashes on the Western Front during the war. Prepare a fact file on these battles. Which nations fought, and where? What was the outcome and impact?

4.2B The failure of the war plans

The race to the sea

By early September 1914, both sides had dug trenches to defend themselves. As neither side could go forward, each tried to get around the back of the other. As the armies moved north, trying to outflank each other, they dug trenches as they went. This part of the war is sometimes called 'the race to the sea'. Several major battles took place during the 'race', for example between 19 October and 22 November, near the Belgian city of Ypres, over 120,000 British, French and Belgian soldiers were killed or wounded while stopping the Germans from outflanking them. By November, both sides had reached the English Channel. The lines of trenches soon stretched the other way too, eventually reaching from the coast to Switzerland, a distance of over 400 miles. For the next four years, these positions hardly changed. This situation was soon referred to as a '**stalemate**' – a complete inability to move forward any great distance and a solid determination not to be pushed back. The war of movement was over and trench warfare had begun.

▼ **C** *The line of trenches of 1914, later known as the Western Front*

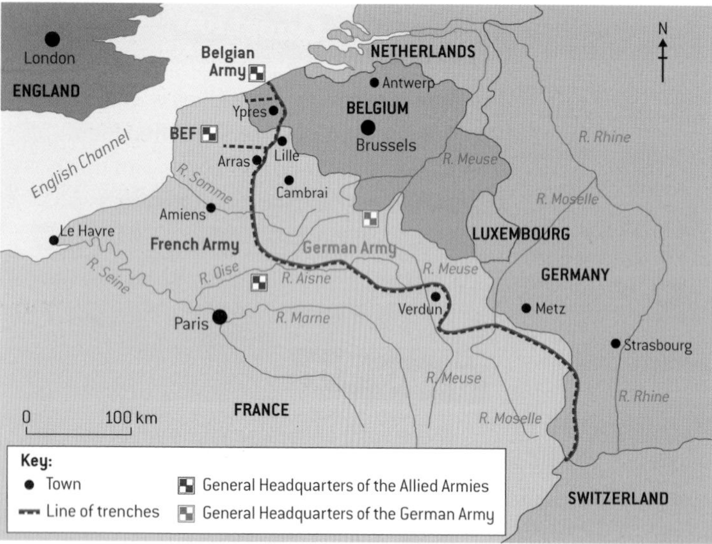

The war on Germany's Eastern Front

The Russian Army, which was ready for action much sooner than had been assumed in the Schlieffen Plan, marched towards Germany and Austria-Hungary within days of the start of the war. The huge Russian Army of over one million soldiers was nicknamed the 'steam-roller' and by mid-August had advanced several hundred miles into German territory. However, the Russians were poorly equipped and badly led. They were also up against two of Germany's most experienced war leaders, Ludendorff and Hindenburg, who were put in place to lead the German Army.

The Germans, now with better leaders and the latest military equipment, beat the Russians at the Battle of Tannenberg (26–30 August 1914) and the Battle of the Masurian Lakes two weeks later. At Tannenberg the Russians lost 125,000 men, the Germans lost 13,000. The Russians lost a further 100,000 at the Masurian Lakes.

▼ **SOURCE D** *German soldiers in trenches during the Battle of Tannenberg*

Russia vs Austria-Hungary

The Russians had more success against Austria-Hungary. In late August, the Austro-Hungarians had followed their own war plan (Plan R) and advanced well into Russian territory. However, when faced with the sight of nearly half a million Russian soldiers, the Austro-Hungarian soldiers turned and fled. In less than a week, the forces of Austria-Hungary retreated over 120 miles, leaving guns and ammunition behind. It has been estimated that 100,000 Austro-Hungarian soldiers were killed, 220,000 wounded and 100,000 captured. The Russians eventually crossed the border into Austria-Hungary but were halted by the Carpathian mountain range.

▼ **SOURCE E** *A British cartoon from September 1914; the front of the steamroller says 'Russia'*

"THE STEAM-ROLLER."

AUSTRIA. "I SAY, YOU KNOW, YOU'RE EXCEEDING THE SPEED LIMIT!"

Over the next few months, the eastern 'front-line' (the area where the two sides faced each other) began to take shape. At around a thousand miles, it ran from the Baltic Sea near Riga (in modern day Latvia), to the shores of the Black Sea in Ukraine. This was known as the **Eastern Front**. There were trenches in places, but as it was longer than the **Western Front**, it was less fortified and more thinly manned. This meant that there was more movement because when one side attacked another it could gain 50 or 60 miles before being pushed back.

Extension

GCSE

The Battle of Ypres in October and November 1914 is commonly known as the First Battle of Ypres today. There were several other major battles in this area – carry out some research and prepare short fact files on the other Ypres battles.

Key Words

stalemate   Eastern Front   Western Front

Work

1 Test your understanding by defining the following terms:
   a 'race to the sea'
   b outflanking.
2 In no more than 100 words per alliance, sum up how the war is going so far for the following:
   a Triple Alliance
   b Tripe Entente.
3 a Look at **Source E**. Who is the emperor pictured in the cartoon?
   b Why do you think Russia has been drawn as a steam-roller?
   c Do you think this is an accurate portrayal of Russia? Explain your answer.

Practice Question

Write an account of how trench warfare developed all along the Western Front. **8 marks**

Study Tip

Remember you are trying to explain how the stalemate of trench warfare spread from the English Channel to the Swiss border.

5.1A What was trench warfare?

The brief war of movement on the Western Front in August and September of 1914 ended when neither side managed to outflank the other during the 'race to the sea'. The opposing armies dug themselves into trenches. Occasionally, one side would attack the other and try to gain ground, but this often ended in failure. For nearly four years, the long line of trenches hardly moved. This stalemate became known as 'trench warfare'. What were the trenches like? How were they built? Why was it so difficult to fight trench warfare?

Objectives

- **Examine** the trench systems on the Western Front.
- **Assess** why it was so difficult to capture enemy trenches.

The trench system

To begin with, trenches were simply holes in the ground that soldiers dug to protect themselves from bullets and bombs. Soon, these trenches developed into a more complex defensive system, protected by barbed wire, sandbags and machine guns. There were usually three lines of trenches on each side, with the land in between known as '**no man's land**'. Where possible, the trenches were built in a zigzag pattern so the blast from exploding bombs would be confined to a small part of the trench. This also stopped enemy soldiers from firing straight down the line if they reached a trench.

The lines of trenches on each side consisted of a front-line (which directly faced the enemy), followed by support and reserve trenches. The three lines of trenches were linked by lots of communication trenches that allowed each side to quickly bring soldiers up to the front-line without being exposed to enemy fire (see **Source F** on page 49). The two enemy front-lines were often only 50 to 200 metres apart.

▼ **A** *The trench system*

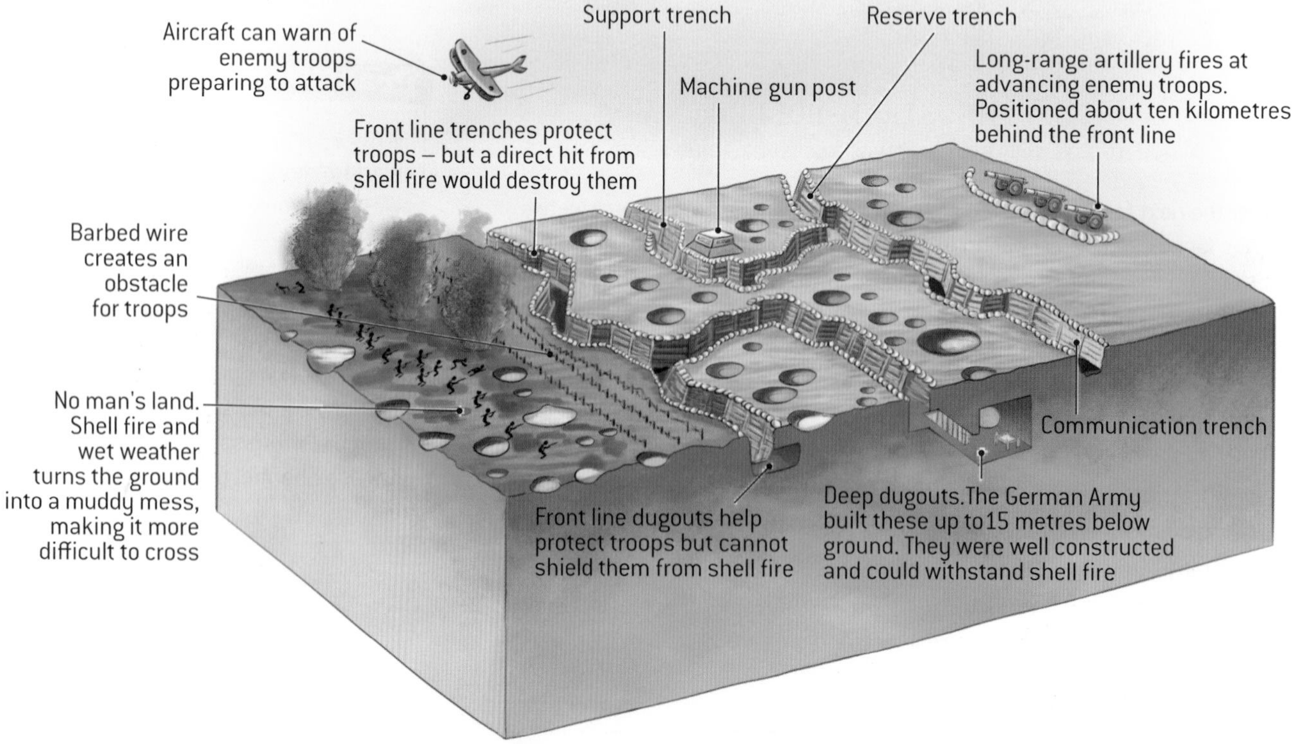

Aircraft can warn of enemy troops preparing to attack
Support trench
Reserve trench
Machine gun post
Long-range artillery fires at advancing enemy troops. Positioned about ten kilometres behind the front line
Front line trenches protect troops – but a direct hit from shell fire would destroy them
Barbed wire creates an obstacle for troops
No man's land. Shell fire and wet weather turns the ground into a muddy mess, making it more difficult to cross
Communication trench
Front line dugouts help protect troops but cannot shield them from shell fire
Deep dugouts. The German Army built these up to 15 metres below ground. They were well constructed and could withstand shell fire

Different types of trench

There were differences in the quality of trenches between the countries. The German trenches were often much deeper and better built. The German generals realised quickly that the war of movement had passed, and the soldiers might be in the trenches for a long time. They tried to provide a reasonable standard of comfort for the soldiers, sometimes with underground living areas (known as 'bunkers' or 'dugouts') more than 10 metres below the surface. These trenches had electricity, beds, and some even had wallpaper.

The British and French, on the other hand, thought that the trenches might only be temporary, so they did not put as much effort into their design to begin with. Only after some months did this approach change.

Fact

During the First World War, several young boys joined up to serve as soldiers before they were eighteen, the legal age to serve in the Army. The youngest British soldier to join up was Sidney Lewis. He was just 12 years old when he lied about his age to join the Army. He fought at the Battle of the Somme in 1916 and survived the war, dying in 1969.

▼ **B** *A cross-section of a trench*

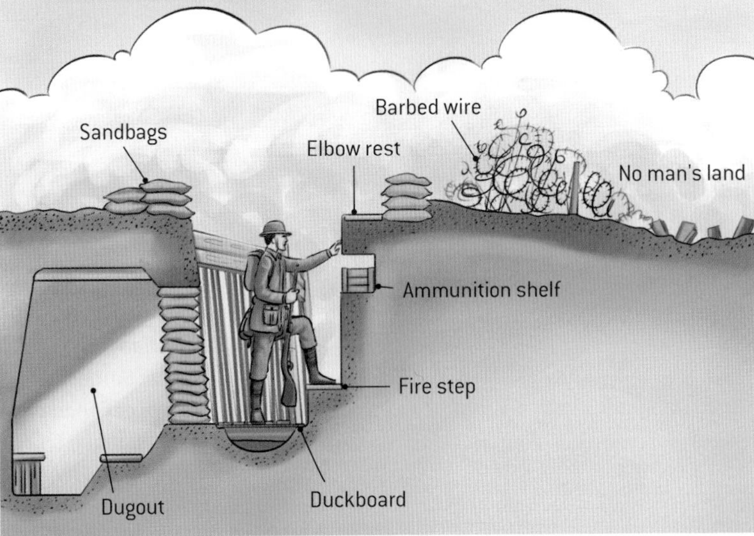

Work

1. Why were trenches built in a zigzag pattern?
2. Where was no man's land?
3. To begin with, how and why were German trenches different from British and French trenches?
4. a Read **Source C**. For what reasons does the writer think that the war will last for a long time?
   b What evidence is there that the writer has personally been to visit the trenches?

Key Words

no man's land

▼ **SOURCE C** *Adapted from an article written by Robert Donald for the British newspaper the* Daily Chronicle*, August 1915; Donald was the editor of the newspaper, and visited the Western Front several times, reporting back on his findings*

The soil is soft clay, suitable for building trenches, tunnelling, and mine warfare – when it is dry. As an outside observer, I do not see why the war in this area should not go on for a hundred years, without any decisive result. What is happening now is precisely what happened last year. The only difference is that the trenches are deeper, dug-outs better made, tunnels are longer, and the charges of explosives heavier.

Everywhere there are trenches, barbed wire, machine guns where they are least expected, and all the complicated arrangements for defence. The trenches are very deep, very narrow, and very wet. Streams of water run at the bottom.

The nearer one gets to the front the more mysterious and wonderful become the methods of defence. You are allowed to peer through an observation post towards the German trenches a few hundred yards away. You see absolutely nothing but a mass of broken trees, hanging branches and barbed wire.

5.1B What was trench warfare?

Attacking the enemy

Different military tactics were used during the war. When the decision was made to try and capture enemy ground and attack the enemy, it usually followed this plan:

1. Large guns behind the trenches would fire shells (large bombs) at the enemy positions. The aim was to smash the enemy trench system and blow holes in their barbed wire so that the attackers could run through.
2. The attacking soldiers would 'go over the top', which meant climbing out of their trenches with their guns and grenades and heading towards the enemy trenches, across no man's land.
3. The soldiers would jump into the enemy trenches and shoot (or fight in hand-to-hand combat) any soldiers that had not been killed by the earlier shellfire.

However, this plan rarely worked. In reality, the shells hardly ever destroyed the enemy trench system in the way it was hoped. German trenches were especially strong with many built using concrete. As a result, the enemy lay in wait for the attacking soldiers and shot them down easily. Also, instead of tearing gaps in the enemy barbed wire, the shellfire often made it more tangled and even harder to get through.

▼ **SOURCE D** *Adapted from a book called* All Quiet on the Western Front, *written in 1929 by a German soldier, Erich Maria Remarque, who fought in the trenches*

> We can see the attackers coming. Our big guns fire, machine guns rattle, rifles crack. They are working their way towards us. They are French, we recognise their helmets. They have already suffered badly before they reach our trench. Our machine gun wipes out a whole line of them, but then it starts to jam, and they move in.
>
> We retreat, and throw grenades at them as we leave. We get to the protection of the support trench and turn to face the enemy.
>
> Our artillery fires furiously, stopping the enemy attack. We counterattack and drive them back through our original trench and beyond it. We are on the heels of our retreating enemy and reach their trenches almost at the same time as they do. But we cannot stay there long and we retreat back to our own position

◀ **SOURCE E** *A painting by the Canadian artist William Barnes Wollen, of Canadian troops fighting on the Western Front in May 1915; when all the other officers had been killed, Lt Hugh Niven, in the centre of the painting, took command to beat back repeated German attacks; at the end of the day only 150 Canadian soldiers remained alive*

War of attrition

The First World War is often referred to as a 'war of **attrition**'. 'Attrition' means to wear away. Attrition warfare is an attempt to win a war by wearing down the enemy to the point of collapse through their continuous losses in men, equipment and supplies. The war is usually won by the side with the greater resources.

On the Western Front, there were occasional breakthroughs where a large group of soldiers (at a cost of many thousands of lives) might push an enemy back a few hundred metres, or even several miles.

Key Words

attrition   counter-attack

But the retreating forces usually just withdrew to another set of trenches that had been built further back. Then, perhaps a week or a month later, the enemy might **counter-attack** and re-occupy their original trench. This was stalemate. At the end of 1915, the man in charge of the British Army, Earl Kitchener, summed up the stalemate when he said, 'I don't know what is to be done, but this isn't war.'

▼ **SOURCE F** *An aerial view of British and German trenches*

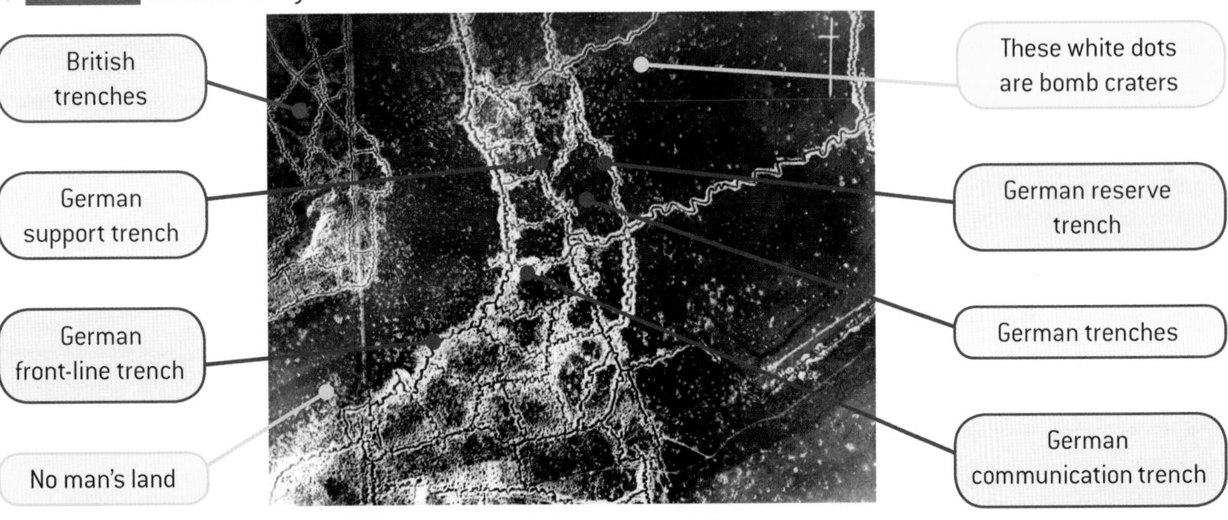

Work

1. Define the following terms:
   a. 'go over the top'
   b. counter-attack
   c. war of attrition.
2. Describe the plan that was followed when one side decided to attack the other.
3. Using information from pages 46–49, suggest as many reasons as you can why there was a stalemate on the Western Front.
4. Read **Source D**.
   a. Draw a simple diagram to show what happened in this attack.
   b. Why do you think it was easy for the Germans to win their trench back quickly?
5. What do you think Kitchener meant when he said '...this isn't war'?

Practice Question

Study **Sources D** and **E**. How useful are these sources to a historian studying trench warfare?

Explain your answer using **Sources D** and **E** and your contextual knowledge. **12 marks**

Study Tip

Explain why it is valuable to have both German and Allied accounts about trench fighting that were produced at different times. How does the text source help when combined with the visual source?

Extension

Trench warfare was mainly fought on the Western Front, but there were other areas of conflict where trenches were built. Carry out some research on other areas of the world where trench warfare was fought between 1914 and 1918.

5.2 Life in the trenches

Many of the soldiers were in their early twenties and none had experienced anything like trench warfare before. The trenches were probably the dirtiest, unhealthiest, most frightening and most dangerous places in the world. What was life like in the trenches? What did the soldiers do when they weren't fighting? How did they cope with their day-to-day lives?

Objectives

- **Examine** the everyday routine of trench life.
- **Consider** how soldiers coped with life in the trenches.

The everyday routine

When soldiers were not fighting, they lived a rather boring life in the trenches. They rotated duties in front-line trenches which meant that one third of the men were on guard duty while another third repaired the trench and collected food, water, letters, ammunition and first aid supplies. The other third would rest, write letters, draw, paint, play cards or cook.

The monthly routine

In a typical month, a soldier might serve four days in the front-line, four days in a support trench, eight days in the reserve trenches and the remainder of his time behind the lines in the local town. Life in the trenches varied – in some places there was little fighting while in others there were regular attacks and counterattacks. The type and nature of the trenches varied too, depending on the local conditions. For example, the ground around the River Somme in France is chalky and easily dug, but trench sides would crumble easily after it had rained. So, the soldiers would build up the sides with wood and sandbags to keep the trench stable.

Stand to

Soldiers on both sides were up before sunlight for a time known as **stand to**. They were on their highest state of alert, with guns loaded, and on the lookout for enemy attacks. It was thought that dawn and dusk were the most dangerous times of day because the changing light made it difficult to spot attacks.

Trench humour

Some soldiers used humour to cope with the stress they were under. They made up rude songs, told naughty jokes and drew funny pictures and cartoons. *The Wipers Times* is a good example of this. In 1916, in the bombed-out ruins of the Belgian town of Ypres (pronounced 'Wipers' by British troops), a group of British soldiers found an old printing press and started an 'unofficial' newspaper for the ordinary soldier. At 12 pages long, it was full of funny stories and cartoons, and lots of cleverly disguised criticisms of the senior commanders.

Health

The trenches could be boiling hot in the summer and freezing cold in the winter. Many soldiers suffered from illnesses like pneumonia, tuberculosis, bronchitis and diarrhoea. Spending weeks on end with cold, wet feet could lead to **trench foot**, a painful condition where the foot swells up and develops open sores.

Luxuries

Soldiers looked forward to the arrival of letters and parcels from home. Every week, around 12 million letters and parcels were sent by family, friends and girlfriends. The parcels contained toiletries, tobacco and sweets, for example. The soldiers sent letters home too, but would usually not mention the horrors of trench warfare to avoid upsetting their loved ones. Most letters sent home were first read by a commanding officer, who checked that the contents of the letters did not give away any army secrets or show low morale. This was a precaution taken in case letters were intercepted by the enemy.

▼ **SOURCE A** *A British look-out in a captured German trench in 1916; note the other soldiers asleep in the trench*

Mental health

A condition known as **shell shock** was common. This was caused by the constant fear of death, the relentless noise of the bombs and witnessing close friends being killed in terrible ways. Some people shook uncontrollably while others became paralysed despite suffering no physical injury.

Key Words

stand to | trench foot | shell shock

Hygiene

Keeping clean was almost impossible, and almost all soldiers were infested with lice. There were no toilets, so a bucket was used and emptied whenever possible. Rats were a constant problem too, trying to get at food supplies and feeding off the dead corpses in no man's land.

Food

Food was basic: stew, bread and hard biscuits. However, for the soldiers from very poor backgrounds, this was the best they had ever had. Bacon, cheese and jam were treats. The water tasted of chlorine, which killed most germs. British troops received a drink of rum in harsh weather and the Germans drank beer and brandy.

Work

1. What word or phrase does each of these definitions describe?
   - a A time at dawn and dusk when all soldiers were on high alert
   - b A painful condition of the feet caused by prolonged exposure to cold and wet
   - c Mental illness caused by experiences of war
2. Choose five adjectives to describe life in the trenches. For each word, write a sentence or paragraph to explain your choice.
3. Suggest reasons why *The Wipers Times* was so popular.

The weapons of trench warfare

In the years leading up to the outbreak of war, there had been major advances in science and technology. Trains, motorcars and aeroplanes had been invented and there were great breakthroughs in physics and chemistry. However, this scientific knowledge and understanding was now used to create terrifying new weapons of war, the aim of which was to kill and maim as many of the enemy as possible.

Objectives

- ▶ **Identify** the most commonly used weapons on the Western Front.
- ▶ **Explain** why the weapons were so deadly.

Artillery

Artillery is the name given to the large guns that fire bombs (or shells) over long distances. It was used extensively in the war as a way of 'softening up' the enemy before a big attack. The enemy trenches would be pounded for hours, even days, before an assault, in the hope of destroying their positions. In 1915, 400,000 artillery shells (some as big as men) were fired every month on the Western Front. There were different types of artillery shells – some contained high explosives, other contained gas or smoke. Shrapnel shells, when they exploded, contained red-hot pieces of metal (shrapnel) that could cut an enemy soldier to pieces. Artillery was responsible for about 60 per cent of all wounds.

▼ **SOURCE A** *British artillery in action in France in 1916; note the soldiers on the left preparing the shells before taking them to the gun*

Machine guns

Machine guns, invented in the mid-1800s, became well-known as deadly weapons during the First World War. They could fire up to ten bullets per second and, in the first two weeks of the war, the French reported losses of over 200,000 men, mostly through machine gun fire. Although they were heavy and needed a crew of between two and four, one machine gun was equivalent to around a hundred rifles. According to British estimates, machine guns caused around 40 per cent of all wounds inflicted on British troops during the war.

Gas attacks

The first use of poison gas was in April 1915, when the Germans released gas from cylinders and allowed the wind to carry it over French soldiers on the front-line. The French panicked and ran, and a six-kilometre gap opened up in the French front-line. However, the Germans did not have enough troops ready to mount a serious attack, the gas soon died down, and soldiers moved back to fill the gap. An opportunity like this never happened again, and despite being an unreliable weapon because it often changed direction with the wind, gas proved its worth as a weapon of terror. Soon both sides were using gas. There were several different types; one would suffocate a victim's lungs and leave them gasping for air while another would burn, blind and eventually kill a soldier over a period of days.

▼ **SOURCE B** *German soldiers with a machine gun, waiting for a British attack, in 1916*

▼ **SOURCE C** *From a poem by Wilfred Owen, one of the best-known war poets; he served on the Western Front*

> Gas! GAS! Quick, boys!—An ecstasy of fumbling
> Fitting the clumsy helmets just in time,
> But someone still was yelling out and stumbling
> And flound'ring like a man in fire or lime.—
> Dim through the misty panes and thick green light,
> As under a green sea, I saw him drowning.
>
> In all my dreams before my helpless sight,
> He plunges at me, guttering, choking, drowning.
> If in some smothering dreams, you too could pace
> Behind the wagon that we flung him in,
> And watch the white eyes writhing in his face,
> His hanging face, like a devil's sick of sin;
> If you could hear, at every jolt, the blood
> Come gargling from the froth-corrupted lungs,
> Obscene as cancer, bitter as the cud
> Of vile, incurable sores on innocent tongues,—
> My friend, you would not tell with such high zest
> To children ardent for some desperate glory,
> The old Lie: Dulce et decorum est
> Pro patria mori. [How sweet and proper it is to die
> for your country]

Rifles, bayonets, grenades and flamethrowers

A **rifle** was the standard weapon given to all soldiers. It was lightweight and deadly accurate up to a distance of about 600 metres. A soldier could fire between 15 and 20 bullets per minute. A 40-centimetre knife, called a **bayonet**, was fitted to the end, and could be used in close combat if a soldier ran out of bullets. Soldiers also carried small, hand-held bombs called grenades that could be thrown into enemy trenches or at advancing troops. Some soldiers were also trained to use flamethrowers to create a wall of fire that could reach about 15 metres. These were deadly in small spaces like dugouts.

Tanks

A British invention, tanks were bulletproof vehicles that could travel over rough ground, crush barbed wire and cross trenches. They were first used in 1916 and by the end of the war the British had produced 2636 and the French 3870. The Germans were not convinced of their value and only produced 20. Part of Germany's unwillingness to make tanks was the issue of reliability. Although tanks caused panic and terror, they could only travel at around five miles per hour and broke down easily. It was not until the Second World War that tanks became a battle-winning weapon.

Key Words

machine gun — rifle — bayonet

▼ **SOURCE D** *A broken down British tank stuck in a trench in France in 1917; troops are attempting to dig it out*

Work

1 Rank the weapons used in the war from most effective (or deadliest) to least effective. Give some reasons for your ranking decision.

2 Do you think the weapons used in the war made it easier for an army to attack or defend? Explain your answer.

3 a Read **Source C**. What were the effects of gas on the victim in this poem?

  b Gas attacks only accounted for around 4 per cent of all combat deaths in the war. So why do you think that gas was one of the most feared weapons?

  c What point do you think Owen was making when he wrote the lines 'Dulce et decorum est / Pro patria mori'?

Practice Question

Write an account of how effective the weapons of trench warfare were. **8 marks**

Study Tip

Explain how different weapons would be effective in different situations.

Key battles on the Western Front: Verdun

Over the next few pages you will explore three epic battles on the Western Front: the battles of Verdun, the Somme and Passchendaele (pronounced 'passion-dale'). You will examine the reasons why each of the battles took place, their key events and their importance.

Objectives

- **Describe** three major Western Front battles of the First World War.
- **Outline** the tactics and technology used in each battle.
- **Assess** the impact each battle had on each side.

Verdun: the longest battle

The Battle of Verdun was fought from 21 February to 18 December 1916. It took place in the hills north of Verdun-sur-Meuse in northeastern France, as French troops defended against a major German attack. It was the longest battle of the First World War.

The plan

The German attack was planned by General Erich von Falkenhayn, commander of the German Army. The city of Verdun was selected as the place to attack French lines because the city has special historic significance for the French. It was ringed by twenty major forts and forty smaller ones that had protected France's eastern border for many years. It was regarded as the strongest city in France. Falkenhayn believed that since Verdun was an important symbol of French pride, the French would do anything to protect it. He did not even think that a German breakthrough at Verdun was actually needed to beat the French – instead he simply wanted to 'bleed France white' because so many men would die defending the city. This was the 'war of attrition' in action.

The attack

The German assault began at 7.15am on 21 February 1916, when German artillery guns began shelling French trenches on the north side of Verdun. Throughout the day around two million high explosive shells were fired by 1400 guns. In late afternoon, a million troops, led by Prince Wilhelm (the German Kaiser's eldest son), attacked about 200,000 French defenders. The next day, the French retreated to their reserve trenches and by 24 February they had retreated once more to a third line of trenches that were only 8 kilometres from Verdun. It seemed as if Verdun was about to fall.

French tactics

Up until now, the French commander at Verdun had been General Joffre, who had overseen the successful defence of the River Marne in September 1914. After a frantic and heated meeting with French Prime Minister Aristide Briand, Joffre was replaced by General Philippe Pétain. The orders went out to all troops saying, 'Ils ne passeront pas', meaning 'They shall not pass'.

Pétain realised that the defence of Verdun would result in many French casualties, so he was determined to inflict the maximum damage on German troops too. Firstly, he ordered every spare French soldier to Verdun. In fact, of the 330 infantry regiments of the French Army, 259 fought at Verdun. He also made sure that food and ammunition could easily reach these soldiers down the one road into Verdun that was still open. Over the course of the next five months, tons of supplies and thousands of soldiers poured into Verdun along this road. It was used by 6000 vehicles a day (an average of one every 14 seconds) and nicknamed the 'Sacred Way'.

The battle continues

The German advance was brought to a halt in late February. On 6 March, a new German attack saw them advance another 3 kilometres, but in April the French began a series of counterattacks. This was the pattern over the next few months – attack by one side, then counterattack by the other. In early June, the Germans took one of the large forts after very tough fighting, but this proved to be their final success.

From Verdun to the Somme

Further fighting continued throughout the summer and early autumn. However, the size of German attacks was reduced; on the Western Front, the British had launched a major attack on German positions at the River Somme and the Germans needed to transfer troops to defend the front-line there. An attack by the Russians on the Eastern Front meant that German troops were needed there too. The weakening of German forces at Verdun meant that the French were able to retake two forts and push the Germans back several kilometres.

Results of the battle

By the time the Germans called off their attacks, they had fired over 23 million shells, destroying the city of Verdun in the process, and killed around 315,000 French soldiers. The Germans had lost around 280,000 soldiers. Despite losing more men, the French thought of themselves as the winners, yet neither side had made any real military gains.

After the war, an area of farmland around the city, covering 170 square kilometres, was declared a Zone Rouge ('Red Zone') owing to the number of unexploded bombs left in the ground. Also, nine villages around Verdun were entirely destroyed. The French decided not to rebuild them and to leave them as memorials known as the 'villages that died for France'.

A *The area where the Battle of Verdun took place*

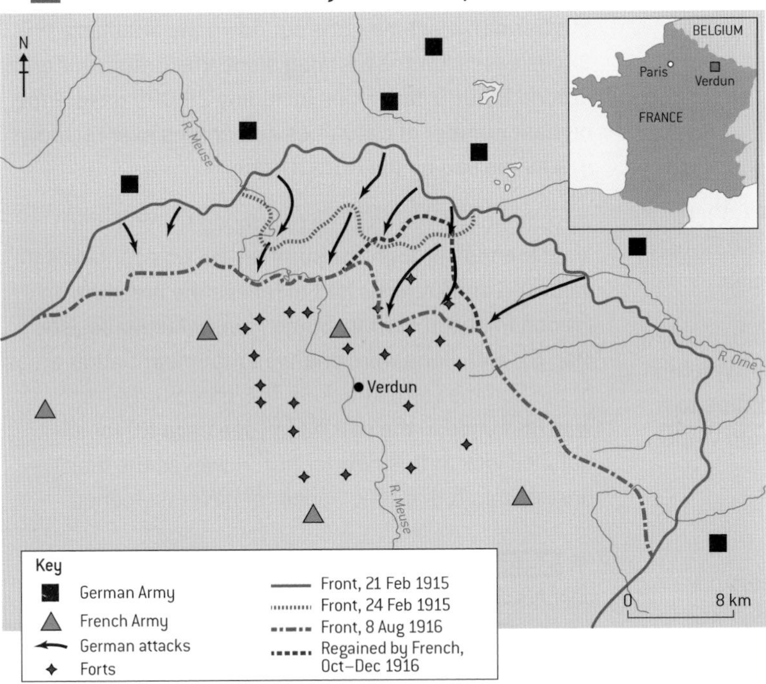

SOURCE B *Written by a Swiss observer of the battle*

> The battle is now at its fiercest phase. But what will have been gained even if the French or the Germans manage to break through? I guess that the Germans have pushed 800,000 men into Verdun. By now they must have lost 300,000 killed, wounded or taken prisoner. Why do they go on? The explanation I've heard makes little sense. They are trying to tire out the enemy. What a mistake – you lose more men attacking than defending.

SOURCE C *From a British newspaper, May 1916; it shows the Kaiser and his son; in the caption Prince Wilhelm says, 'Father, we need a higher pile to see Verdun'*

Work

1 Describe the role played in the battle by:
   a General Erich von Falkenhayn
   b Prince Wilhelm
   c Aristide Briand
   d General Philippe Pétain
   e 'the Sacred Way'.
2 Explain why the Battle of Verdun is a good example of 'attrition warfare'.
3 More French soldiers were killed than German soldiers and Verdun was destroyed. Why do you think the French view the battle as a victory?

Practice Question

Study **Source C**. The source supports the French fighting at Verdun. How do you know?

4 marks

Study Tip

Say what the cartoonist thinks the Germans have achieved at Verdun.

Key battles on the Western Front: the Somme

The Somme: the largest battle

The Battle of the Somme (also known as the Somme Offensive) took place between 1 July and 18 November 1916. It was fought near the River Somme in northern France by the armies of the British and French against German forces. It was the largest battle of the First World War on the Western Front, with more than three million men taking part. Around one million men were wounded or killed, making it one of the bloodiest battles ever to have taken place in human history.

The plan

Since the summer of 1915, the British and French had been planning a coordinated attack in the hope of breaking the stalemate and pushing the Germans back. The French and British lines of trenches met around the River Somme and this was selected as where the attack would take place. In December 1915, Sir Douglas Haig took command of British forces and warned British politicians that the country needed to prepare for heavy losses if it was going to win the war. As a result, there had been a major recruitment campaign and the British Army had gained about one million fresh recruits.

In February 1916, the Germans attacked Verdun. Instead of sending troops directly to help the French at Verdun, the British decided to lead an attack at the Somme to gain ground and draw German troops away from Verdun to relieve the pressure on the French.

The bombing begins

On 24 June 1916, British and French artillery began a huge bombardment of German trenches. The idea was to destroy their front-lines, allowing the attacking soldiers to walk across no man's land and into German-held territory. Over 1,500,000 shells were fired in eight days. However:

- The Germans knew that an attack was coming because their spotter planes, flying overhead, had seen soldiers and artillery moving into the area.
- The Germans had secretly pulled back from their front-lines and taken shelter in concrete dugouts deep underground.
- The Germans had stretched barbed wire in a 30-metre-wide band in front of their trenches. The French and British shells had simply lifted the wire and dropped it back down in an even more tangled mess.
- Some of the British shells were of poor quality and failed to explode.

As soon as the bombing stopped, the Germans left their well-protected shelters, dragged their machine guns to the front-lines and waited for the attack on foot to begin.

The attack

At 7.30am on 1 July 1916, the first wave of British soldiers went 'over the top'. Several French divisions joined the British attack. They were told there would be no survivors in the German trenches so they could walk safely across no man's land towards the enemy. They carried heavy backpacks and tools, so they could repair the captured German trenches when they got there.

But German machine guns cut down the attacking forces easily. On the first day alone, the British suffered around 60,000 casualties including 20,000 dead – the highest number of casualties and deaths ever recorded in a single day by the British Army.

Despite heavy losses, Haig continued to send men 'over the top' through the summer. He was confident of victory – and knew he had to relieve the pressure on French forces at Verdun. Some gains were made (see Map **E**), and plans were changed that meant other areas of the Somme were attacked. The 'creeping barrage' was first used in the battle too (see page 80 for a detailed look at this new tactic). However, the major breakthrough that Haig hoped for never happened.

▼ **SOURCE D** *The body of a German telephone operator near his dugout at the Somme, 1916*

▼ **E** *The advance of the British and French forces from July to November 1916, near Belgium*

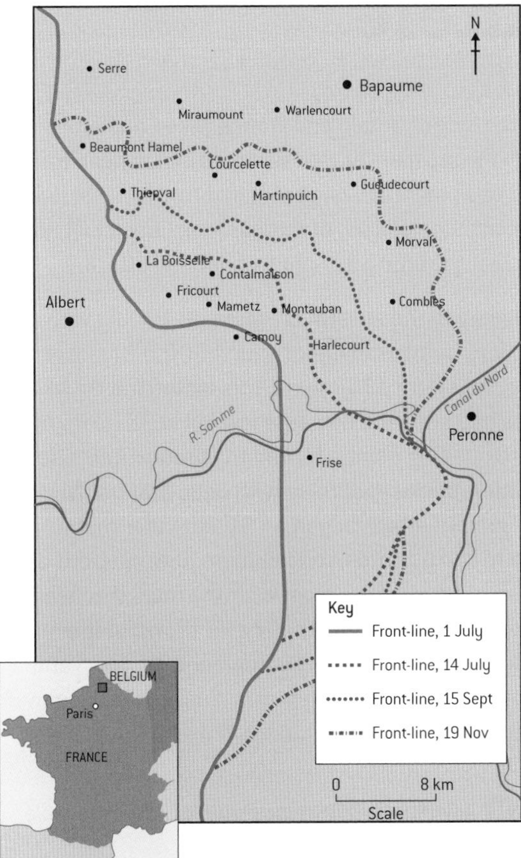

Results of the battle

In November, with winter approaching, the attacks were stopped. British and French troops had gained a strip of land about 25 kilometres long and 6 kilometres wide, and had lost around 620,000 men. The Germans lost around 500,000 soldiers.

After the battle, Haig was widely criticised by politicians, soldiers, and newspapers. He was nicknamed 'The Butcher of the Somme'. Historians have disagreed as to whether Haig deserved such criticism. He certainly misjudged the effectiveness of the eight-day bombardment and continued to send men into battle for months on end. But Haig's actions must be put in the context of the time. None of the military leaders had any experience of trench warfare on this scale. Haig had served in the Boer War (1899–1902) when completely different military tactics were used. Haig himself would also argue that the Battle of the Somme achieved some of its main aims: Verdun had been saved, and hundreds of thousands of German troops had been killed, seriously weakening the German Army.

▼ **SOURCE F** *Adapted from a* Daily Express *newspaper report on 3 July 1916; this report would have been checked by the British military and government before it was printed, and the reporter would have been given limited information from the military*

> The energy and eagerness of the first assault were worthy of the best tradition of the British Army. We had not to wait long for news, and it was satisfactory and encouraging: 'On a front of twenty miles north and south of the Somme, we and our French allies have advanced and taken the German first line of trenches. We are vigorously attacking Fricourt, la Boisselle and Mametz. German prisoners are surrendering freely, and a good many already fallen into our hands.'

▼ **SOURCE G** *Written by George Coppard, a machine gunner at the Battle of the Somme*

> The next morning (July 2nd) we gunners surveyed the dreadful scene in front of us. It became clear that the Germans always had a commanding view of no man's land. Hundreds of dead were strung out like wreckage washed up to a high water-mark. Quite as many died on the enemy wire as on the ground. Machine gun fire had done its terrible work.

Work

1. Why was the attack at the Somme planned?
2. Why were British and French troops told they would be able to walk across no man's land?
3. Why did the plan fail?
4. Why are there different opinions about General Haig?
5. a Read **Sources F** and **G**. In what ways are the sources different?
   b Suggest reasons why the sources are different.

Practice Question

Write an account of how the Somme Offensive earned General Haig the nickname 'The Butcher of the Somme'.

8 marks

Study Tip

Try to give several reasons why so many men died.

5.4C Key battles on the Western Front: Passchendaele

The Battle of Passchendaele: the muddiest battle

The Battle of Passchendaele (also known as the Third Battle of Ypres) took place from July to November 1917. It was fought between troops from Britain and its empire against German forces, for control of the hills south and east of the Belgian city of Ypres. It has become well known not only for the number of casualties, but also for the muddy ground upon which the battle was fought.

The background

In the spring of 1917, several attacks were planned by both the French and British armies in an attempt to break through German lines. The results were mixed. On 9 April, the British attacked German defences near the French town of Arras and pushed the enemy back several kilometres. Fighting as part of British Empire forces, Canadian troops captured Vimy Ridge, an 8-kilometre long, 60-metre high hill near to the town. However, the Germans soon brought up reserve troops and the British advance stopped.

Further south, French troops attacked German lines in the Nivelle Offensive but were cut down by machine guns from a new line of concrete defences that the Germans had just built. After this failed French attack, a **mutiny** began in the French Army. Half of the entire army refused to follow orders and this was only stopped when hundreds of **mutineers** were sentenced to death. Improved food rations prevented further mutiny.

The British then attacked once more in the north at Messines, where miners had been digging under a 140-metre high hill since 1915. By then, they had dug 19 tunnels under the hill and filled them with around a million tonnes of high explosives. On 7 June 1917, the explosives were detonated. The energy released was so great that windows rattled as far away as London – and the hill completely disappeared. Thousands of soldiers attacked, supported by 72 tanks, and pushed the Germans back.

The attack

Encouraged by the success at Messines, General Haig ordered the Army to advance further towards the Belgian town of Ypres. This had been the site of battles in 1914 and 1915. Haig was convinced that he could achieve a quick breakthrough here and then advance north to capture the Belgian ports which were being used by the Germans as submarine bases. America had also just come into the war on the side of Britain and France (see Chapter 7). With the prospect of vast reserves of American troops and equipment arriving soon, and concern that Russia was about to pull out of the war (see Chapter 7), Haig felt that the time was right to mount an attack.

Haig began the assault on Ypres on 18 July with an artillery bombardment of over 4,500,000 shells launched from 3000 guns. This lasted ten days. The area had seen the heaviest rainfall in 30 years and the exploding bombs turned the ground into a sea of thick, sticky mud filled with deep craters. When the ground attack began on 31 July, the troops had to carry boards and lay them down in front of them in an attempt to get over the mud. If soldiers slipped off the boards they could drown in the mud, weighed down by heavy equipment. As men (and horses) died during the battle, their bodies began to rot, and the mud began to stink.

▼ **H** *Advances made at the Battle of Passchendaele (Third Battle of Ypres), 1917*

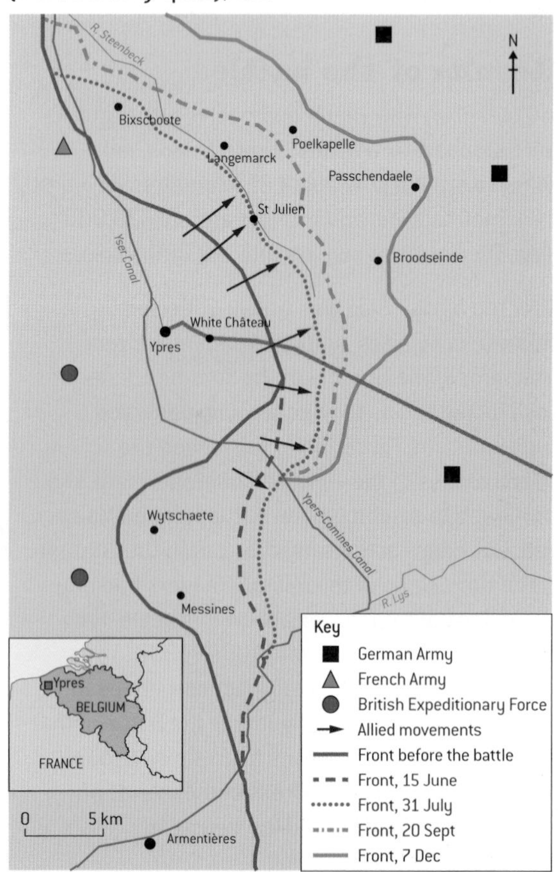

The results

Within a week, the British had lost 30,000 men. The artillery bombardment had failed to destroy the German positions. But the British attacked again and again, and by October the fighting had reached the village of Passchendaele, about 8 kilometres from the starting point. In early November, the village itself was captured and then, because conditions on the battlefield were getting worse in the winter months, the attacks were called off.

In total, 400,000 soldiers from Britain and its empire were killed and injured. The Germans lost over 300,000 soldiers. Haig's reputation was further discredited and, after the battle, when he sent one of his officers to visit the battlefield, he said, 'My God, did we really send men to fight in that?'

▼ **SOURCE I** *An aerial view of the village of Passchendaele before and after the Third Battle of Ypres, 1917*

Key Words

mutiny mutineer

▼ **SOURCE J** *From a book written by English writer R. C. Sherriff who wrote several books and plays based on his experiences as an army officer in the First World War*

The order came to advance. There was no dramatic leap out of the trenches. You had to crawl out through a slough of mud. Some of the older men, less athletic than the others, had to be heaved out bodily. There were no tree stumps or ruined buildings ahead to help you keep direction. The shelling had destroyed everything. As far as you could see, it was like an ocean of thick brown porridge. The wire entanglements had sunk into the mud, and frequently, when you went in up to the knees, your legs would come out with strands of barbed wire clinging to them, and your hands torn and bleeding through the struggle to drag them off.

All this area had been desperately fought over in the earlier battles of Ypres. Many of the dead had been buried where they fell and the shells were unearthing and tossing up the decayed bodies. You would see them flying through the air and disintegrating

Work

1. Describe the events that led to General Haig ordering the Army to advance towards the Belgian town of Ypres in July 1917. You must make sure that your answer contains the following words: Arras, Vimy Ridge, mutiny, Nivelle Offensive, Messines.
2. Compare the Battle of the Somme with the Battle of Passchendaele. What similarities and differences in military tactics can you identify?
3. Look at **Source I**. Describe what has happened in the time between the taking of these two images.

The Gallipoli Campaign

In February 1915, British and French warships began to bomb forts on either side of a stretch of water called the Dardanelles, controlled by Turkey. Within a month, troops from Britain and its empire, supported by French soldiers, began an invasion of the Turkish-owned land next to the stretch of water – the Gallipoli Peninsula. Why was Turkey involved in the war? Why were the British and French so keen to control this stretch of water? Was the Gallipoli Campaign, as these events became known, a success or a failure?

Objectives

- **Examine** the reasons behind the invasion of the Gallipoli Peninsula in 1915.
- **Assess** the effectiveness of the Gallipoli Campaign.

The background

Soon after war broke out in 1914, Turkey joined on Germany's side. During the build up to the war, Turkey had not committed to support either of the alliances. But when Germany promised to help improve Turkey's army and navy, the Turks agreed to an alliance with Germany.

Before long, Turkey and Russia were fighting each other in the Caucasus Mountains region, and Russian generals appealed to their French and British allies for help. The British and French knew that if they could get control of the Dardanelles then they would be able to get supplies by sea to Russia because this stretch of water linked the Mediterranean Sea to the Black Sea. But there was another reason why the British and French wanted to attack the Turks.

The plan

As well as opening up a sea route to get supplies to Russia, the British felt that an attack on Turkey would distract Turkey's allies, especially the Germans. Up until now, Germany and Austria-Hungary had been fighting on two main fronts: the Western and Eastern Fronts. This was putting a great deal of strain on the strongest of those countries, Germany. Winston Churchill, who was head of the British Navy, believed that an attack on Turkey would mean that the Germans would have to send soldiers to help. He thought the Turkish Army was not particularly strong, and when the Germans went to assist the Turks, this would weaken the German front-lines on the Western and Eastern Fronts. This would give British and French troops a chance to mount huge attacks and break through enemy lines. He also hoped that a quick defeat of Turkey would mean that countries near to Turkey, such as Greece, Bulgaria and Romania, would join in on Britain's side and attack Austria-Hungary. A defeat of Austria-Hungary would leave Germany isolated and surrounded.

Approval for the plan

Churchill believed that Britain's navy could beat the Turks, without the need for an invasion by soldiers. He thought the Navy could destroy the Turkish forts guarding the Dardanelles and sail up to the Turkish capital, Constantinople (which today is called Istanbul), and force it to surrender. After all, the British Navy was the most powerful in the world. Many leading politicians of the time thought it was a sound plan. On 15 January 1915 the war council (a group of leading politicians who coordinated Britain's war plans) agreed that the plan should be put into action.

Phases of attack

The Gallipoli Campaign can be divided into three phases. Phases 1 and 2 were naval campaigns, while Phase 3 was a military campaign on land.

Phase 1

On 19 February 1915, British and French ships began their attack on the Turkish forts at the entrance to the Dardanelles. Several forts were hit and abandoned by the Turks. The Turks had put mines in the water so special ships, called minesweepers, were brought forward to clear them. By 25 February the entrance to the Dardanelles was clear of Turkish forts and mines.

Phase 2

The main naval attack was launched on 18 March. Eighteen large battleships, supported by smaller warships and minesweepers, sailed into the Dardanelles but soon came under a hail of shell fire from Turkish forts further up the coast. A new line of mines in the water sunk three ships and severely damaged three more. The rest of the ships retreated.

Phase 3

Churchill was told by naval commanders that they couldn't sail up to Constantinople unless the Turkish forts were destroyed – so this would mean a land invasion of Gallipoli by soldiers. Churchill agreed, and General Ian Hamilton led troops in invading Gallipoli and destroying the Turkish forts. The British were told by Greek army leaders that around 150,000 soldiers would be needed to take Gallipoli – but Lord Kitchener (a leading army general and Minister for War) felt that about half that number were needed. So, Hamilton gathered a force of 70,000 soldiers to begin the invasion on 25 April. These were mainly ANZAC (Australia and New Zealand Army Corps) troops, but they also included soldiers from Britain and its Empire, and France. However, the Turks had received information ahead of the invasion and realised that an attack was coming. They quickly moved 84,000 Turkish troops along the coast and told them to prepare for an invasion from the sea.

▼ **A** *The Gallipoli Peninsula and the Dardanelles Strait*

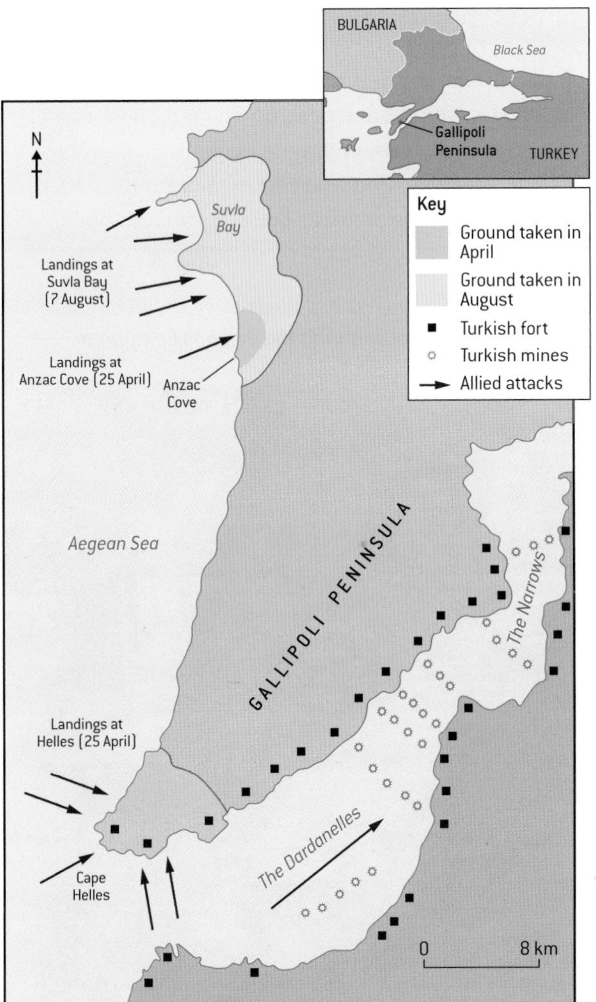

▼ **SOURCE B** *David Lloyd George, then part of the war council, speaking in February 1915*

If we take Gallipoli, then Romania, Greece and probably Bulgaria will declare for us. This would throw an army of 1,500,000 onto the Austrian flank. This would not only relieve pressure on Russia, but indirectly on France. This will give time to re-equip the Russian army.

Work

1 Explain the following terms:
  a the Gallipoli Peninsula
  b the Dardanelles.

2 Explain why Turkey entered the war on Germany's side.

3 What would be the advantages of attacking Turkey for
  a Russia
  b the Allies in Belgium and France
  c support for the Allies from other countries?

4 How would an attack on Turkey weaken Germany?

Key Biography

Winston Churchill (1874–1965)

- In 1893, he joined the Army and served in India and the Sudan. He wrote for newspapers about his time in the Army.
- Went to South Africa to report on the Boer War and was captured by the Boers, but escaped and wrote about his adventures. Came home a hero and in 1900 was elected as an MP.
- Became Home Secretary in 1910 and took charge of the British Navy in 1911 during a time when Britain was in a naval arms race with Germany.

Fact

The British forces also included men from Ireland and Canada, as well as 15,000 Indian troops. Of these Indian troops nearly one third were killed or injured, yet they are often known as the 'forgotten soldiers of Gallipoli'.

6.1B The Gallipoli Campaign

The land invasion

The landings began in the early morning of 25 April when British and French troops, transported in small boats from large battleships out at sea, landed on beaches at Cape Helles. On three of the five beaches, the attacks were successful, but there was heavy fighting on the other two. Further up the coast, the attack by ANZAC troops went badly wrong. At Anzac Cove, the Turks were waiting on the clifftops above the beach. Thousands of ANZAC, troops were gunned down within minutes of leaving their boats. It was said that the sea turned red with blood. Despite their losses, the ANZACs managed to capture some of the enemy positions. But they could not advance any further because the Turkish resistance was too strong. Instead, the British, French and ANZAC troops dug trenches to protect themselves – just like on the Western Front.

Trench life – in Turkey

The conditions in the trenches, in the sweltering heat of a Turkish summer, were terrible. Water was in short supply and food was often contaminated. Around 80 per cent of the ANZAC Army contracted dysentery, an infection of the intestines resulting in severe diarrhoea. In August, the British landed 60,000 troops in Sulva Bay in an attempt to drive the Turks out of Gallipoli, but despite early successes, the soldiers were eventually beaten back.

News reaches home

Back in Britain, the military leaders out in Gallipoli were being heavily criticised. Hamilton had been slow in making decisions – and poor decisions by other commanding officers had cost lives. On 14 October, Hamilton was replaced by General Munro. He immediately went to inspect the situation at Cape Helles, Anzac Cove and Sulva Bay, and recommended that the soldiers should withdraw. By now, the soldiers were facing another enemy – the cold winter temperatures. Soldiers began to get frostbite and even die from the cold. Lord Kitchener, who arrived two weeks after Munro, agreed that troops should be evacuated, and on 12 December groups of soldiers were secretly led away at night to waiting boats. More than 80,000 soldiers escaped without a single death, which was probably the most successful part of the whole campaign.

Fact

Gallipoli was the first major battle in which ANZAC troops took part. Each year, on 25 April, there is a national day of remembrance in Australia and New Zealand – Anzac Day – to commemorate the day of the first landings at Anzac Cove.

▼ **SOURCE C** *Trenches and dugouts of ANZAC troops, protected by sandbags, during the Gallipoli Compaign*

Results

The Gallipoli campaign is regarded by many as a failure.

- Turkey was not knocked out of the war.
- Bulgaria joined the war on the side of Germany.
- Churchill resigned, and it took many years (and another world war) for him to improve his reputation.
- There were over 200,000 Allied deaths (and around 300,000 Turkish deaths).
- The Russians remained short of supplies.

However, it could be argued that there were some achievements.

- The campaign diverted the Turks from helping Germany or Austria-Hungary.
- No troops died during the evacuation.
- A few British submarines managed to get through the Dardanelles, attack Constantinople and sink Turkish warships and supply ships. This seriously affected Turkey's war effort.

▼ **SOURCE D** *A New Zealander named Robert Steele, recalls the landings on 25 April*

I could see Turks along the ridge. I fired eight or nine shots, and each Turk I fired at disappeared. Whether he was hit or had only shifted I don't know. Others fired at me in return, and a New Zealand colonel dropped alongside me, a bullet in his heart. You would just think 'Another gone', and go forward.

The man next to me got one through his leg, just above the ankle. This Australian was bleeding badly. I put a pad on each side of the wound, bandaged it up.

Just finished, and then I felt as if I had been hit with a brick. I saw a hole in my leg, the Australian fixed me up. It did not bleed at all. I fastened up my trouser leg with safety pins, lightened myself as much as I could, and started off for the beach.

Wounded men were all around me, and some were in an awful state. I slept well that night. Hobbled up and watched the warships at work. The troops had dug trenches and fought all night. We left on Tuesday [April 27] and the fight, judging by the row, was still going on. So ended my part. It was an awful day for all, and the toll was heavy.

▼ **SOURCE E** *A German cartoon from November 1915 entitled, 'John Bull beaten at Gallipoli'; John Bull is a character, often used in political cartoons, to represent Britain*

Work

1 Describe the three phases of the Gallipoli Campaign.

2 Why was the campaign eventually called off?

3 Do you think the Gallipoli Campaign was a complete disaster? Explain your answer carefully.

4 Look at **Source E**. Why do you think the cartoonist has drawn:
   - **a** skeletons at the feet of John Bull
   - **b** sunken ships out at sea?

Extension

Research how the Allies managed to evacuate so many soldiers from Gallipoli.

Practice Question

Write an account of how events at Gallipoli became a military failure. **8 marks**

Study Tip

Try to identify key points in the campaign that made the fighting more difficult.

6.2A The war at sea

In the years leading up to the outbreak of war, both sides had spent vast sums of money building up their navies. By the time war broke out, Britain had nearly two hundred large battleships and submarines while the Germans had built over a hundred. How were these weapons used? What major battles happened at sea? How important was the war at sea?

Objectives

- **Explore** the key events and developments in the war at sea.
- **Evaluate** the impact of the Battle of Jutland.

The importance of control

Both sides knew it was vital to try to control the seas. There were two main reasons for this. Firstly, countries do not always have all the supplies they need within their own country (such as food and oil), so they have to import from abroad. So, control of the seas is important for protecting boats bringing supplies in. Secondly, controlling the seas allows a country to stop supplies getting to its enemy, in the hope of starving them into surrender. This tactic is known as a **blockade**.

Impact of the blockade

Germany's coastline is in the northern part of the country and supply ships can only get to it through the North Sea. In November 1914, the British declared that the North Sea was a 'War Zone' and that any ships entering it did so at their own risk. British sailors would stop any ships in the area and confiscate their cargo. Stopping supplies reaching Germany had a devastating effect on the country.

- Coal, oil and steel supplies could not get through, so industry suffered.
- Fertilisers for the crops were in short supply, so there were food shortages. It has been estimated that around 420,000 Germans starved to death during the war.
- A lack of vital medicines and drugs meant that soldiers (and civilians) suffered.
- The impact of the blockade saw a decline in support for the war. There were major protests against the war as early as 1915.

Early clashes

Despite the importance of trying to control the seas, both sides were very cautious with their navies. They had cost so much money to build that neither side wanted to risk losing them in a large-scale sea battle. One of Britain's leading naval commanders, Admiral Jellicoe, even said that 'the war could be lost in an afternoon' if the British Navy was destroyed.

However, this did not prevent sea battles in the early years of the war, although these were only small clashes between a few ships. In August 1914, three German ships were destroyed in the North Sea (Battle of Heligoland), while in November the Germans sank two British ships off the coast of Chile. The British hit back two weeks later and sank four German warships near the Falkland Islands, off the coast of Argentina. Over 2000 German sailors drowned, including the admiral in command and his two sons. Early in 1915, another German warship was destroyed in the North Sea at Dogger Bank.

Stalemate at sea

Despite these few clashes, in the first two years of the war the British Navy spent most of its time patrolling the North Sea or at its main base at Scapa Flow (in the Orkney Islands), while the German ships remained safe in their ports. A measure of the success of the British Navy at this time is the fact that dozens of ships sailed across the English Channel from Britain to France and back every day – and not one was sunk by enemy ships.

A new German approach

There was one major sea battle in the war, at Jutland (near Denmark), in May 1916. In January 1916, Admiral Reinhard Scheer had been put in charge of the German Navy. He felt that the Navy had been too timid in the way they dealt with the British so far – and was eager for action. So, he hatched a plan that aimed to bring the British out into the open, so he could take them on.

- A few German ships would sail into the North Sea to act as bait, commanded by Admiral Hipper.
- The British Navy, as they had done in the past, would sail out to attack the German ships.
- The rest of the German fleet, leaving port an hour and a half after Admiral Hipper, would sail up behind the British ships and attack them.
- The British Navy would be caught in a trap and destroyed by the German fleet.

Fact

In November 1914, German warships sailed close to the British coast and opened fire on the seaside towns of Great Yarmouth and Lowestoft. Houses were destroyed, and several people were killed. In December, Scarborough, Hartlepool and Whitby were also shelled. There were nearly 600 casualties, mostly civilians, of whom 137 died. These attacks caused public outrage and damaged Germany's reputation in world public opinion. There was also much criticism of the British Navy for its failure to prevent the raids.

▼ **A** *War in the North Sea*

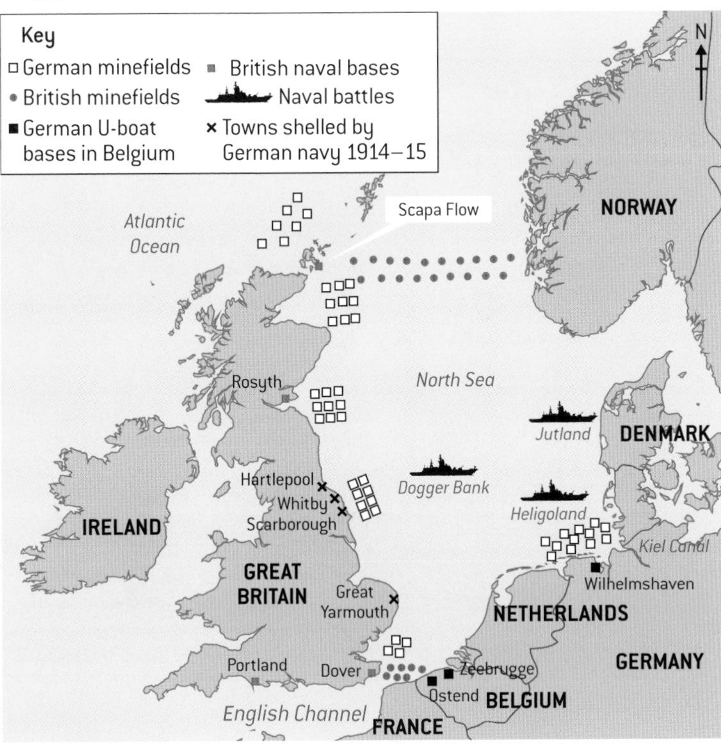

▼ **SOURCE B** *British ship HMS* Inflexible *picking up sailors from a sunken German ship after the Battle of the Falkland Islands*

Practice Question

Study **Source C**. The source supports the British naval blockade of German ports. How do you know? Explain your answer using **Source C** and your contextual knowledge. **4 marks**

Key Word

blockade

▼ **SOURCE C** *A British cartoon from 1917 about the naval blockade of German ports, drawn by the Northern Irish cartoonist, Edwin Morrow, for* Punch *magazine; the title said that it showed the ordinary Germans enjoying their Christmas dinner*

Work

1 a What is a blockade?
  b What was the impact of the British blockade on Germany?
  c Why do you think some historians argue that the war at sea was just as important as the war on the Western Front?

2 Why were the Germans and British so cautious with their navies?

3 Why do you think Admiral Reinhard Scheer, was so keen to attack the British Navy?

Study Tip

How does the cartoonist suggest that the naval blockade has had an impact? Why would he say this?

6.2B The war at sea

The Battle of Jutland

On 31 May, in line with their plan, the Germans sent out a small group of ships into the North Sea under the command of Admiral Hipper. An hour later, Admiral Scheer followed with the rest of the German Navy. However, unluckily for the Germans, the British had captured a German code book in 1914 so could listen in and decode all the radio messages that the German ships were sending to each other.

- The British sent a small fleet of ships from Rosyth, under the command of Admiral David Beatty, to meet Admiral Hipper's 'bait' ships. The two fleets opened fire at a range of 15 kilometres.
- A British ship was destroyed within 20 minutes of the start of the battle.
- Three more British ships were sunk before the rest of the German ships arrived under Admiral Scheer. Another British battleship was destroyed before the rest of the British fleet arrived.
- When the main British fleet arrived from Scapa Flow, the Germans sailed north. Fearing it was another trap, the British did not follow, but instead tried to intercept the German ships on the route they thought the German ships would take home.
- Twice more the two sides opened fire on each other before the Germans finally fled back to their naval base.

Who won the Battle of Jutland?

The Germans immediately claimed victory based on the number of ships destroyed and the casualties inflicted (see Chart **D**).

However, the British pointed out it was the Germans who fled the area of battle first, and that the British fleet was ready to sail again immediately, whereas the German fleet needed major repairs. The Germans also failed to make any impact on the blockade and Germany's warships stayed in their ports for the rest of the war.

▼ **D** *Total losses at the Battle of Jutland*

	Britain	Germany
Battleships	0	1
Battle cruisers	3	1
Cruisers	3	4
Destroyers	8	3
Sailors killed	6100	2550

▼ **E** *The Battle of Jutland*

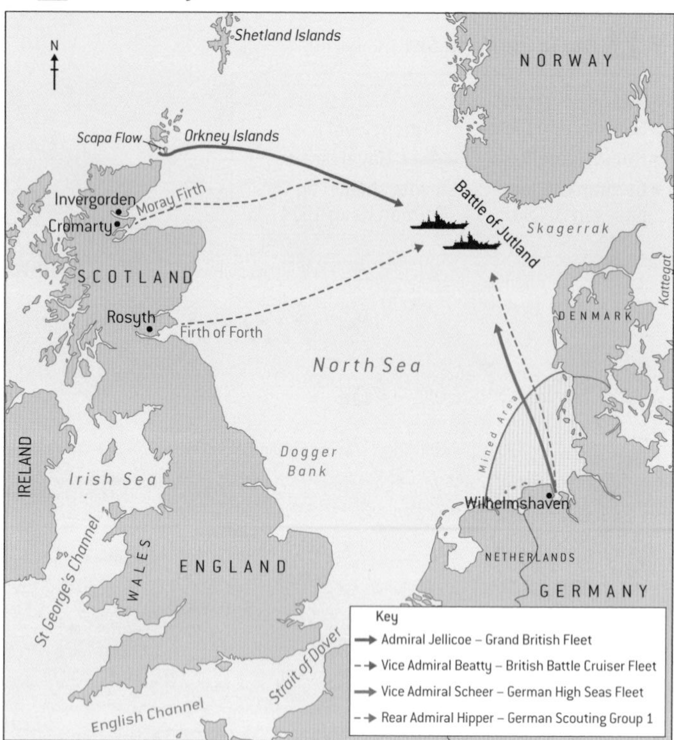

War under the sea

After Jutland, there were no more large naval battles for the rest of the war. Instead, the Germans relied more and more on their submarines (**U-boats**) to wage an underwater war against their enemy.

In the early stages of the war, the Germans announced that all ships entering British waters would be attacked by one of Germany's U-boats. They called this 'unrestricted submarine warfare'. The British responded by laying minefields around Britain to protect the coast and prevent U-boats from using the English Channel. The British also used **Q-ships** to trick the Germans. These were heavily armed warships disguised as supply ships that lured U-boats into attacking before firing upon them.

However, despite the use of minefields and Q-ships, the German U-boat campaign had an important impact on Britain. U-boats sank an average of two supply ships a day and hundreds of thousands of tonnes of supplies failed to get through to Britain.

The sinking of the *Lusitania*

In May 1915, a German U-boat sank a British passenger liner, the *Lusitania*, sailing from New York to Liverpool. Over 1000 passengers drowned, including 128 Americans. The Germans (perhaps correctly) said that the ship was carrying military supplies but there was a huge outcry over the sinking, and tension between the US and German governments increased. The Germans scaled back their U-boat attacks for a while after this but the USA remembered this attack, referring to it when declaring war on Germany in 1917.

A second U-boat campaign

By February 1917, the Germans had built over a hundred U-boats, and another series of U-boat attacks began. Five hundred supply ships heading for Britain were destroyed in eight weeks. By April, the U-boat campaign had been so successful that Britain was said to only have six weeks' food supply left.

The convoy system

The British responded to the renewed threat by introducing a **convoy system**. This meant that supply ships sailed close together in large groups, protected by British warships. **Depth charges** (bombs dropped into the water that exploded at certain depths) were used to attack the U-boats. Also, long-range aircraft had also been developed that could fly overhead looking for U-boats near to the surface of the water. This was so successful that between July and August 1917 only five of the eight hundred ships bringing supplies to Britain were sunk.

▶ **SOURCE F** *This appeared in a newspaper five days before the* Lusitania *set sail*

NOTICE!

TRAVELLERS intending to embark on the Atlantic voyage are reminded that a state of war exists between Germany and her allies and Great Britain and her allies; that the zone of war includes the waters adjacent to the British Isles; that, in accordance with formal notice given by the Imperial German Government, vessels flying the flag of Great Britain, or of any of her allies, are liable to destruction in those waters and that travellers sailing in the war zone on ships of Great Britain or her allies do so at their own risk.

IMPERIAL GERMAN EMBASSY
WASHINGTON, D. C., APRIL 22, 1915.

Key Words

U-boat | Q-ships | convoy system | depth charge

◀ **SOURCE G** *A cartoon from Italian satiricial weekly magazine* Il Pasquino; *it has the caption of Uncle Sam (the US) saying to Germany's Kaiser, 'To make you look closely at your victory, I must hold your head under water.'*

Work

1 a Why do you think both the British and the Germans claimed they had won the Battle of Jutland?
  b Who do you think won the battle? Give reasons for your answer.

2 a What did the Germans hope to achieve with their policy of 'unrestricted submarine warfare'?
  b How did the British try to fight 'unrestricted submarine warfare'?

3 What does **Source G** suggest will be America's reaction to the sinking of the *Lusitania*?

Practice Question

'The main result of the war at sea was the naval blockade of Germany'. How far do you agree with this statement? Explain your answer.

16 marks

SPaG: 4 marks

Study Tip

You should also refer to other results of the war at sea, for example the Battle of Jutland, U-boat war, and the convoy system.

6.3 The war in the air

When war broke out, it had been just over ten years since the invention of the aeroplane in 1903. So, perhaps it is surprising to discover that aeroplanes played a part in the First World War. However, aeroplanes had developed rapidly since their invention and a military role had been found for them by 1914. What role did they play? How did aviation technology develop during the war?

Objectives

- **Examine** the role played by aircraft in the war.
- **Outline** how aviation technology developed.

The first aeroplanes in warfare

When the fighting began, aeroplanes were very slow, clumsy and unreliable. They were mainly used for **reconnaissance** (keeping an eye on what the enemy was doing and spotting artillery). In August 1914, for example, two British pilots spotted thousands of German soldiers preparing to surround British troops on the Western Front. The British Army leaders ordered their soldiers to withdraw from the area – a move that might have saved the lives of 100,000 British troops. In September, during the First Battle of the Marne, aeroplanes spotted a gap in the German lines. French and British troops attacked the gap and were able to split the German Army and drive it back.

Fighter planes

Enemy pilots would fight each other in the air. At first, they fired pistols and even threw bricks at each other, but this wasn't very effective. Machine guns fitted to the front of aeroplanes would often shoot away the propellers so a special mechanism was developed that allowed machine guns to be fired between the blades of the propeller. Pilots would take part in '**dogfights**' in the skies above the trenches. Every time a pilot shot down another plane, he claimed a 'kill' and those with the most kills were known as 'aces'. Aces kept track of their kills and were great heroes with the public at home. News of their dogfights was recorded in newspapers and used to boost morale at home and among the troops.

▼ **SOURCE A** *A recruitment poster from 1918 asking for volunteers to join the Royal Air Force; the image shows a 'dogfight' between German and British fighter planes*

▼ **SOURCE B** *Adapted from the diary of Manfred von Richthofen, the 'Red Baron', a German First World War fighter pilot, 1917*

When we passed above Arras I saw planes approaching from the other side. We caught them up. I attacked the man to the rear. His comrades deserted him. My opponent did not make matters easy for me. He was a good shot but he discovered that I was not an easy target. So he plunged and disappeared in a cloud. He had nearly saved himself. I dived after him and at last I hit him. I noticed a ribbon of white benzene vapour. He had to land for his engine had stopped. He was a stubborn fellow. I dropped to 900 feet. However he fought until he landed. I flew over him at 30 feet in order to see whether I had killed him or not. What did the rascal do? He took his machine-gun and shot holes into my machine. Afterwards, my friend told me he would have shot the airman on the ground. I ought to have done so for he had not surrendered. He was one of the few fortunate fellows who escaped with their lives.

Bomber planes

Both sides used aircraft to drop bombs on enemy positions. But these 'bomber planes' could only carry small bombs that the pilots dropped over the sides, so military engineers worked tirelessly to develop aeroplanes that could fly for a long period of time and bomb enemy cities. By 1917, the Germans had developed the Gotha bomber and began bombing British towns and cities. In one raid, in June 1917, a 20-bomber raid on London killed 162 people, including 18 children at a primary school in Chelsea. The British hit back with their own long-range bomber (the Handley Page) and by the end of the war these planes had flown more than 200 bombing raids over Germany.

Airships

The war in the air was not just fought by aeroplanes. Airships were used for both reconnaissance and bombings. The Germans made the most use of airships and developed one known as a **Zeppelin**. Zeppelins bombed French, Belgian and British cities. In 1915, in Britain, there were 20 raids, resulting in 188 deaths. However, as aeroplanes improved it became easier to shoot down Zeppelins and the use of them declined.

Key Words

reconnaissance   dogfight   Zeppelin

Extension

Prepare fact files on some of the famous fighter pilots of the war. Manfred von Richthofen was the best known (see Source B), but you might want to look up Edward Mannock (British), Billy Bishop (Canada), René Fonck (French), and Eddie Rickenbacker (American).

▼ **C** *Zeppelins were about 200 metres long (two football pitches) and could carry 27 tons of bombs; in total, they made 57 raids on British towns, killing 564 people and injuring over 1300*

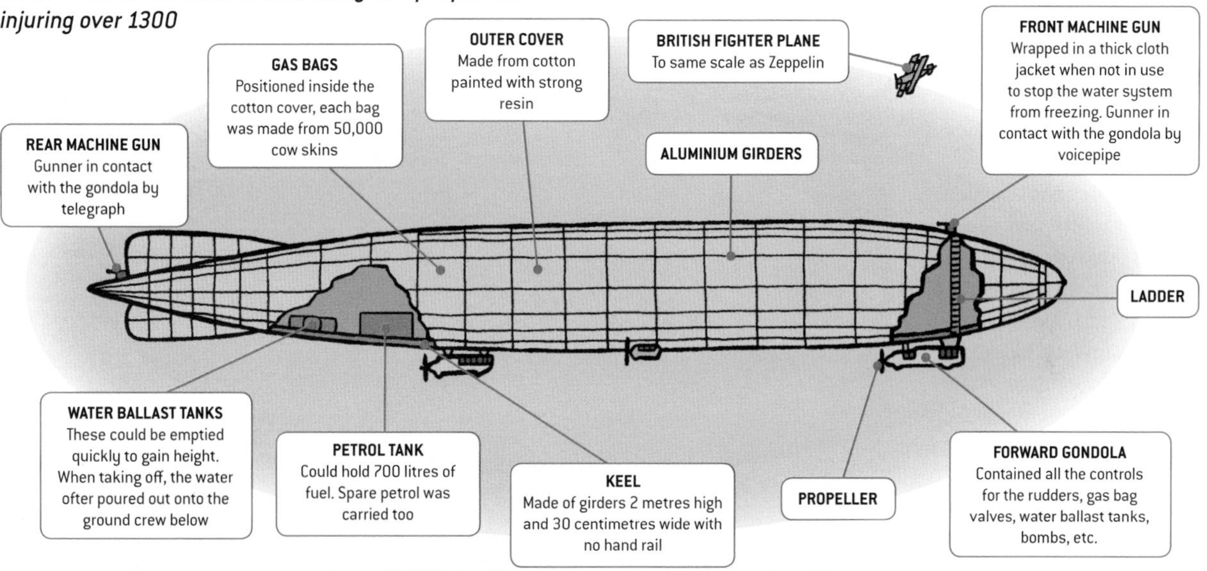

Work

1 Explain the following terms.
   a Reconnaissance
   b Dogfights
   c Gotha bombers
   d Fighter aces
   e Zeppelins

2 Look at **Source A**. How does the poster try to persuade people to join the RAF?

3 a Read **Source B**. How did the British pilot try to escape?
   b What attitude to his enemy does the Red Baron show?

Practice Question

Study **Sources A** and **B**. How useful are **Sources A** and **B** to a historian studying air warfare of the time?

Explain your answer using **Sources A** and **B** and your contextual knowledge. **12 marks**

Study Tip

Consider the purpose of each source in your answer.

6.4 The war in the wider world

When war broke out in August 1914, Austria-Hungary attacked Serbia, the Germans launched the Schlieffen Plan in the west, and the Russians attacked in the east. But the First World War was not just confined to Europe. Many of the countries involved ruled colonies beyond Europe. The war quickly spread around the world as fighting took place in some of these colonies, and many soldiers from these places fought in Europe.

Objectives

- **Recall** areas and regions of the world outside Europe where fighting took place.
- **Justify** why the war is commonly called a 'world war'.

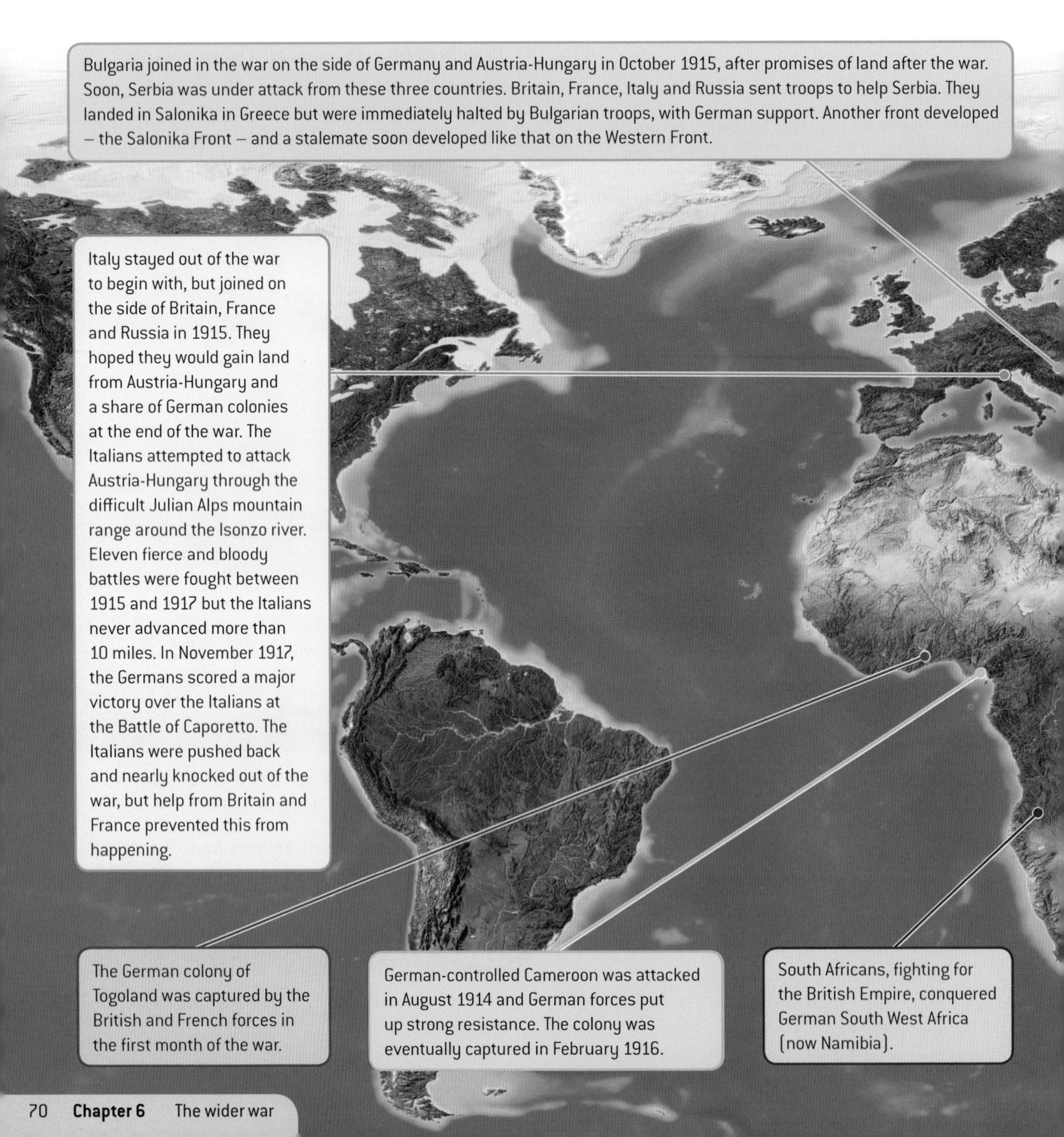

Bulgaria joined in the war on the side of Germany and Austria-Hungary in October 1915, after promises of land after the war. Soon, Serbia was under attack from these three countries. Britain, France, Italy and Russia sent troops to help Serbia. They landed in Salonika in Greece but were immediately halted by Bulgarian troops, with German support. Another front developed – the Salonika Front – and a stalemate soon developed like that on the Western Front.

Italy stayed out of the war to begin with, but joined on the side of Britain, France and Russia in 1915. They hoped they would gain land from Austria-Hungary and a share of German colonies at the end of the war. The Italians attempted to attack Austria-Hungary through the difficult Julian Alps mountain range around the Isonzo river. Eleven fierce and bloody battles were fought between 1915 and 1917 but the Italians never advanced more than 10 miles. In November 1917, the Germans scored a major victory over the Italians at the Battle of Caporetto. The Italians were pushed back and nearly knocked out of the war, but help from Britain and France prevented this from happening.

The German colony of Togoland was captured by the British and French forces in the first month of the war.

German-controlled Cameroon was attacked in August 1914 and German forces put up strong resistance. The colony was eventually captured in February 1916.

South Africans, fighting for the British Empire, conquered German South West Africa (now Namibia).

Work

1 Briefly explain why there was fighting:
   a on the Isonzo Front
   b in Africa
   c in Greece
   d in the Middle East
   e in the Far East and Pacific region.

2 a Who was Lawrence of Arabia?
   b Why do you think Lawrence's tactics were so successful against the Turks?

3 Based on all the work you have done so far in your studies on the topic, do you think that it is correct to call it a *world* war? Give reasons for your answer.

Extension

The Victoria Cross (VC) is the highest award for bravery for members of the British armed forces. It recognises acts of extreme bravery carried out under direct enemy fire. Find out how many soldiers were awarded a VC in the First World War. What nations of the empire were they from? Research the soldier who was awarded it *twice*.

British and Indian troops fought the Turks in Mesopotamia (modern day Iraq, Kuwait, parts of Syria and southeast Turkey). After a Turkish victory at the Siege of Kut (December 1915 to April 1916), a new British-Indian force was joined by ANZAC troops and began to drive the Turks back out of Mesopotamia and towards Turkey. The Turks also faced opposition from Arabs in the region, who wanted independence from Turkish control. Helped by a British army officer named T E Lawrence (known as 'Lawrence of Arabia'), the Arabs waged a 'hit and run' war against the Turks. They attacked Turkish positions and blew up railway lines used by the Turks. At the same time, British and ANZAC troops pushed the Turkish Army further back and defeated the Turks at the battles of Beersheba and Megiddo.

In the Pacific region, troops from Australia and New Zealand (ANZACs) captured German colonies Western Samoa (now Samoa) and New Guinea within a few weeks of the outbreak of war.

In German East Africa (now Rwanda, Burundi and Tanzania) German forces, under the leadership of Paul von Lettow-Vorbeck, amounted to 12,000 men (3000 German and 9000 African), but they managed to keep around 200,000 Allied troops occupied until the end of the war.

Japan and Britain had been allies since 1902. In August 1914, Japan declared war on Germany and captured German colonies in the Pacific Ocean (the Mariana, Caroline and Marshall Islands) and German-controlled territory in eastern China (Kiaochow).

How to... analyse sources

Below is an example of a question that asks you to evaluate how useful two sources are.

▼ **SOURCE A** *A British poster from 1915, advertising cigarettes; Mitchell's introduced the 'Golden Dawn' cigarette in 1901; many companies used images from the war in their advertising*

▼ **SOURCE B** *Adapted from a letter written in the Allied trenches on the Western Front by a British soldier, Lieutenant Bernard Pitt, writing home to his parents 25 December 1915*

What is life like in the trenches? Well, muddy, cramped and filthy. Everything gets covered with mud; you can't wash, for water has to be fetched for a mile. There is no room, and if you walk upright in many of the trenches, you risk being shot; and you sleep, huddled together, unable to stretch. All day long shells explode and rifle bullets whistle past; at night the Germans fire rifles and machine guns, and throw grenades at us.

Practice Question

Study **Sources A** and **B**.

How useful are **Sources A** and **B** to a historian studying trench warfare in the First World War?

Explain your answer using **Sources A** and **B** and your contextual knowledge.

12 marks

Study Tip

This is the **provenance** of the source. It gives the place and date of publication, and the type of source it is. In this case, it's an advert for cigarettes. Knowing this will help you to assess its usefulness.

Study Tip

The **content** of the source is the image. What can you see in the image? Does this reflect what you know about life in the trenches?

Study Tip

This is the provenance. Remember that to assess the usefulness of a source, you could write about the type of source it is (in this case, it's a letter home to parents from a British soldier), the author and their role, and the place and date of the publication, as well as the content of the letter itself.

Over to you 

The usefulness of a source is what it can tell you about the history and how that might help us understand more about what was happening. A source might be useful because it reveals something new, why events turned out the way they did, or why people acted or thought in a particular way at the time.

This question asks about perspectives of life in the trenches during the First World War. Remember this as you consider both sources and work through the following questions.

1. Start with a basic analysis of the content of each source. What can you see in Source A? What is the point of the source? What does the writer say in Source B?
2. Remember that the question is asking you *how useful* both sources are. You could begin by saying, 'Source A is useful because …' or 'Both sources are useful to a historian because …'.
3. You should also consider the provenances for each source, how they differ, and what that means to the usefulness of the sources. The provenance should lead you to think about the purpose of each source. Why was each source created? Does this make an impact on its value?
4. Having worked through what you can see and what is said, remind yourself of the question.
5. What are the strengths and weaknesses of this part of an answer? When you have looked through it, continue this answer by evaluating Source A.

Source B is very useful for a historian studying trench warfare, in particular the Allied trenches on the Western Front. It gives a vivid description of the conditions in the trenches that the men had to endure, such as the muddy conditions, crowded living areas and difficulties in keeping clean. The soldier also mentions the dangers he faces from the enemy attacks. He is writing on Christmas Day too, showing that the war continued relentlessly, despite the time of year. It is of particular use because the soldier was actually there in the trenches, so it is a first-hand account and written by someone who actually lived in the conditions he describes. Interestingly though, he did find time to write, which demonstrates to a historian that the fighting was not non-stop, all the time.

The source is interesting because it is such a shocking account of the conditions in the trenches. Letters home were censored. It is surprising that such an alarming account of conditions would be allowed through. It might have been allowed because he was an officer though, or he might have given the letter to a soldier returning home to post.

Study Tip

The answer refers to the provenance here.

Study Tip

The student uses knowledge of the period here.

Study Tip

The student uses the provenance of the letter here.

Study Tip

The answer refers to usefulness throughout.

7.1 Russia leaves the war

In November 1917, a new government in Russia announced that they would make peace with Russia's enemies. In early December, a peace conference began between Russia, Germany and Austria-Hungary and, on 15 December, the fighting stopped on the Eastern Front. Why was there a new government in Russia? How did Russia's withdrawal from the war affect Germany's strategy?

Objectives

- **Examine** why Russia withdrew from the war.
- **Explore** the effect of Russia's withdrawal on Germany's strategy.

The early stages of the war

To begin with, the Russians won some important battles against both Germany and Austria-Hungary. But a shortage of decent military equipment and poor leadership meant they suffered two major defeats in the battles of Tannenberg and the Masurian Lakes (see pages 44 and 45).

The effects of war on Russia

Russia's Tsar made things worse by going to the front to lead the Army – he was a poor leader, and was personally blamed for the Army's defeats. With the Tsar away from Petrograd (the Russian capital's name was changed from St Petersburg during the war), the government was now in the hands of his German wife (the Tsarina) and her divisive and unpopular adviser, a monk called Rasputin.

Ordinary Russians were soon suffering. Over 15 million men had joined the Army and left fields, mines and factories without workers. This led to shortages of food and fuel. Russia's railway system also couldn't cope with the extra demands of war, and fuel could not get to the cities, leading to power failures. Neither the Tsar, his wife, her adviser, or the government seemed to have any solutions to these problems. By 1916, over a million Russians had been killed in the fighting, and both soldiers and civilians had completely lost their enthusiasm for the war.

Revolution

By the beginning of 1917, discontent had turned to open opposition. Riots and strikes broke out all over Russia. When the Tsarina ordered soldiers to fire at the rioters, they refused and joined the protests. Soldiers on the front-lines were also refusing to follow orders, and many **deserted**. In the capital city, workers and soldiers set up their own council – the Petrograd Soviet – to coordinate what was now a revolution. In March, the Tsar returned from the front and saw the chaos in Petrograd, but it was too late for him to do anything about it. No soldiers were loyal to him and he **abdicated** on 15 March. Immediately, the Tsar and his family were seized and imprisoned.

▼ **SOURCE A** *Adapted from the diary entry of an English nurse, Florence Farmborough, who worked at the Russian Front during the war; she describes events taking place during the revolution in Russia*

> 23 Jan 1917: Sabotage – railroads destroyed, workshops looted. Mobs shouting, 'Peace and bread'. They are aware that the war is at the root of their hardships. The Tsar wishes to please everybody and pleases no one. We are amazed at newspapers criticising the government. A few months ago the writers would have been arrested. Things cannot continue as they are.

A new leadership

A provisional (or temporary) government replaced the Tsar. The new leaders promised to hold elections and divide the land among the peasants. But they did not promise to end the war. In fact, they ordered a new attack on Germany in July 1917, which ended in a heavy defeat for the Russians. After this, whole sections of the Russian Army deserted.

Another revolution

Meanwhile, the Germans were quietly smuggling a man named Vladimir Lenin back *into* Russia. He had been exiled by the Tsar for many years because of his revolutionary ideas. The Germans thought that getting him back into Russia might destabilise the weak provisional government and start another revolution. They were right.

In November 1917 Lenin and his supporters (the **Bolsheviks**) staged a second revolution, overthrew the provisional government, and set up a new government. Lenin declared that Russia was going to make peace with its enemies.

The Treaty of Brest-Litovsk

In March 1918, the Russians signed the Treaty of Brest-Litovsk with Germany and its allies. The treaty was harsh on Russia, which lost some of its best farmland and natural resources. The British and French were angry that the Russians had broken the alliances made before war broke out. And the treaty gave the Germans a sudden advantage.

Advantages to Germany

Russia's withdrawal from the war meant that the Germans could pull their troops away from the Eastern Front and move them to the Western Front. Germany no longer had to fight a war on two fronts. They could concentrate all their military power into beating the British and French. Also, the Germans had gained valuable farmland and raw materials in the Treaty of Brest-Litovsk, so this would help ease the shortages in Germany that had been caused by the British blockade.

▼ **SOURCE B** *From British magazine* Punch, *12 June 1918; the title was, 'A German "Peace" (For the instruction of our pacifists)'; it comments on the Treaty of Brest-Litovsk; German troops were stationed in the territory Russia had to give up*

Key Words

desert abdicate Bolshevik

▼ **C** *The Treaty of Brest-Litovsk; Russia lost some of its richest areas, totalling 26% of its population, 27% of its farmland, 26% of its railways, and 74% of its coal and iron ore*

Work

1. Describe the impact of the war on:
   a ordinary Russians b the Tsar.
2. Why were there two revolutions in Russia in 1917?
3. Read **Source A**. How does this source help you understand:
   a the effects of the war
   b a method the Tsar used to control Russia before the revolution?
4. a Look at Map **C**. What land had Russia lost?
   b What impact do you think these losses would have had on Russia?
   c What advantages would they give to Germany?

Practice Question

Study **Source B**. This source supports the continued fighting by British and French armies on the Western Front. How do you know? Explain your answer using **Source B** and your contextual knowledge. **4 marks**

Study Tip

After four years of fighting, many people in Britain wanted, like the Russians, to end the war. How does this cartoon warn against that?

7.2 The USA enters the war

Russia's exit from the war was a major blow to Britain and France. It meant that German troops would no longer be needed to fight the Russians, so they could be sent to strengthen the German Army on the Western Front. However, the loss of Russia was balanced when the USA entered the war on the side of Britain and France. What were the reasons for America's entry into the war? Why had America avoided the conflict up to this point? What was the impact of America's entry?

Objectives

- **Outline** the reasons for the USA's entry into the war.
- **Assess** the impact of the USA's entry into the war.

American neutrality

When war broke out in 1914, the USA refused to take sides or support any particular alliance. This is known as **neutrality**. The British felt that the Americans should join in on their side; after all, they spoke the same language and had strong cultural, religious and historical links. However, the Americans had never been involved as an ally in a major European war before, and felt that this was a distant European conflict. Also, many Americans were of German descent and approved of the policy of neutrality.

The business of war

American neutrality did not mean that the USA remained totally unconnected to the war. American companies sold food, weapons and other goods to Britain and its allies. This created many jobs in America and made lots of business people very rich. American banks also lent money to Britain and its allies (around two billion dollars), which was used to buy weapons and food, mainly from the USA. So, in the first three years of the war, the USA was financially involved in the war.

Submarine attacks

Ships transporting American weapons, foods and other goods to Europe were a target for German submarines (U-boats). In America, anti-German feeling grew as increasing numbers of ships were sunk by German U-boats. In May 1915, the Germans sank the passenger liner *Lusitania*, sailing from New York to Liverpool, killing over a 1000 passengers, including 128 Americans. There was a huge outcry over the sinking, and tension between the US and German governments increased. Many Americans demanded that the USA declare war on Germany, but President Woodrow Wilson refused to get drawn into the war. In fact, the Germans decided to cut back their U-boat attacks for a while after this.

The end of neutrality

By 1917, the Germans were in a desperate situation and felt that one of their best chances of victory was to starve Britain and France into surrender. To do this, they needed to attack ships of any country that were sailing in British waters. Within a few months, German U-boats had sunk eight American ships, and the demands in America to declare war on Germany grew louder once again.

Then, in March 1917, the Americans discovered that the Germans were trying to forge a secret alliance with Mexico. The plan was that Germany would provide money and weapons to the Mexicans, so they could attack the USA. Mexico would then claim the US states of Texas, New Mexico and Arizona. This was the final straw and America declared war in April 1917.

▼ **SOURCE A** *Adapted from President Woodrow Wilson's declaration of war, 2 April 1917*

> Germany has committed repeated acts of war against the people of the USA; therefore, we declare that a state of war exists between the United States and the Germany. This war has been thrust upon the United States. The President is authorised and directed to use the entire naval and military forces of the United States and the resources of the Government to carry on war against Germany

▼ **SOURCE B** *An American army recruiting poster from 1917*

Impact of the entry of the USA

The entry of America was a great boost for Britain and France. They were one of the richest countries in the world with huge supplies of coal, oil, iron, cotton and wheat. And even though it would take a few months for the American soldiers to arrive, the news came at a time when Russia's commitment to the war was in doubt. There had been a revolution, the Tsar had abdicated, and Russian soldiers were deserting. The arrival of US troops would help to balance the loss of the Russians.

For the Germans, Russia's withdrawal from the war would be good news, but America's entry was a devastating blow. Although Germany would no longer be fighting a war on two fronts, it was racing against time to mount a concentrated attack on the Western Front against Britain and France before the American troops arrived.

Fact

By the end of the war, America had sent nearly 90,000 tonnes of meat and 600,000 horses to Europe.

Key Words

neutrality

Work

1. a Define 'neutrality'.
   b Do you think America was really a neutral country in the first three years of the war?
2. Read **Source A**. What do you think Wilson was referring to when he said, 'Germany has committed repeated acts of war against the people of the USA'?
3. Look at **Source B**. What impression of Germany does the artist give?
4. What happened in 1917 that made the USA abandon its neutrality?
5. What benefits did the USA bring to its new allies after April 1917?

Extension

The President who took America into war was named Woodrow Wilson. Prepare a fact file on him. Summarise the President's reasons for entering the war on the Allied side. What were his ideas for the post-war world? What role did he play in the peace conferences after the war? Interestingly, when Wilson was elected in 1916, he campaigned with the slogan 'He Kept Us Out of War'.

Practice Question

Study **Sources A** and **B**. How useful are these sources to a historian studying why Americans fought in the First World War?

Explain your answer using **Sources A** and **B** and your contextual knowledge. **12 marks**

Study Tip

Make sure you use both sources in your answer. Try to think about the impact of these sources on American citizens.

8.1A The impact of new tactics and technology

There were important advances made in both tactics and technology during the First World War. Soldiers fighting in 1918 would use weapons on the battlefield that were different from those used in 1914. They would also use different tactics when fighting. What were the main changes? What caused these changes and what impact did they have?

Objectives

- **Examine** the development of new tactics and technology during the First World War.
- **Identify** the impact of the new tactics and technology.

Advances at sea

Some of the main developments related to the threat of German submarine attacks. The U-boat campaign sank millions of tonnes of cargo and killed thousands of sailors and civilians. New tactics to defend ships against U-boat attacks included using minefields, depth charges and Q-ships, and the introduction of the convoy system (see pages 66–67).

The hydrophone was a new technological breakthrough that helped to locate submarines. A hydrophone is a microphone that can be used underwater to listen for underwater sound. By 1918, hydrophones could detect submarines several miles away.

Another new development towards the end of the war was the creation of the first aircraft carrier. As early as 1912, some of the larger battleships carried small 'floatplanes' (aeroplanes fitted with floats instead of wheels). These were launched by catapults from the ship's deck, and then recovered by a crane from the water after landing.

In October 1918, a British ship became the world's first aircraft carrier when an aeroplane landed on the deck of HMS *Argus*. However, the war ended a month later and the ship played no part in the conflict.

Fact

The hydrophone was invented in 1914 by Canadian inventor Reginald Fessenden, who began work on the idea after the Titanic disaster (1912) which highlighted the need to protect ships from collisions with icebergs.

▼ **SOURCE A** *HMS* Argus*, the larger ship in the photograph; note how the ship was painted; this technique using bold shapes, lines and contrasting colours was called 'dazzle'; the aim was not to camouflage the ship, but to distort a submarine commander's view of the ship and make it difficult for them to assess its size, shape and range; over 2000 British ships were painted like this*

Developments in air warfare

At the start of the war, aeroplanes were mainly used for reconnaissance. However, over the next four years, air warfare developed at a fast pace.

- Aeroplanes were constructed with stronger materials and so became more manoeuvrable. A Dutch engineer working for the Germans, Anthony Fokker, developed the first synchronised mechanism that allowed machine guns mounted in front of the pilots to fire between the propeller blades.
- Stronger planes meant they could have larger fuel tanks so they could travel greater distances. They could hold larger bombs and 'bomb racks' (for multiple bombs). This meant that long-range bombing attacks were possible. Aeroplanes could even carry torpedoes to attack enemy submarines or warships.
- Fighter and bomber planes supported troops as they attacked enemy trenches. They could also help slow down enemy attacks, as they did in 1918 when British aeroplanes attacked the German advance.
- Air warfare tactics developed during the war. At first, aeroplanes flew either alone, or in small groups of two or three. By 1917, pilots were flying in large patrols or formations. Patrol leaders would try to surprise enemy fighters by positioning themselves above the enemy before attacking.
- By 1917, pilots could communicate with ground troops by radio, rather than by dropping them weighted messages about the effectiveness of their artillery fire, as they did at the start of the war.

▼ **SOURCE B** *A German Gotha bomber is loaded with large bombs*

Tank power

The first ever tanks were used by the British at the Battle of the Somme in 1916. But they were very slow and most of them broke down before they even got to the German trenches. A year later, at the Battle of Cambrai, over 400 tanks crossed no man's land, crushed German machine gun positions and gained 8 kilometres of land for a fraction of the usual troop losses. At the Battle of Amiens in August 1918, around 600 tanks led an attack on German positions that saw British and French troops advance 32 kilometres. However, by the fifth day of the advance, fewer than 50 tanks were still working.

By 1918, the Germans had developed guns that could punch a hole through the side of a tank and long-range 'anti-tank guns' that could blow them up from a distance. The Germans also dug 'anti-tank trenches', which were ditches wide enough and deep enough to prevent a tank from crossing.

▼ **SOURCE C** *An image from 1917 that demonstrates how tanks, troops and planes would coordinate attacks*

Work

1. a Read **Source A**. What new development in sea warfare does this show?
   b Explain why the ship is painted this way.
2. Look at **Source C**. Describe what is happening in the image. Use the information on the 'Development of air warfare' and 'Tank power' to help you.
3. How did the Germans deal with the threat posed by tanks?

8.1B The impact of new tactics and technology

Powerful artillery

Several improvements were made to artillery guns, shells and tactics. By the end of the war:

- special shells were developed that could destroy barbed wire and explode on contact with the ground (rather than get buried in the mud)
- the 'creeping barrage' was perfected. This slow-moving artillery attack acts as a defensive 'curtain' for the troops following closely behind. Although not entirely successful (failure to get the timing right would result in the artillery killing their own soldiers), it was used effectively in several of the final advances of the war
- anti-aircraft guns were developed to shoot down enemy planes
- guns became a lot bigger and more accurate. By March 1918 the Germans had developed guns that could fire a 106-kilogram shell up to 130 kilometres (80 miles). These were used to fire shells into Paris, and were known as 'Paris Guns'
- mine warfare or mining had become increasingly used. Tunnels were built, usually by ex-miners, under the enemy's trenches, so that explosives could be placed and blown up to destroy a key location.

▼ **D** *In a creeping barrage, artillery guns aim shells just in front of a line of ground troops; as the line of shelling slowly moves closer towards the enemy's front-line, the troops follow behind, ready to attack*

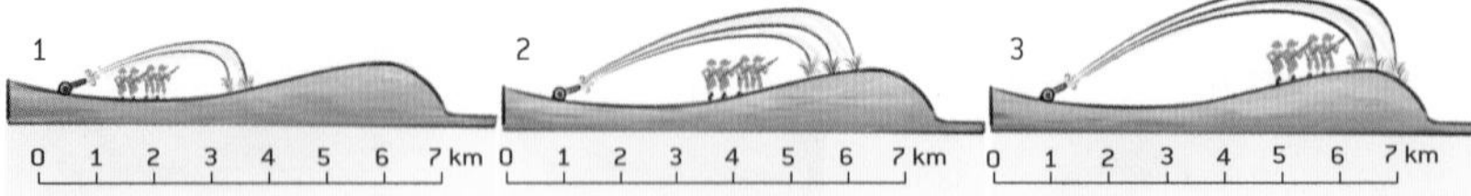

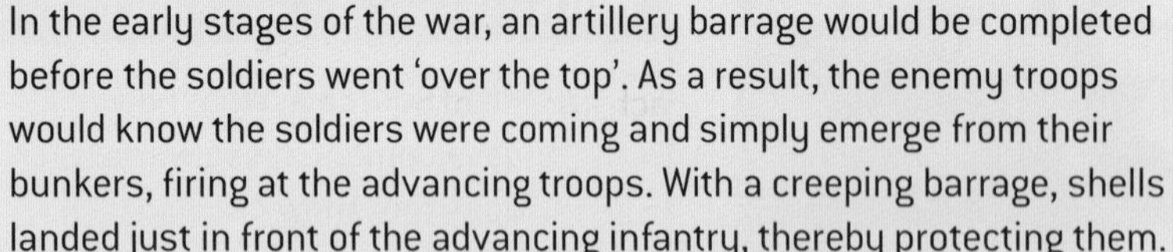

Fact

In the early stages of the war, an artillery barrage would be completed before the soldiers went 'over the top'. As a result, the enemy troops would know the soldiers were coming and simply emerge from their bunkers, firing at the advancing troops. With a creeping barrage, shells landed just in front of the advancing infantry, thereby protecting them.

◀ **SOURCE E** *A German 'Paris Gun', July 1918; these guns were in service from March to August 1918*

Infiltration tactics

In the early stages of the war, the standard method of attacking a trench was to bombard the enemy with shells (hoping to destroy their positions), followed by a rush forward of troops in an attempt to overwhelm any remaining defenders. This process was not very successful and, at most, gained only a small amount of ground, whilst incurring heavy casualties.

In the later stages of the war, a new technique developed. First suggested by the French, it was proposed that a specially trained team of elite soldiers, armed with light machine guns, grenades and flamethrowers, should advance shortly ahead of the main attack to locate and destroy any German machine guns. However, the French and British were not the first to try this new tactic – the Germans were first after they translated a captured copy of a booklet detailing the technique.

To begin with, this new tactic required the soldiers to advance as fast as they could towards the enemy, but this resulted in high casualties. A later version of this tactic saw soldiers sneaking towards the enemy, often crawling, in an attempt to get as near to the enemy as possible before attacking key areas, such as control centres or artillery placements.

▼ **SOURCE F** *German stormtroopers at work on the Western Front*

In 1917, the Germans began training small units of soldiers in this new method of attack. The Germans called them *Sturmmann*, which means 'storm man' (but is usually translated as 'stormtrooper'). In September 1917, the Germans successfully used their stormtroopers at the Battle of Riga, on the Eastern Front. The Germans used them again during the battles of Caporetto (see page 71) and Cambrai. Troops from other countries soon adopted similar tactics, known as 'infiltration tactics'.

Commanding the troops

In March 1918, as the massive German attack – the Ludendorff Spring Offensive – threatened to completely overwhelm the British and French lines, a crucial decision was made. It was clear that better coordination between the different commanders was essential to deal with the German breakthrough. In a series of meetings, Allied generals and politicians agreed that there would be a 'commander-in-chief' who would plan and direct all of the British, French and American troops against the German Army. This was known as a 'unified command structure'. Ferdinand Foch, an experienced and well-respected French general, was chosen.

Almost immediately, Foch acted to stop the German attack and halt their advance by coordinating the French, British and American troops and organising a great counterattack.

Key Biography

Ferdinand Foch (1851–1929)

- Ferdinand Foch was born in 1851 in southwestern France.
- He fought in the Franco-Prussian War of 1870–1, becoming an artillery specialist.
- When war broke out in 1914 he commanded troops that halted the German advance on the French town of Nancy. He also commanded French troops at the Battle of the Marne (the battle that stopped the German advance on Paris) and led the French troops that took part in the Battle of the Somme.
- Although he retired in 1916, Foch returned to the Army in 1917 to coordinate all Allied forces in France.
- He retired again in 1919 and died in 1929. There is a statue of Foch in central London in honour of his contribution to the war effort.

Work

1. Explain each of the following:
   a. a creeping barrage
   b. unified command structure
   c. stormtroopers.
2. a. Write a report or prepare a presentation that summarises how tactics and technology changed during the war. Include the following headings: War in the air, War at sea, The battlefield, Communications, Command.
   b. For each section of your report, state what impact the changes had on the war.

Practice Question

Write an account of how new technology and tactics tried to solve the problems of trench warfare. **8 marks**

Study Tip

Say what the problem was the new technology tried to solve.

8.2A Ludendorff's Spring Offensive

In late 1917, the Russians dropped out of the war. The Germans were no longer fighting a war on two fronts. They could now send all the soldiers that had been fighting the Russians on the Eastern Front to fight the British and French on the Western Front. By now, however, the USA had entered the war on the side of Britain and France. But the USA needed time to build up its army and transport the soldiers to Europe. So, before the Americans arrived in huge numbers, the Germans decided to gamble everything on an all-out attack to win the war.

Objectives

- **Examine** the plan for Ludendorff's Spring Offensive.
- **Assess** the reasons for the failure of the offensive.

The German plan

General Ludendorff devised a plan to attack at several points along the British and French lines. The main attack would happen near Arras, where the British had recently taken over a section of the front-line from the French. Here, the trenches were not particularly well built, and the Germans hoped to exploit this weak spot.

The attack would start with an intense, five-hour artillery bombardment, known as a **hurricane bombardment**. The Germans planned to fire one million artillery shells at the British lines – over three thousand shells per minute.

- The Germans would then use their specially-trained, elite stormtroopers to burst through the enemy lines and create panic amongst the enemy troops.
- Attacks would take place in three other places, and the gaps in the lines would allow a larger German force to break through and surround the British, forcing their surrender.
- The French would also surrender because they could not fight on without British support.

The Germans had high hopes for their plan. They named it '*Kaiserschlacht*', the 'Emperor's Battle'. It is sometimes known as the Spring Offensive because the attack would begin on the first day of spring, 1918.

▼ **SOURCE A** *Early success for the Germans; here, a group of German soldiers stand in front of several captured British tanks*

Ludendorff's Spring Offensive begins

The artillery bombardment began at 4.40am on 21 March 1918. An area of 150 square miles was hit by one million shells, fired from six thousand guns in five hours; it was the heaviest bombardment of the entire war. This was followed by the release of poison mustard gas, and then a massive attack by thousands of stormtroopers. These fast-moving soldiers were not weighed down with heavy kit – they carried only light machine guns, grenades and flamethrowers.

The British were totally outnumbered and confused. Thousands fled or surrendered. By the end of the first day, 20,000 British soldiers had been killed, 35,000 had been wounded, and another 21,000 had been taken prisoner. This was to become the biggest breakthrough on the Western Front for three years. The stalemate had been broken.

▼ **SOURCE B** *A cartoon from* Punch *magazine on 31 July 1918; it shows General Ludendorff and had the title, 'A Champagne counteroffensive'*

Practice Question

Study **Source B**. The source supports the Allies. How do you know? Explain your answer using **Source B** and your contextual knowledge. **4 marks**

Key Words

hurricane bombardment

▼ **SOURCE C** *A report from the British newspaper, the* Daily Express, *22 March 1918*

> An attack which appears to be the beginning of the great German offensive, was made against the British front west and south-west of Cambrai today.
>
> If this battle proves to be the real German effort against the British front we must expect hard and continuous fighting. The enemy has trained his troops well in open warfare, and they are well supported by light and heavy artillery and a host of trench mortars intended to move forward steadily with the advancing infantry.

Work

1. Explain why the Germans were so keen to mount an attack on the Western Front in the spring of 1918.
2. When asked to describe his plan, Ludendorff said, 'We chop a hole. The rest follows.' Explain what he meant.
3. a Write a brief report, from either a British or German point of view, describing the early stages of the Spring Offensive.

   b In what ways would your report be different if you were writing it from the other point of view?

Extension

Stormtroopers played a major role in Germany after the war. Carry out some research into the role of the post-war stormtroopers.

Study Tip

What do you think the pliers and the bottle label mean?

8.2B Ludendorff's Spring Offensive

Unstoppable?

The German advance had been spectacular. In some places, they had pushed forward over 60 kilometres. The Germans regained control of the region around the River Somme – where so many soldiers had been killed in the great battle of 1916 – and reached as far as the River Marne. But they had paid a high price. Between March and April 1918, the Germans had lost over 220,000 men and did not have enough soldiers in reserve to replace those that had been killed or injured. At this rate, before long, the Germans would run out of men.

▼ **D** *Ludendorff's Spring Offensive, March – July 1918; at the River Marne, the advance got to within 120 km of Paris; this meant that the German Army could fire shells at the French capital from the world's largest artillery gun; in total, 183 shells hit Paris and many Parisians fled the city in fear*

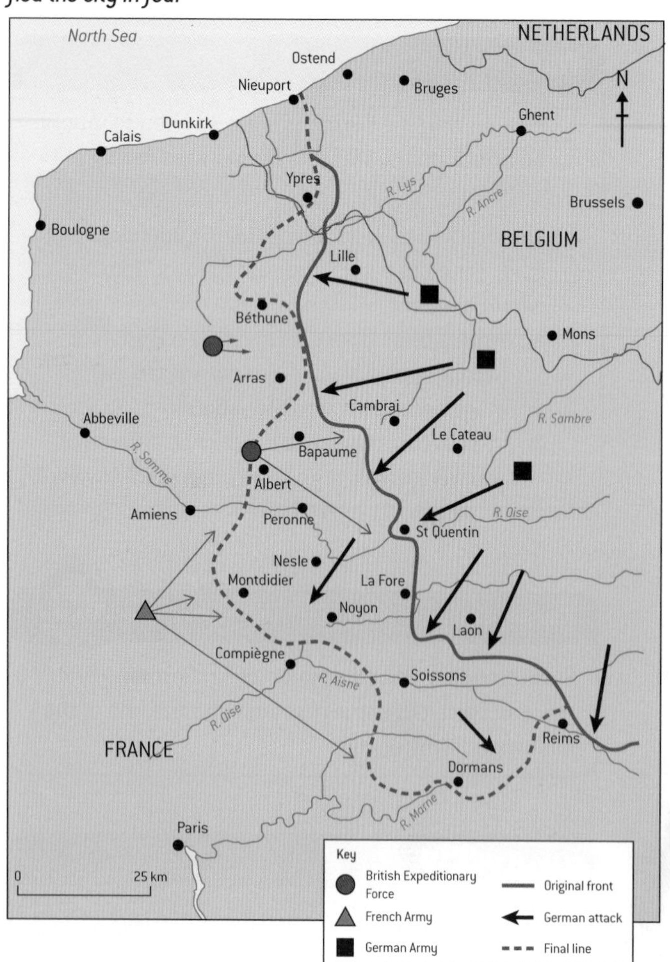

▼ **SOURCE E** *Adapted from the notice issued by British Army leader General Haig on 11 April 1918*

In spite of throwing already 106 Divisions into the battle and enduring the most reckless sacrifice of human life, the enemy has as yet made little progress.

We owe this to the determined fighting and self-sacrifice of our troops. Words fail me to express the admiration which I feel for the splendid resistance offered all ranks of our Army under the most trying circumstances.

Many amongst us now are tired. To those I would say that Victory will belong to the side which holds out the longest. The French Army is moving rapidly and in great force to our support.

There is no other course open to us but to fight it out. Every position must be held to the last man: there must be no retirement. With our backs to the wall and believing in the justice of our cause each one of us must fight on to the end. The safety of our homes and the Freedom of mankind alike depend upon the conduct of each one of us at this critical moment.

Problems with the rapid advance

Another problem for the Germans was that the stormtroopers had performed too well! Put simply, Ludendorff had sent too many men deep into French territory. As a result, supplies of food and weapons were taking too long to get to the troops, and they were running out of both. The German advance began to slow down as troops stopped in captured French villages to loot for supplies. The British and French forces also began to fight back, and finally the first American troops began to arrive.

The response

In the panic and confusion of the German advance, the British and French military leaders had decided to place their armies under the command of one person, French general Ferdinand Foch. Before this, the British and French armies had acted independently of each other, but now the plan was to act as a unified force. It was to be an inspired decision.

The fightback

As you can see from Map **D**, the German advance meant there was a bulge in their front-lines. In warfare, this is often called a **salient**. It meant that they could be attacked from different sides – and this is exactly what Foch did. By June, American soldiers were arriving at a rate of 50,000 per week, and Foch had also kept other soldiers in reserve. On 15 July, Ludendorff ordered one final attack, which ended in disaster. The Germans advanced only two miles before once again running short of supplies. At this point, Foch ordered his fresh troops to counterattack, and they soon pushed the Germans back to the River Marne. The German attack on 15 July was their last major attack of the war. The Ludendorff Offensive had cost the Germans around half a million men – and now the Allies were about to launch their own huge attack.

Key Words

salient

▼ **SOURCE F** *Adapted from an account by a German officer, Hartwig Pohlmann, 1918, describing the last days of Ludendorff's Spring Offensive*

> In July 1918 we tried to cross the River Marne but after three days we had to fall back. The resistance of the enemy was too heavy and there we met first American troops. We knew more and more American troops will come to the front-line and the enemy will become overwhelming for us. But we knew that we had to do our duty as soldiers for as long as we could. We had very heavy losses in that year and the units became smaller and smaller, we had to combine to form one company out of two and so on. The number of our guns diminished.

Key Biography

Erich Ludendorff (1865–1937)

- Born in 1865, in Prussia.
- He helped revise the Schlieffen Plan.
- Together with another military leader he masterminded Germany's victories over the Russians at the battles of Tannenberg (1914) and the Masurian Lakes (1915).

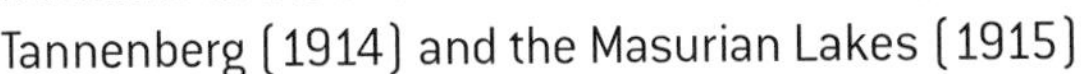

- He supported the policy of 'unrestricted submarine warfare' – a major reason why America entered the war in 1917.
- He played a key role in organising the terms of the Treaty of Brest-Litovsk after Russia's withdrawal from the war.

Work

1. a. Read **Source E**. In what ways does Haig praise the British and French soldiers?
   b. This notice was issued on 11 April. Haig wrote that the Germans had 'made little progress' in their attack. Do you agree with Haig?
   c. Why do you think Haig did not tell the soldiers how far the Germans had advanced?
   d. Why do you think Haig issued this notice?
   e. Do you think it had a positive or a negative effect on the morale of the troops? Explain your reason.
2. a. Write a brief report, from either a British or German point of view, describing the later stages of the Ludendorff Offensive.
   b. Why did the Ludendorff Offensive fail? List as many reasons as you can.

Practice Question

'Appointing General Foch as the Supreme Allied Commander was the main reason for the failure of Ludendorff's Spring Offensive.' How far do you agree with this statement? Explain your answer.

16 marks **SPaG: 4 marks**

Study Tip

As well as the appointment of General Foch for the Allies, why did the German plan fail?

8.3 The Hundred Days

By August 1918, the German Army was close to defeat. Despite their stunning advances in the spring, the German Army had ground to a halt and was running short of food and weapons. Starting on 8 August, the Allies launched a final decisive series of attacks on the Germans all along the Western Front. It is a period known as 'The Hundred Days' and marks the last stage of the First World War.

Objectives

- **Recall** Foch's strategy during 'The Hundred Days' offensive.
- **Explore** the impact of Foch's new strategy.

A new approach

After stopping Ludendorff's Spring Offensive, the Allied armies quickly began to prepare for their own attack. The arrival of fresh American troops was not only a morale boost for the soldiers in the trenches, but the Americans brought new military equipment, food and supplies.

General Foch, the new unified 'Commander-in-Chief' of the Allied armies, decided on a new approach. Instead of focusing a large attack on a single, concentrated area of the front-lines, he decided to launch a series of attacks at different points, which would stretch the enemy and wear them down to breaking point. British, French, Belgian and other Allied forces would attack along the northern part of the front-lines, while the French and the Americans would attack in multiple places along the eastern part of the Western Front (see Map **A**).

8 August 1918

The attacks began at Amiens on 8 August when British, Australian, Canadian and French forces (supported by over 400 tanks) broke through German lines and took 11 kilometres of enemy-occupied territory on the first day. Over the next week, another 8 kilometres of ground was taken as the Germans retreated. Allied losses were reported at 6500, while the Germans lost 30,000 men. Around 300 German guns were captured and a further 17,000 Germans were taken prisoner. General Ludendorff called it 'the black day of the German Army'.

Fact

Tanks were used very effectively at Amiens. Heavy tanks were used to attack well-defended German positions, while the smaller, quicker 'Whippet' tanks were used to support advancing infantry patrols as they probed German defences.

The Second Battle of the Somme

As well as the attack at Amiens, British and Australian forces attacked and captured the city of Albert. The French captured the town of Noyon while another British attack saw them take Bapaume. Collectively, these battles are often referred to as the Second Battle of the Somme.

Battles of the Hindenburg Line

After these multiple breakthroughs, the Germans were gradually pushed back to a line of concrete trenches they had built in 1917, called the Hindenburg Line. In September 1918, French and American forces began their attack on this defensive line with the Meuse-Argonne Offensive. This was to be the largest attack that American troops had ever carried out in their history, involving 1.2 million US soldiers. It also became one of America's deadliest attacks, costing over 26,000 American lives.

▼ **A** *The Hundred Days offensive*

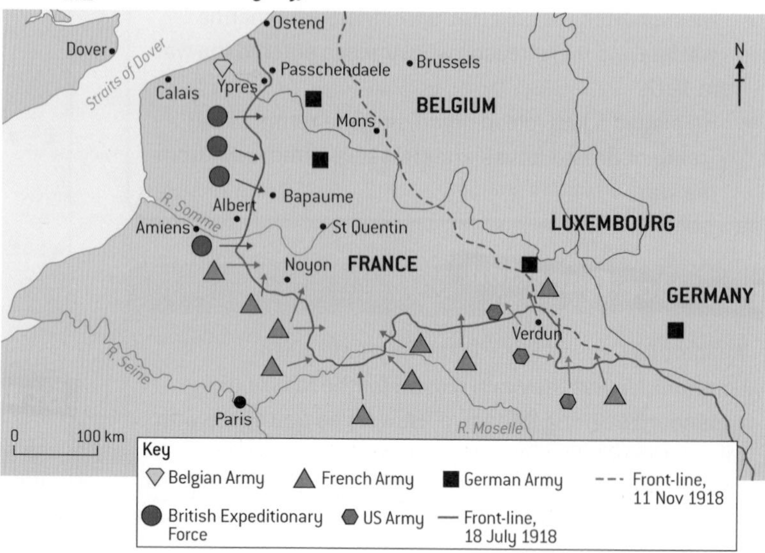

Two days later, Belgian, British and French troops, attacked near Ypres in Belgium (this was now the *Fifth* Battle of Ypres), while soldiers from Britain, the British Empire, Australia and America fought at the Battle of St Quentin Canal. Meanwhile, the French continued with the assault on parts of the Hindenburg Line and by early October the Allies had completely broken through the defences and the Germans were in retreat. As they retreated, the Germans burned bridges, destroyed roads, cut down trees and poisoned water wells so advancing enemy forces could not use them. But they also left heavy guns, equipment and supplies behind in their panic. This collapse forced most of the German military leaders to accept that the war should be ended.

▼ **SOURCE B** *A cartoon from the British magazine* Punch, *21 August 1918; the caption has the German soldier saying, 'Heavens, Ludendorff spoke the truth – the worst is behind us.'*

▼ **SOURCE C** *Adapted from* My War Memories *by General Ludendorff (joint German Commander-in-Chief 1916–18), published in 1919*

> Early on 8 August, in a dense fog, English and French attacked with strong squadrons of tanks, but otherwise in no great superiority. Between the Somme and the Lys they penetrated deep into our positions. By mid-morning I had gained a complete impression of the situation. It was a very gloomy one. I was told of deeds of glorious valour, but also of behaviour which, I openly confess, I should not have thought possible in the German army. Groups of men had surrendered to single troopers. Retreating troops, meeting a fresh division going bravely into action, had shouted things like, 'You're prolonging the war'. The officers in many places had lost their influence and had allowed themselves to be swept along with the rest. Everything I had feared had here, in one place, become a reality. Our war machine was no longer efficient.

Work

1. In what way did Foch's attack strategy during The Hundred Days offensive differ from earlier strategies?
2. Write a summary of The Hundred Days Offensive in no more than 50 words.
3. a Look at **Source B**. Describe what you can see happening in the cartoon.
   b Why do you think there is so much time between the Battle of Amiens and the appearance of the cartoon?
4. a Read **Source C**. Write down something positive that Ludendorff says about his troops.
   b Write down a negative statement.
   c Who does Ludendorff appear to blame for the poor performance of the troops?

Practice Question

How useful are **Sources B** and **C** to a historian studying The Hundred Days offensive? Explain your answer using **Sources B** and **C** and your contextual knowledge. **12 marks**

Study Tip

Write about the things that occur in both sources to explain what happened in the Hundred Days Offensive.

Extension

One of the most successful tanks used on the Western Front was the British Whippet. This was the tank that German forces were especially keen to capture. Prepare a fact file on the Whippet. In what military battles did it feature? In what ways was it different from earlier tanks?

9.1 The impact of war on the home fronts

Many people in Europe were enthusiastic about the war when it broke out in 1914. A wave of patriotism swept through most countries as men rushed off to join the Army, and crowds cheered as they waved them off to war. However, this enthusiasm did not last long and the impact of war was soon felt in each of the countries involved in the conflict.

Objectives

- **Define** what is meant by 'home front'?
- **Explore** the impact of the war on civilians in some of the main countries involved in the conflict.

The home fronts

The First World War was fought on many fronts – on land, on sea and in the air, for example. But it also affected ordinary civilians left back at home. This 'front' is known as a '**home front**'. One of the most direct ways that ordinary civilians were involved in the conflict was when they were the victims of enemy bomb attacks. Within a week of war breaking out, a German Zeppelin airship bombed the Belgian city of Liège, for example. By the end of the first month, Britain had also been targeted by German airships.

▼ **A** *The best available estimates of First World War military casualties; deaths were listed in newspapers, searched everyday by anxious families; by 1917–18 the British government was acutely conscious of how costly and destructive the war had been so far*

	Total mobilised forces	Killed and died	Wounded
Allied Powers	42,188,810	5,142,631	12,800,706
Central Powers	22,850,000	3,386,200	8,388,448

How the war changed the home fronts

The soldiers, sailors and airmen not only needed vast supplies of guns, bullets and shells, they also needed ships, aeroplanes, trucks and tanks. As a result, countries had to find ways to increase production.

- In some countries, such as Germany and Britain, the government took over certain industries to make sure enough of what was needed was produced. Mines, railways, weapons factories and shipyards were controlled by the government and high production targets were set for the workers.
- With so many men away fighting, women were needed to do their jobs. Thousands of women found work in weapons factories, shipyards and steelworks, and with the police force and ambulance services. In Germany and Russia for example, women were especially important in agriculture for completing the farming jobs that the men had left to join the Army.

Food shortages

In most countries, there were shortages of food. Both Britain and Germany tried to starve each other by using their navies to block food supplies reaching each country by sea. In Germany, by 1916, soap, cheese, butter and eggs were unavailable, while coal and shoes were scarce. With goods in short supply, prices went up.

The German government responded by setting maximum prices on certain products, including sugar and potatoes. They even introduced special compulsory 'meatless' days when meat consumption was banned. The German winter of 1916–17 was nicknamed the 'Turnip Winter' because turnips were one of the only foods available after a very poor harvest. The blockade of Germany continued after the war ended and was not completely lifted until the final peace treaty (the Treaty of Versailles) was signed in June 1919 (see Source C). In Britain, the government introduced rationing to make sure that food was equally shared out. Each person was allowed only a set amount of butter, sugar, bacon, ham and so on.

▼ **SOURCE B** *A butcher's shop, looted in a food riot, 1919*

SOURCE C *A German Government poster from 1919; the caption said, 'Farmers, do your duty! The cities are starving'*

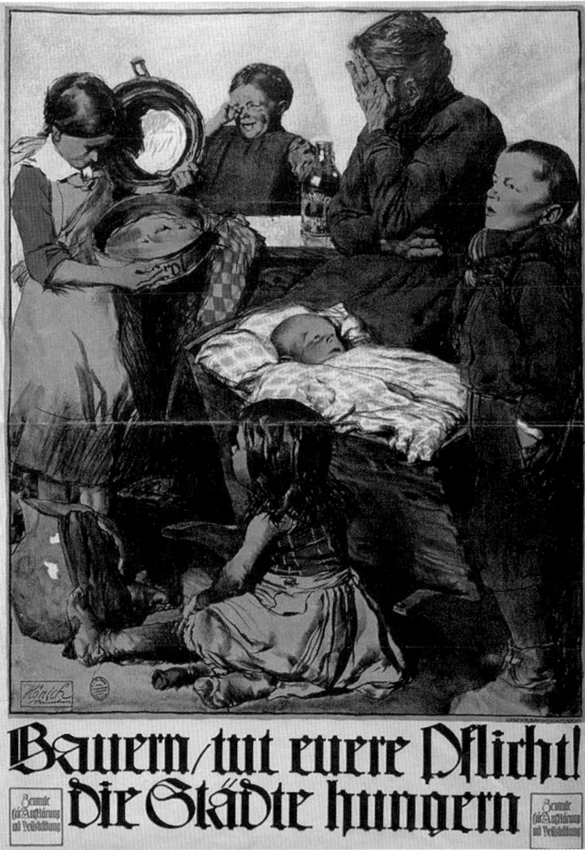

Devastated landscapes

It must also be remembered that there was a significant impact on the countries in which the fighting took place. In France, for example, over two million people were made homeless because 750,000 houses had been destroyed. Over 20,000 factories, 1000 bridges, 48,000 kilometres of road, 2000 breweries and 1600 kilometres of railway line had been wrecked too. An area the size of Wales had been devastated as high explosive shells ripped up the rich soil into useless mud. Even today, some of the soil cannot be used because of the dangers of unexploded shells just below the surface.

Anger

After many months of fighting, the high casualty rates and the shortages of food and fuel made people increasingly angry with their rulers. In Germany in 1915, 500 women collected in front of the Reichstag (Parliament) buildings and said that they wanted their men back from the trenches. A year later, 10,000 workers assembled in Berlin's city centre to shout 'Down with war, down with the government'. Eventually, in Russia in 1917 and in Germany in 1918, this anger fuelled a revolution which destroyed the old systems of government.

Key Word

home front

SOURCE D *By the end of the war, hunger was widespread in Germany; this image from January 1919 shows people cutting pieces from a dead horse lying in the street, to get meat for a meal*

Work

1 Explain what is meant by the term 'home front'

2 Why did governments need to take direct control of factories, shipyards and steelworks during the war?

3 a Why did Germany suffer such severe shortages during the war?

b What impact did these shortages have on Germany?

Practice Question

Study **Source C.** The source criticises the effects of the Allied blockade. How do you know? Explain your answer using **Source C** and your contextual knowledge. **4 marks**

Study Tip

Use your historical knowledge to explain why the Germans criticised the Allied blockade after November 1918.

The end of the war

On 9 November the Kaiser abdicated and secretly left Germany. On 11 November 1918 German representatives, led by Matthias Erzberger, were told to sign a piece of paper which officially ended the First World War. How did the war end for Germany, and why did it end this way?

Objectives

- **Examine** the reasons why Germany surrendered in November 1918.
- **Outline** the terms of the armistice.

The impact of war on Germany

By September 1918, Germany was close to collapse. The British naval blockade (see page 89) had stopped vital supplies getting into the country. German people were so short of food that they were surviving on turnips and bread – and a deadly 'flu epidemic was sweeping the country, killing thousands already weak from a poor diet.

On the battlefields, Germany and its allies were close to defeat. On 29 September, General Ludendorff told shocked German politicians and generals that he thought Germany should 'abandon the war as hopeless'. In response, the Kaiser reluctantly allowed the main political parties to form a new government, which took away some of his powers and gave them to the German parliament. But the changes came too late to satisfy the German people. Large demonstrations were held against the war and some protesters even talked of overthrowing the Kaiser in a revolution.

Mutiny, revolution and abdication

On 28 October, the German Navy, based in Kiel, northern Germany, was ordered out to sea to attack British ships. Sailors on the ships refused to follow orders – they just did not want to fight any more. News of their mutiny began to spread. In ports nearby, other sailors refused to follow orders. Workers in the towns supported them. Soldiers, sent to deal with the protests, joined in with the sailors and workers. Soon they began to take over more towns and set up special councils to run them. In just six days, workers' and soldiers' councils were governing towns and cities all over Germany, such as Hamburg, Cologne, Frankfurt, Munich, and finally, Berlin. The country was in chaos and there was little the Kaiser could do; he had lost control and his army generals refused to support him. On 9 November 1918, he abdicated and secretly left Germany. He went to live in Holland, never to return.

▼ **SOURCE A** *Adapted from a letter written by General Hindenburg to a member of the German royal family in October 1918*

> The Supreme Command demands an immediate despatch of a peace offer to our enemies. There no longer exists any hope of forcing peace on our enemies. The enemy can bring in new and fresh reserves. The German army holds fast and repulses all attacks with success. But we must stop fighting to save the German people further useless sacrifices.

The end of the war

Friedrich Ebert, one of the leaders of Germany's largest political party (the SDP), took the Kaiser's place as leader of Germany on a temporary basis. He promised to hold elections soon. If ordinary German people wanted him as their leader, they would get the chance to vote for him if they wished. Meanwhile, he gave the people what they really wanted – an end to the war.

The armistice: Germany surrenders

Ebert sent a small group of representatives, led by Matthias Erzberger, to France to negotiate an **armistice** (ceasefire). The Germans hoped to sort out a fair deal but the British, French and Americans were in no mood to negotiate. Marshal Foch, the Allied Commander-in-Chief, met the Germans in a railway carriage at Compiègne, northern France, and instructed them to agree to the terms of the armistice. The main terms included:

- all fighting on land, sea and in the air, should end within six hours
- all land occupied by German troops in Belgium, Luxembourg, and France (plus Alsace-Lorraine, held since 1870 by Germany) were to be evacuated within 15 days
- the Allies were to occupy land in Germany to the west of the River Rhine up to a distance of 30 kilometres

Key Words

armistice

- German troops had to withdraw from Austria-Hungary, Romania, and Turkey
- Germany must immediately hand over ten battleships, six battle cruisers, eight cruisers and submarines, give up its largest weapons and hand over railway trains, railway carriages and rail trucks
- the naval blockade would continue
- Germany would pay a financial settlement for all damage caused.

When the terms of the armistice were read out, one of the German representatives began to cry. But Erzberger had been told that they must sign, whatever was placed in front of them, because the situation back in Germany was so chaotic and the new German government needed an end to the war. So, at 5.10am on 11 November 1918, the German representatives signed to agree to the terms. The war was to end at 11.00am later that day. Immediately after the paper was signed, Foch left the carriage, without shaking hands. The First World War was over.

▼ **SOURCE B** *From a speech made in the German parliament by General Hindenburg in November 1919*

> In spite of the superiority of the enemy in men and materials, we could have brought the struggle to a favourable conclusion if determined and unanimous cooperation had existed between the army and those at home. The Germany Army was stabbed in the back. It is plain enough on whom the blame lies.

Practice Question

Study **Sources B** and **C**. How useful are these sources to a historian studying the reasons why Germany asked for a ceasefire in 1918? **12 marks**

▶ **SOURCE C** *In 1919, Hindenburg gave evidence to a German government enquiry about why Germany lost the war; this cartoon from the humorous German magazine* Simplicissimus, *November 1919, comments on his evidence; the cartoon shows him revealing a theatrical performance*

Work

1. a Explain what is meant by the word 'abdicate'.
   b In your own words, explain why Germany's Emperor, Kaiser Wilhelm, decided to abdicate.
2. a Read **Source A**. Who was General Hindenburg?
   b Sum up his view of Germany's current situation in October 1918.
3. a Read **Sources A** and **B**. In what ways do the two sources differ?
   b Can you explain why Hindenburg might be saying different things about the end of the war?
4. Describe the role played in the armistice by:
   a Matthias Erzberger
   b Friedrich Ebert
   c Marshall Foch.
5. Why do you think one of the German representatives cried when the terms were read out to him? Explain your answer.

Extension

In January 1919, the winning nations in the war met up in Paris to discuss what to do with the defeated countries. The result was a series of treaties which severely punished Germany, Austria-Hungary, Bulgaria and Turkey. Prepare fact files on each of these treaties, detailing the main points and punishments and the long-term impact each had.

Study Tip

What does the magazine think of Hindenburg's explanation of why Germany lost the war?

9.3A Why was Germany defeated?

The First World War came to an end at 11am on 11 November 1918. By this time, Germany was fighting alone because its allies – Austria-Hungary, Bulgaria and Turkey – had all withdrawn from the war in the weeks before. But there is no clear single reason (or factor) why Germany was defeated in November 1918. Instead, there are several reasons that combined to contribute to its defeat. It is the role of a historian to explore and assess these reasons, in order to draw conclusions as to why Germany surrendered in 1918.

Objectives

- **Assess** the factors that contributed to Germany's defeat in November 1918.
- **Explore** the contribution of Haig and Foch to Germany's defeat.

The war at sea and the British naval blockade of Germany

As early as 1915, Germany was only able to import half the amount of goods as before the war. This severely damaged both the German war effort, and the living standards of ordinary Germans. For example, German industry ran short of fuel and chemicals for explosives and gas, and agriculture was severely hit due to a lack of fertilisers for the crops. There were food riots in German cities in 1916 because so many people were going hungry. It has been estimated that about 120,000 people died of starvation in 1916, rising to as many as 420,000 by 1918. The continued shortages and hunger gradually eroded support for the war and, by 1918, there were riots and strikes as civilians demanded an end to the conflict.

The USA enters the war

The USA's decision to enter the war was a great morale boost for the Allied soldiers in the trenches. Also, the economic and military strength of America meant that around 2 million soldiers and millions of tonnes of food, equipment and weaponry arrived in support of the Allies, while German supplies and forces were weakening. The arrival of the USA also forced the Germans to put a huge effort into Ludendorff's Spring Offensive (see pages 82–85), which ultimately failed.

Failure of the Ludendorff Spring Offensive

The failure of Germany's last major attack was the sign to their military leaders that they could not win the war. The Germans lost around 800,000 troops during the whole course of the attack, and Ludendorff calculated that he needed 200,000 fresh troops each month to continue the war. However, he was told that he could only be supplied with about 300,000 for the *whole* of the next 12 months. At this point, the German war leaders knew that defeat was near. The Allied counterattack that followed quickly pushed the Germans back, and it was clear that an armistice needed to be agreed upon soon.

Impact of the Bolshevik (Russian) Revolution

Russia's withdrawal from the war was a bonus for Germany to begin with. It allowed Germany to pull together all its forces and concentrate them on one huge attack on the British and French (before the US troops arrived). But Ludendorff's Spring Offensive failed, and the revolution in Russia began to have an impact on Germany. Some Germans with the same political ideas as the Russian revolutionaries wanted to remove the Kaiser, just as the Russians had removed their tsar. There was an increasing number of riots and strikes in 1918, and like in Russia, workers' and soldiers' councils were set up across Germany. This chaos across Germany was one of the factors that led the Kaiser to abdicate – and the government that replaced him ended the war.

The development of the tank

The Germans were not convinced of the value of the tank, and only produced 20. The British and French, on the other hand, believed tanks could help to break the stalemate on the Western Front, and so they produced thousands. They were first used to great effect at the Battle of Cambrai in November 1917, and then on a larger scale at the beginning of the Battle of Amiens on 8 August 1918. Success on that day marked the beginning of the final attack that led to the military defeat of Germany.

The defeat of Germany's Allies

During September and October 1918, Germany's allies collapsed. The Bulgarian Army surrendered on 29 September after being driven back by Serbian and French forces. In late October, Turkish forces surrendered to combined British and Arab troops, and on 3 November Austria-Hungary pulled out of the war after a devastating defeat against Italian troops at the Battle of Vittorio Veneto.

▼ **SOURCE A** *A cartoon drawn in 1916 by a Dutch artist Louis Raemaekers; it shows the Kaiser (in the centre) hand-in-hand with war (on the left) and hunger (on the right)*

Work

1 How is the time and date of the end of the First World War remembered every year?

2 a Look at **Source A**. Describe what you can see in the cartoon. In your description, write about the way the cartoonist has drawn the images.

  b What do you think the cartoonist wanted people to think about Kaiser Wilhelm II? In your answer, think whether the image shows the Kaiser in a positive or a negative way.

Fact

The last soldier to be killed during the war was an American named Henry Gunther. He was shot whilst charging at a German machine gun post at 10.59am, one minute before the armistice was to take effect at 11am. He was the grandson of German immigrants to the USA.

9.3B Why was Germany defeated?

The German Revolution

When news of the failure of the Ludendorff Spring Offensive and the advance of the Allies reached Germany, the morale of the German people dropped quickly. This, combined with the worsening food shortages and a deadly flu epidemic which killed thousands led to a revolution in Germany. German sailors at the Kiel naval base mutinied and refused to follow orders, and soon the rebellion spread over Germany. It was clear that the Kaiser had lost control of his country as workers and soldiers began to set up their own councils to run the different German states. The Kaiser left Germany on 9 November and the war was over by 11 November.

The role of Foch and Haig in Germany's defeat

▼ **B** *Ferdinand Foch*

There are different views about Ferdinand Foch and Douglas Haig, the two best-known French and British generals. Some argue that they were reckless with their troops' lives and stubbornly followed their plans when alternative ideas were possible. Others argue that no matter what you think about their tactics, they did, after all, win the war. The following interpretations demonstrate a variety of views.

▼ **C** *Douglas Haig*

▼ **INTERPRETATION D** *From an article by S Warburton in* Hindsight *magazine, 1998*

Blaming Haig the individual for the failings of the British war effort is putting too much of a burden of guilt on one man. Haig was the product of his time, of his upbringing, education, training and previous military experience. One argument goes that he was, ultimately, victorious and, even if he had been replaced, would there have been anyone better for the job? Even on the Somme a German officer called the battlefield 'the muddy grave of the German army'. This was the same battle in which Haig's numerous mistakes contributed to the half a million casualties suffered by the Allies.

▼ **INTERPRETATION E** *Adapted from a biography about Haig by Alfred Duff Cooper, 1935*

Was it stupid to fight at the Somme? Surely there can be only one opinion. If we had not attacked at the Somme, the Germans would have beaten the French at Verdun and the French and British alliance could have been broken.

▼ **INTERPRETATION F** *From a 2017 article by Kennedy R Hickman, a historian specialising in military and naval history*

As fighting continued into 1915, [Foch] oversaw French efforts during the Artois Offensive that [Autumn]. A failure, it gained little ground in exchange for a large number of casualties. In July 1916, Foch commanded French troops during the Battle of the Somme. Severely criticised for the severe losses sustained by French forces during the course of the battle, Foch was removed from command in December.

Key Biography

General Sir Douglas Haig (1861–1928)

- Born in Edinburgh in 1861 into a wealthy family, he went on to study at Oxford University and at the Royal Military Academy at Sandhurst.
- In 1906, he became director of military training for the British Army. He was responsible for organising the British Expeditionary Force (BEF) in case of war with Germany.
- He successfully commanded troops at the battles of Mons and Ypres in 1914 and was promoted to commander of the whole British Army in December 1915.
- In July 1917, another attack at Ypres resulted in more heavy casualties, but in 1918 he oversaw a series of victories against German forces.
- He helped set up the Royal British Legion (known for its Poppy Appeal).
- He retired from the military in 1921 and died in 1928.

Extension

Recently, historians have suggested that General Haig's reputation as 'The Butcher of the Somme' is undeserved. Research the reasons for this reinterpretation.

Work

1 Write a brief summary of the way in which the following contributed to Germany's defeat in the war:
   - a the war at sea and the British naval blockade of Germany
   - b the Bolshevik Revolution
   - c the USA entering the war
   - d the failure of Ludendorff's Spring Offensive
   - e the tank, and the use of new technologies and tactics
   - f the defeat of Germany's allies
   - g the German Revolution
   - h General Haig
   - i Commander-in-Chief Foch

2 Which three factors do you think played the most important role in Germany's defeat? Explain your choices.

3 Read **Interpretations D** to **F**.
   - a Make two lists, one outlining positive ways in which Haig and Foch contributed to Germany's defeat and the other outlining criticisms.
   - b Why do you think historians have disagreed so much about the roles of Haig and Foch in Germany's defeat? Explain your answer.

Practice Question

'The failure of Ludendorff's Spring Offensive was the main reason for Germany's surrender in the First World War.' How far do you agree with this statement? Explain your answer.

16 marks
SPaG: 4 marks

Study Tip

Write a paragraph about the failure of Ludendorff's Spring Offensive and other factors that influenced Germany's surrender in 1918.

How to... respond to statements

Below is an example of a question that asks you to explain how far you agree with a statement.

Practice Question

'The entry of the USA on the Allies' side was the main reason for Germany's defeat in the First World War.'

How far do you agree with this statement?

Explain your answer. **16 marks** **SPaG: 4 marks**

Study Tip

Your extended writing is tested in this type of question. Don't forget you get marks for SPaG (spelling, punctuation and grammar). Make sure that you know how to spell key words correctly and check your answer at the end for mistakes.

Over to you

This type of question begins with a statement that contains a judgement, and it asks you to explain the *extent* to which you agree with the statement. In this case, the judgement states that America's entry into the war was the main reason for Germany's defeat. Your answer is about whether you agree with that or not.

1 Analyse the statement provided. It says that the main reason Germany lost the war was because the USA joined on the Allied side. This assumes that the USA played a role in Germany's defeat. Do you agree with this? What do you know about America's arrival in the war and the role it played in Germany's defeat?

2 Remember that the question is about the reasons for Germany's defeat in the war. By stating that the USA's arrival was the *main reason*, this implies that there are other reasons too. The word 'main' qualifies the judgement and makes the question more complex. So, which other factors played a role in Germany's defeat in the war? Copy and complete the diagram below by adding detail to the titles provided.

3 Looking at your completed diagram, which of the reasons for Germany's defeat do you think is most important?

4 When you choose a reason as the most important one for Germany's defeat, you must write about other reasons as well. Your choice of the 'main' reason is not as important as the reasons you give for choosing it.

5 The question continues by asking 'How far do you agree ...?', which means that you need to offer an opinion.

6 What are the strengths and weaknesses of the following answer? Does it include the impact of America joining the war on Germanys' defeat? Is there supporting evidence for the factors mentioned? Does it come to a judgement about whether America's entry into the war was the main reason (or not) for Germanys' defeat?

The entry of America into the war on the Allies' side in 1917 played a key role in Germany's defeat in the First World War, but it was not the most important factor. There were more important factors, for example, the naval blockade of Germany by British ships and the revolution in Germany that was one of the consequences of this blockade.

The entry of the USA was important because it boosted the morale of the Allied soldiers. Also, America's economic and military strength meant that around two million soldiers and millions of tonnes of food, equipment and weapons arrived in support of the Allies, whilst these were denied to Germany.

However, one of the main reasons the Americans joined in the war was because of the German policy of unrestricted submarine warfare, which meant that their U-boats were sinking many American ships sailing to Europe. This provoked America into the war, but the reason for Germany's attacks was because of the British naval blockade of German ports. The blockade meant that as early as 1915, Germany was only able to import half the amount of goods as before the war. This damaged both the German war effort and the living standards of ordinary Germans. It also led the Germans to try to sink American ships in an attempt to starve Britain into surrender and win the war. As a result, the blockade was the more important reason because without it, Germany would not have tried to sink American ships – which brought them into the war.

The blockade also led to food riots in German cities and deaths from starvation. Eventually Germans demanded an end to the war and a revolution led to the Kaiser's abdication. This saw a new government take over and call for an armistice.

Study Tip

The answer deals with the question straight away.

Study Tip

You should try to write about the 'named factor' in your answer. In this case, the entry of the USA.

Study Tip

Think about the way reasons interact with each other. Here, the student has shown how the naval blockade led to America joining the war.

Study Tip

The answer contains precise and detailed knowledge.

7 Could you add any more factors in Germany's defeat? What about a conclusion? Why not finish off the answer?

Practice Questions for Paper 1: Conflict and Tension: The First World War, 1894–1918

The examination questions on Conflict and Tension will be varied but there will be some questions on sources (AO3), a question on your knowledge and analysis of the period using historical concepts (AO1 and AO2), and an extended writing question (AO1 and AO2). Below is a selection of these different kinds of questions for you to practise.

Answer **all four** questions. You are advised to spend 50 minutes on these four questions.

Source A A French cartoon, published in 1915. It comments on the Kaiser's foreign policy. The caption reads 'too hard for a glutton'. A 'glutton' is someone who is greedy.

Source B Kaiser Wilhelm II speaking in an interview to the *Daily Telegraph,* a British newspaper, published in October 1908.

> Germany is a young and growing empire. She has world-wide trade which is rapidly expanding. Germany must have a powerful fleet to protect that trade and her many interests in even the most distant seas.
>
> Who knows what might happen in the Pacific in the days to come. Look at the rise of Japan; think of the possible national awakening of China.
>
> Only those powers that have great navies will be listened to with respect. It is for this reason that Germany must have a powerful fleet. It may even be that England herself will be glad that Germany has a fleet when they speak together on the same side in the great debates of the future.

Source C A cartoon published in a British newspaper, the *Daily Mirror,* in 1914. It shows the Kaiser spying on the British fleet.

Answer **all four** questions below

1 Study **Source A**.

Source A criticises the Kaiser's foreign policy. How do you know?

Explain your answer by using **Source A** and your contextual knowledge. **4 marks**

2 Study **Sources B** and **C**.

How useful are **Sources B** and **C** to a historian studying the Anglo-German naval race?

Explain your answer using **Sources B** and **C** and your contextual knowledge. **12 marks**

3 Write an account of how the U-boat campaign led to America's entry into the war. **8 marks**

4 'The failure of the Ludendorff Spring Offensive was the main reason Germany asked for an armistice.'

How far do you agree with this statement?

Explain your answer. **16 marks**
SPaG: 4 marks

Glossary

abdicate to give up a throne

alliance an agreement between two countries to support each other

armistice a ceasefire, after which, the terms of a treaty are negotiated

arms race when rival nations attempt to outdo each other in the size and quality of their armed forces

assassin a person who kills someone for political or religious reasons

attrition to wear away an enemy to the point of them collapsing

boyonet a 40-centimetre knife used for close combat

blockade the stopping of supplies reaching an enemy country

Bolshevik a member of a political party that believed in violent revolution and followed the ideas of Karl Marx

colony a country or area under the full or partial control of another country

convoy system supply ships sailing close together in large groups, protected by warships

counter-attack when a group of soldiers try to drive back an enemy attack

depth charge a bomb dropped into the water that exploded at certain depths to destroy U-boats

desert abandon a duty or post without permission

dogfight air battle

Eastern Front the 1000-mile front-line between Russian troops and the soldiers of Germany and Austria-Hungary in Eastern Europe

empire a group of nations or people ruled over by an emperor, empress, or other powerful government

ethnic group people who share a distinctive culture, race, religion or nationality

foreign policy the action and strategy taken by a leader or government in dealing with other nations

home front the civilian population of a nation whose armed forces are involved in a war abroad

hurricane bombardment a short, intense artillery bombardment

imperial relating to an empire or an emperor

July Crisis the term used to describe the chain of events from the assassination of Franz Ferdinand to the declarations of war by the major powers from late June to early August 1914

machine gun an automatic gun that fires bullets in quick succession for as long as the trigger is pressed

mobilise prepare for war

mutineer soldier who takes part in a mutiny

mutiny when soldiers refuse to follow orders

nationalist a person with great love for their nation. Nationalist can also mean a person or group within a country that desires political independence

neutrality not supporting or helping either side in a conflict

no man's land an area of land between two countries or armies that is not controlled by anyone

outflanked when an army has moved around the side of an enemy to outmanoeuvre them

pan-Slavism the idea of uniting all Slavs into one country

province a large section of a country with its own government or administration

Q-ship heavily armed warship disguised as a supply ship that lured U-boats into making attacks, before firing upon them

reconnaissance the observation of an area to spot an enemy

Reichstag part of the German parliament

rifle a portable long-barrelled gun for precision shooting

salient a bulge in the front-lines that allows enemy forces to attack from several sides

semi-independent an area that controls some parts of its rule, but is mainly ruled by the controlling government or nation

shell shock psychological illness caused by prolonged exposure to the sights and sounds of warfare

Slavs an ethnic group of eastern, south-eastern, and central Europe, including Russians, Bulgars, Serbs, Croats, Slavonians, Poles, Czechs, Slovaks

Splendid Isolation Britain's position in the late 1880s and early 1900s, meaning it was 'isolated' from alliances with other nations

stalemate a deadlock, when neither side can win

stand to a time at dawn and dusk when all soldiers were on high alert

trade union an organization of workers formed to bargain with the employer

treaty an official agreement or deal between two or more nations

trench foot a painful condition of the feet caused by prolonged exposure to cold and wet

tsar the male ruler or emperor of Russia up to 1917; the female ruler was called the tsarina

two-power standard the idea that Britain's navy should be at least equal in size to the combined strength of the next two largest navies in the world

U-boat underwater boat or submarine

ultimatum terms or demands presented by one power (or group of powers) to another

Weltpolitik meaning 'world policy'. Used to describe Kaiser Wilhelm II's desire to be a world power

Western Front the 400-mile line of trenches running from the English Channel to Switzerland

Zeppelin large bomber airship

Index

N

O

Acknowledgements

The publisher would like to thank the following for permissions to use their photographs:

Cover: IWM/Getty Images;

Artworks: QBS Learning

Photos: p8: Grenville Collins Postcard Collection/Mary Evans Picture Library; **p9:** Chronicle / Alamy Stock Photo; **p10:** Wikipedia Commons; **p12:** © Illustrated London News Ltd/Mary Evans Picture Library; **p14:** Sueddeutsche Zeitung Photo/Mary Evans Picture Library; **p16:** Lebrecht Music and Arts Photo Library / Alamy Stock Photo; **p19:** Pictorial Press Ltd / Alamy Stock Photo; **p20:** German emperor William II during a visit in Tangier in Morocco in april 1905 / Tallandier / Bridgeman Images; **p22:** The Awakening of the Eastern Crisis; Bulgaria proclaims its independence, Austria annexes Bosnia-Herzegovina, cover of 'Le Petit Journal', 18th October 1908 (engraving) (colour photograph), French School, (20th century) / Private Collection / Roger-Viollet, Paris / Bridgeman Images; **p24:** Paul Fearn / Alamy Stock Photo; **p25:** Mary Evans Picture Library; **p27:** World History Archive / Alamy Stock Photo; **p28:** Archive Farms Inc / Alamy Stock Photo; **p29:** Der Wahre Jacob, 5th January 1909, cover, - CC-BY-SA 3.0/ Heidelberg University Library; **p6 & p31 (L):** © Illustrated London News Ltd/Mary Evans Picture Library; **p31 (R) & p99:** Mirrorpix.com; **p32:** Paul Fearn / Alamy Stock Photo; **p34:** Chronicle / Alamy Stock Photo; **p7 (L) & p35 (TL):** Mary Evans Picture Library; **p35 (BL):** dpa picture alliance / Alamy Stock Photo; **p35 (TR):** Pictorial Press Ltd/Alamy Stock Photo; **p37:** Photo 12 Stock Photo/Alamy Stock Photo; **p40:** Granger Historical Picture Archive / Alamy Stock Photo; **p42:** Mary Evans Picture Library; **p44:** Sueddeutsche Zeitung Photo/Mary Evans Picture Library; **p45:** Punch Cartoon Library; **p48:** David Cohen Fine Art/Mary Evans Picture Library; **p49:** WORLD WAR I: TRENCHES Aerial view of trenches and no man's land in Europe during World War I. Photograph, c.1917. / Granger / Bridgeman Images; **p50-p51:** PRISMA ARCHIVO Stock Photo/Alamy Stock Photo; **p52 (L):** © Illustrated London News Ltd/Mary Evans Picture Library; **p52 (R):** Everett Historical/ Shutterstock; **p53:** Stuck Tank, Arras, France, April, 1917 (b/w photo) / Underwood Archives/UIG / Bridgeman Images; **p55:** "Father we must have a higher pile to see Verdun", c.1916 / Private Collection / Bridgeman Images; **p56:** The body of a German telephone operator in his shelter at the Somme, 1916 (b/w photo), Moreau, Jacques (b.1887) / Archives Larousse, Paris, France / Bridgeman Images; **p59:** Wikipedia Commons; **p61:** John Frost Newspapers / Alamy Stock Photo; **p62:** World History Archive / Alamy Stock Photo; **p63:** Mary Evans Picture Library; **p65 (L):** Fotosearch/Getty Images; **p65 (R):** Sueddeutsche Zeitung Photo/Mary Evans Picture Library; **p67 (T):** Wolfsonian–Florida International University Library; **p67 (B):** German advertisement warning travellers of RMS Lusitania. May 1, 1915. The liner was torpedoed off the Irish coast by a German submarine only five days later. (BSLOC_2012_4_99) German submarine on five days later. (BSLOC_2012_4_99) German submarine on five days later. (BSLOC_2012_4_99) German submarine on five days later/ Everett Collection/Bridgeman Images; **p4 & p68:** IWM/Getty Images; **p70-p71:** AridOcean/Shutterstock; **p72:** Mitchell's Golden Dawn Cigarettes', 1914-18 (colour litho), English School, (20th century)/Private Collection/Peter Newark Military Pictures/ Bridgeman Images; **p75:** Punch Cartoon Library; **p77:** DeAgostini/ Getty Images; **p78:** PJF Military Collection / Alamy Stock Photo; **p79 (L):** Robert Hunt Library/Mary Evans Picture Library; **p79 (R):** Grenville Collins Postcard Collection/Mary Evans Picture Library; **p80:** INTERFOTO / Alamy Stock Photo; **p81 (L):** WWI German stormtroopers on the Western Front, 1918 (b/w photo), German Photographer (20th Century) / Private Collection / Peter Newark Pictures / Bridgeman Images; **p81 (R):** Everett Historical/ Shutterstock; **p82:** INTERFOTO / Alamy Stock Photo; **p83:** Punch Cartoon Library; **p85:** INTERFOTO / Alamy Stock Photo; **p87:** World History Archive / Alamy Stock Photo; **p88:** The LIFE Images Collection/Getty Images; **p89 (L):** World History Archive / Alamy Stock Photo; **p89 (R):** Albert Harlingue/Roger Viollet/Getty Images; **p91:** Kladderadatsch', 72.1919, p655 - CC-BY-SA 3.0/ Heidelberg University Library; **p93:** Louisiana State University ; **p95:** Everett Historical/Shutterstock; **p98:** (c)Robert Hunt Library/Mary Evans Picture Library;

We are grateful to the following for permission to include copyright material:

AQA for practice questions from the *AQA GCSE History: Paper 1B/A*, 'Conflict and Tension: The First World War 1894–1918', copyright © 2018 AQA and its licensors, reproduced by permission of AQA.

Curtis Brown Group Ltd, London on behalf of The Estate of R C Sherriff for extract from *No Leading Lady* by R C Sherriff (Little Hampton Books, 1968), copyright © R C Sherriff 1968.

Daily Express/ N&S Syndication for extract from John Irvine's report, *Daily Express*, 3 July 1918.

The Orion Publishing Group, London for extract from *With a Machine Gun to Cambrai* by George Coppard (Cassell, 1999), copyright © George Coppard 1999.

Philip Allan Publishers for Hodder Education, for extract from article by S Warburton: *Hindsight: GCSE Modern History Review*, April 1998 Vol 8.

John Wiley & Sons Inc, via CCC Republication for extracts from *The First World War* by Barry Bates (Basil Blackwell, 1984), copyright © 1984.

We have made every effort to trace and contact all copyright holders before publication, but if notified of any errors or omissions, the publisher will be happy to rectify these at the earliest opportunity.